Gender and the Rhetoric of Modernity in Spanish America,
1850–1910

UNIVERSITY PRESS OF FLORIDA

Florida A&M University, Tallahassee
Florida Atlantic University, Boca Raton
Florida Gulf Coast University, Ft. Myers
Florida International University, Miami
Florida State University, Tallahassee
New College of Florida, Sarasota
University of Central Florida, Orlando
University of Florida, Gainesville
University of North Florida, Jacksonville
University of South Florida, Tampa
University of West Florida, Pensacola

Gender and the Rhetoric of Modernity in Spanish America, 1850–1910

LEE SKINNER

University Press of Florida

Gainesville · Tallahassee · Tampa · Boca Raton

Pensacola · Orlando · Miami · Jacksonville · Ft. Myers · Sarasota

Library of Congress Cataloging-in-Publication Data
Names: Skinner, Lee Joan, author.
Title: Gender and the rhetoric of modernity in Spanish America, 1850–1910 /
  Lee Skinner.
Description: Gainesville : University Press of Florida, [2016] | Includes
  bibliographical references and index.
Identifiers: LCCN 2016015351 | ISBN 9780813062846 (cloth)
Subjects: LCSH: Rhetoric—Latin America—History. | Gender identity—Latin
  America. | Latin American literature—History and criticism. | Philosophy,
  Modern.
Classification: LCC PQ7081 .S59 2016 | DDC 860.9/3521—dc23
LC record available at https://lccn.loc.gov/2016015351

The University Press of Florida is the scholarly publishing agency for the State
University System of Florida, comprising Florida A&M University, Florida Atlantic
University, Florida Gulf Coast University, Florida International University, Florida
State University, New College of Florida, University of Central Florida, University of
Florida, University of North Florida, University of South Florida, and University of
West Florida.

University Press of Florida
15 Northwest 15th Street
Gainesville, FL 32611-2079
http://www.upf.com

For Phoebe and Natalie
Beloved daughters

Contents

Figures

Acknowledgments

Several institutions provided funding for this book at different stages. I am grateful to Claremont McKenna College for supporting my work with a sabbatical and the Gould Center for Humanistic Studies at Claremont McKenna for additional summer funding. The University of Kansas awarded me a Summer General Research Fund Grant, which allowed me to do necessary research, as well as a sabbatical, and the Hall Center for the Humanities Center at the University of Kansas funded additional leave.

A portion of chapter 3 previously appeared in "Constructions of Domesticity in Nineteenth-Century Spanish America" in *Hispanic Journal* 21.2 (Fall 2000): 409–20. Permission to reprint is gratefully acknowledged.

It has taken a long time for this project to come to fruition, and I am fortunate to have had many people offering me support along the way. Space doesn't allow me to name every one of the colleagues and friends who have been so helpful; please know that I'm deeply appreciative of all of you. I especially want to acknowledge the generous encouragement, helpful advice, intellectual engagement, and constructive feedback of Carolina Alzate, Danny Anderson, Christopher Conway, Juan Carlos González Espitia, Montserrat Ordóñez, Karen Stolley, and Vicky Unruh. The original idea for the book came to me when I asked Carlos Alonso a question. To this day it remains the only question I have seen him unable to answer immediately. This book is my effort to suggest an answer. For that, as for so much else, I am immensely grateful to him. My colleagues at the University of Kansas and at the Claremont Colleges have been invaluable supporters. I am also particularly thankful to Mary, Diana, Friederike, and Laura for helping me find the impetus I needed to finish this book and to stay balanced in the process.

Thank you.

1

Introduction

In 2014, Latin America boasted a record number of women presidents. Michelle Bachelet was elected to a second, nonconsecutive term in Chile, after her first stint in office from 2006 to 2010; Cristina Fernández de Kirchner of Argentina, first elected in 2007, won reelection in 2011; Brazilians selected Dilma Rousseff as president in 2011 as well; and Laura Chinchilla concluded her four-year term in Costa Rica. Journalists, pundits, and analysts described these elections as signaling progress not just for women in those countries but for the entire continent. Women's progress was tied to national progress and, implicitly, to an idea of modernity that has held sway in Latin America for over a hundred years.

In Chile, Michelle Bachelet's 2006 campaign deliberately made use of the "outsider" status that being a woman gave her, as well as of the stereotype of women as trustworthy, warm, and empathetic. Her communication strategy included the conscious decision not to be confrontational or aggressive, in marked contrast to her opponent, Silvio Piñera. What her campaign sought to use as strengths were turned against her as weaknesses when Piñera's strategists also tried to take advantage of gender stereotypes to represent their candidate as decisive and capable and Bachelet as sympathetic yet weak.[1] In the case of Fernández de Kirchner, Gabriela Azzoni, writing in *La Nación*, notes that the president makes use of a variety of discursive strategies based on gender and that it is her emotional connection with voters that wins her popularity. Fernández de Kirchner uses her status as former president Néstor Kirchner's widow to great effect, positioning herself as the traditional "humilde mujer sufriendo" or "humble, suffering woman"; she also has described herself as "la madre del país, la madre de todos los argentinos" (the mother of the country, the mother of all Argentines). Meanwhile, in *RPP Noticias* Nadine Heredia, the wife of Peruvian president Ollantay Humala and the head of the Partido Nacional, calls upon women to work with the government to improve the health and well-being of Peruvian children and praises women's constructive power, saying, "El poder de las mujeres en el Perú es un poder de hacer una diferencia. . . . Nunca excluyente, sino complementario" (Women's power in Peru is the power to make a difference. . . . Never exclusive, but rather complementary). Heredia is careful to note that women do not exclude others, implying that they do not threaten male privilege but rather seek to amplify and assist others. Such invocations of women's traditional roles as mothers and helpmeets to male partners, used to justify the women's movement into public life, politics, and activism, have deep roots in long-standing discourses about women and their connection to the nation. A vision of women's increasing participation in political life as a token of national progress in general also finds its origins in ideas that won popularity in much of Latin America in the nineteenth century and that were used by men and women alike to further their own political and social agendas for their countries. In what follows, I trace the ways that nineteenth-century intellectuals thought and wrote about gender, modernity, and the nation as they initiated debates and established discursive models that set the stage for future imaginings of engendered possibilities.

Attitudes toward gender and gendered norms served to condition responses to ideas about modernity and progress in nineteenth-century Spanish America. Looking at writings by both men and women, including novels, stories, poetry, essays, and magazine and newspaper articles, this book analyzes such efforts to create and respond to discourses about modernity. Throughout much of the nineteenth century in Spanish America, men and women took advantage of the rhetoric of modernity in order to attach their own, sometimes very different, agendas to those discourses about modernity. Indeed, it is precisely the rhetorical nature of modernity in Spanish America that, I argue, allowed nineteenth-century intellectuals to affix such differing, even contradictory, interpretations to it. Crucially, biological sex in and of itself does not directly correlate to a particular response to modernity; that is, it does not follow that men held conservative beliefs about modernity and women held progressive ones. Rather, men and women responded to modernity in great part based on their attitudes about gender. There were progressive male thinkers who wanted to further a liberalization of women's roles and tied that to the overarching narrative about national progress, just as there were conservative women who argued against women's participation in the public sphere.

This book makes several assumptions about the status of modernity and modernization in nineteenth-century Latin America. Briefly, those are that there is a meaningful distinction between the physical realities of modernization and the rhetoric connected to those realities; that modernization was and is a complex process that has taken place differently in South America than in the supposed model of Great Britain and the United States; that modernization processes vary throughout South America and that modernization occurs at different rates both within and among countries; that while the role of Great Britain and the United States as a model for the physical processes of modernization can be and is disputed, Latin American intellectuals were influenced to a greater or lesser degree by ideas about modernity stemming from those countries; and that there are similarities crossing national and regional boundaries in Latin America pertaining to the rhetoric of modernity, just as there are differences among and within countries.

There is, of course, a distinction to be made between the material conditions of modernization and the discursive practices stemming from and responding to those material conditions, or modernity, a distinction about which Carlos J. Alonso has written extensively. According to Alonso, the two master narratives of novelty and futurity were at play in the complex relationships between Europe and America; the metropolis advanced the image of America as novel and new because such an image furthered the Old World's conceptual mastery of the New World, while the concept of America as incarnating the future "posited a break in the absolute continuity" that Europe sought to establish (10). Identifying America as constantly "future" enabled the imaginative creation of multiple discursive versions of that future and created the conditions in which modernity existed as a rhetorical condition. Alonso has argued that beginning in the nineteenth century, the newly formed Spanish American nations embraced the rhetoric of modernity as a means of nation-building and differentiation from

Spain: "Hence, modernity became from the outset the cri de coeur for the Spanish American republics because the former's narrative repertoire dovetailed perfectly with the rhetorical demands of the cultural myth of futurity that had been forged to oppose the discourse of Spanish hegemony" (18). The rhetoric of modernity offered the economically and politically marginalized Spanish American countries the possibility of imagining themselves as important players on the global stage, equal to the other nations with which they hoped to ally themselves, or to which, at least, they aspired to liken themselves. By deploying the discourse of modernity, Latin American intellectuals hoped to force, persuade, coax, and imagine their countries into actually becoming modern. Alonso is chiefly concerned with demonstrating that the case of Spanish America is unique due to this discourse of futurity and that, while Spanish American intellectuals took advantage of these narratives of futurity and modernity, they also ran the risk of being figured as the objects of the very rhetoric that they wielded as subjects (25), a phenomenon which Alonso refers to consistently as a crisis with numerous discursive consequences. He explores the intellectual consequences of these understandings of modernity, subject position, and discursivity in canonical writers of the nineteenth and twentieth centuries. His thorough explication of the foundations of Latin American modernity as crucially rhetorical in nature undergirds much of my approach in this book. Nonetheless, despite Alonso's emphasis on the historical specificity of the Latin American situation, his analysis rarely places the texts he discusses within their specific regional and historical contexts. More notably still, Alonso does not address gender issues or, in general, take into account the ways in which members of groups that historically have not enjoyed the same privilege as elite, white men experience, think, and write about modernity, nationhood, and identity. Such topics form a vital component of my own thinking about nineteenth-century Latin Americans' understanding of their sociopolitical contexts and their consumption of and reaction to ideas about modernity and progress.

As Peter Osborne has written, there is a complex and meaningful "relation between the meaning of 'modernity' as a category of historical periodization and its meaning as a distinctive form or quality of social experience." What Osborne calls the "category of historical periodization" can also be productively thought of as the historical period during which the physical processes of modernization occur with sufficient momentum to cause lasting changes in their society. Modernization may be conceived of as "complete" in some places and as ongoing and contingent in others. The traditional model for thinking about the relationship between modernization and modernity is provided by the example of Great Britain and the United States, where widespread industrialization and its accompanying phenomena, the rise of a large middle class and the penetration of capital, are seen as the material conditions that led to the development of an ideology of modernity. As economic production and growth shifted from a predominantly agricultural base in the country to factories in cities, there was a corresponding massive shift of population from the rural environment to urban areas. With the concentration of populations in geographically compressed cities, and with the move away from rural areas where families and small villages were largely self-sufficient, cities became places where services were centralized, encouraging the growth of stores and restaurants, for example. The middle class expanded as commerce and trade opportunities developed, and the growing bourgeoisie's higher income and leisure time allowed for the consumption of material luxuries and the development of service industries. As the middle class gained more widespread access to education, there was a larger base of literate consumers than had existed previously, spurring the popularity of cultural products such as magazines, novels, and entertainment such as museums, galleries, opera, and theater. The rhetoric of modernity was thus closely associated with the accompanying physical phenomena of modernization. This is, at least, the narrative of modernization and modernity typically associated with the industrialized areas of Europe, Great Britain, and North America.

In Latin America, however, the rhetorical phenomenon of modernity arrived prior to the rise of the material conditions of modernization upon which that rhetoric depended. For a variety of reasons, industrialization in Latin America did not take place in the same ways or at the same time as it did in Western Europe, parts of the United States, and Great Britain. As Julio Ramos sums up succinctly:

> En Europa la modernización literaria, el proceso de *autonomización* del arte y la profesionalización de los escritores bien podían ser procesos sociales primarios, distintivos de aquellas sociedades en el

umbral del capitalismo avanzado. En América Latina, sin embargo, la modernización, en todos sus aspectos fue—y continúa siendo—un fenómeno muy desigual.

In Europe literary modernization, the process of *autonomization* of art, and the professionalization of writers could well be primary social processes, distinctive of those societies on the threshold of advanced capitalism. In Latin America, on the other hand, modernization, in all its aspects, was—and still is—a very unequal phenomenon. (11–12)

Modernization in Latin America occurred well after modernization in the countries that served as Latin America's models for both modernization *and* modernity, due in great part to factors stemming from the colonial period. During most of the colonial period, roughly 1500–1800, Spain imposed a trading monopoly on the colonies, which could only send exports to Spain and, furthermore, could only send commodities that did not compete with Spanish producers. The colonists produced raw goods rather than refined products, a pattern that would continue well into the twentieth century in much of the continent. Only beginning in 1759 under the Bourbon reforms were the colonies permitted to trade with other parts of Europe as well as with one another.

Although the Bourbon reforms resulted in economic gains for the colonies, those gains were halted by the resource-sapping, prolonged struggle for independence. While the newly independent nations anticipated being free from Spanish colonial economic control, the very creation of those nations imposed some barriers to free trade in the form of increased tariffs and protectionism that stymied the growth of the export economy and disincentivized local producers. Lack of capital, the collapse of the fiscal system, and new expenditures, such as re-creating infrastructure that had been destroyed during the war and paying pensions to veterans of those wars, were also immense disadvantages to sustained and steady economic growth. At the same time, the land-tenure system, which concentrated large tracts of land in the hands of a few landowners, persisted from the colonial period through the nineteenth century. After the abolition of slavery, debt peonage of indigenous and mestizo laborers continued but had little impact on the labor shortage from which the colonies and now the new nations suffered; a lack of willing workers also impeded economic development.[2]

José Joaquín Brunner has described the challenges to modernization thus:

> Mientras [la modernización] existe sólo en la cabeza de las élites [...] su advenimiento se mantiene latente, contrarrestada en su potenciali-dad por la hegemonía de la vida rural, la organización segmentada de las culturas, el predominio de la distinción aristocrática u oligárquica, el peso de la parroquia, [y] el analfabetismo extendido.

> While [modernization] exists only in the minds of the elite, its ar-rival is latent, halted in its potential by the hegemony of rural life, the segmentation of cultures, the dominance of aristocratic or oligarchic privileges, the weight of the Church, [and] widespread illiteracy. (51)

Some countries met these challenges with greater apparent success than others. For example, Chile achieved political stability relatively quickly after independence, overcoming or avoiding disputes over borders with its new neighbors that would have diverted attention away from other economic issues and managing to institute national fiscal policies that resulted in a steady flow of income in the form of taxes to the new government. Chile also benefited from the discovery of readily accessible deposits of silver and copper that did not require a large upfront investment in infrastructure. Mexico, on the other hand, was racked by political turmoil and fiscal cri-ses throughout much of the nineteenth century and, while possessing rich mines, lacked the capital investment needed to develop them.

To speak of the physical processes of modernization in Latin America is to run the risk of collapsing together a host of historical, chronological, and socioeconomic differences. It is beyond the scope of this project to engage in a historical analysis of the processes of modernization in each Latin American country. At the same time, it is not my intent to erase the very important differences among the new Latin American nations, and even within them as various regions experienced modernization at differ-ent times, but to examine some of the ways in which such variations in modernizing processes related to the deployment of discourses of moder-nity. Nor is it my intent to suggest that modernization in Latin America is delayed, incomplete, or lacking when compared with modernization in Great Britain or North America. Any comparison runs the risk of assuming an inequality, implicit or explicit, of worth; when the processes of modernization are perceived to be desirable, the fact that those processes appear in one country earlier than in another may convey an implicit value judgment. Similarly, framing the topic in terms that establish a chronology, however loose, may invoke discourses about the center versus the periphery that assume the center's superiority. I strive to avoid making those judgments and invoking those discourses; when I state that modernization takes place unevenly, I do not mean that countries or areas that achieved modernization earlier are superior to others, nor are their inhabitants superior to the inhabitants of places where modernization took place differently.[3]

Nonetheless, in the nineteenth century many Latin American intellectuals consciously looked to North America, Great Britain, and much of Western Europe, modeled their ideas about what their societies should do and how their inhabitants should act, and drew comparisons between Latin America and other areas, often to the detriment of their societies. This is the process by which discourses *about modernization*—that is, the discourses *of modernity*—circulated in much of Latin America. That process and the formation of and response to discourses about modernization as conditioned by attitudes toward gender form the focus of this investigation.

If modernization is the concrete set of material practices outlined above (industrialization, urbanization, the accumulation of capital, the rise of a substantial middle class), modernity is the set of discursive practices connected to modernization. Those discursive practices include an orientation toward the future and things and ideas perceived to be new rather than traditional; a focus on progress, often associated with science, rationality, and secular education; and a fascination with logical systems and the regularization of political, economic, and social policies. Vivian Schelling proffers a description of the various features that characterize societies typically referred to as modern, writing that in terms of the economy, "modern societies are seen as governed by instrumental rationality, defined by criteria of efficiency and productivity" (2), and have a "profane, rationalist culture [. . . and] a scientific world-view which claims privileged access to truth" (3).

In Sarah Radcliffe's formulation, modernity "defines itself in relation to the future, and invokes planning, projects, and regularization" (22). Modernity's associations with the future and with newness were attractive to Latin Americans who wanted to emphasize the break with the colonial Spanish past that the Wars of Independence had wrought. Moreover, as Alonso argues, the attachment to "the narrative of futurity" helps to explain why "the idea of recovering or returning to indigenous cultural ways [did not] play a significant role" in nation-building rhetoric after independence (15). Modernity's forceful projection of and toward the future has problematized discursive and material relations with the past, be it the pre-Encounter indigenous world or the colonial era.

Key features of modernity, according to Néstor García Canclini, include extending "the knowledge and possession of nature" as well as the "production, circulation, and consumption of goods" (12); these aspects are related to societal growth and the expansion of the urban sphere. Modernity also conveys strong associations with the process of secularization; over and over again, nineteenth-century liberal intellectuals decried the retrograde influence of the Catholic Church and sought to diminish that influence. Modernity's drive toward constant innovation and the importance placed on education and specialized knowledge as a means to "achieve rational and moral evolution" (García Canclini 12–13) led to increasing governmental intervention in education at all levels and to the production of knowledge systems that were divorced from religious influence.

Secularization meant a rift not only with the Catholic Church but also with indigenous religious-based traditions, and intellectuals in countries with significant surviving indigenous populations struggled with questions about the role that indigenous peoples and their history and culture were to play in the new nations. Many nineteenth-century Latin Americans emphasized the importance of rationality and logic and created a classification system in which all that was not rational, logical, or scientific was deemed negative, anti-modern, and retrograde, while everything categorized as rational and scientific was lauded and embraced. At the same time, writers and thinkers disputed the boundaries of those categories. Throughout the nineteenth century, discourses about modernity were never stable but rather were always in contention. While it is possible to establish some general parameters for what most people understood by the terms *modernidad* and *lo moderno* in the nineteenth century, those terms were in flux, allowing for a variety of definitions, categories, and ideas to be attached to them.

This process was magnified by the ways in which discourses of modernity were received and processed in Latin America. Agustín Martínez explains,

> La modernización social no respondió a una evolución interna y espontánea de la sociedad latinoamericana, sino primordialmente a un reclamo externo proveniente de las metrópolis europeas y norteamericanas.

> Social modernization did not respond to an innate, spontaneous evolution of Latin American society, but primordially to an external demand coming from the European and North American metropolis. (79)

At the same time, Martínez calls attention to the fact that

> señalar el origen externo de la modernización de la sociedad latinoamericana, no significa reducir este proceso a una mera recepción pasiva de los modelos externos por más que, en efecto, los comportamientos miméticos se hayan intensificado durante el período.

> signaling the external origin of the modernization of Latin American society does not signify reducing that process to a mere passive reception of external models, no matter how much, in effect, mimetic behaviors [of Latin Americans] may have intensified. (80)

Latin American thinkers were actively engaged in shaping a rhetoric of modernity rather than passively absorbing the modern ideas coming from Europe and North America. The discourses of modernity that began to emerge from Latin America were disconnected from the material context of modernization, but that does not mean that they were any less powerful than they were in the European or North American contexts. In short, as Alonso succinctly avers, "one does not have to *be* modern in order to appropriate discourses deemed 'modern'" (45–46). The processes by which male and female Latin American intellectuals appropriated, reproduced, and revised ideas about modernity and its relations to such topics as national consolidation, racial identities, and gender were continual, shifting, multivalent, sometimes contradictory, and often contentious. They were *processes* rather than *products*. What constituted "modernity" was always being called into question, and multiple interest groups participated in the discussions that sought to establish—or attack—viable definitions of modernity.

It is in these junctures, or disjunctures, the places where rhetoric and reality do not coincide and where people strive to shape rhetoric in order to shape their reality/ies, that my project inserts itself. This book puts into dialogue narratives by both male and female writers working throughout Spanish America in the second half of the nineteenth century and into the beginning of the twentieth in order to tease out some of the key differences and similarities. That is, while each country and, indeed, each region within each country experienced modernization and modernity differently, there were at times some striking similarities. Both the differences and the similarities provide valuable insights into how Latin Americans perceived and lived first the rhetorics of modernity and then the processes of modernization, as well as into the ways in which gender affected responses to and creations of discourses of modernity.

Pierre Bourdieu's work on the field of cultural production emphasizes understanding the "structural relations—invisible, or visible only though their effects—between social positions that are both occupied and manipulated by social agents which may be isolated individuals, groups, or institutions" (29) and defines the literary field as "a field of forces, but [...] also a field of struggles tending to transform or conserve this field of forces" (30). While elsewhere some of Bourdieu's statements about the struggles within the literary field seem to imply a binary vision, I extend his vision to understand nineteenth-century Spanish American cultural production as a series of moments, or spaces, in which intellectuals attempted to stake out political and ideological positions that were by necessity contingent on each other as well as on the discourses emanating from the European and North American metropolis. Moreover, while in the twentieth century it is possible to speak of a dominant ideology or discourse in the Latin American countries and of attempts to override that hegemony, the nineteenth-century field of cultural production is more open and less hierarchical, in the way that Bourdieu's opening statements assert. For instance, because national governments were often decentralized or unstable, in many countries the state as a dominant entity capable of producing and enforcing regulations and controls did not exist until well into the twentieth century, which allowed for the free circulation of multiple understandings of the role of government in public and private life. Instead of a hegemonic ideology against which oppressed discourses must struggle, usually in vain, nineteenth-century Spanish America functions as a "field of struggles"—of attempts to establish hegemony made by contesting equals or near-equals.

Male intellectuals tended to respond to the ideology of modernity in two distinct ways: either they embraced it, seeing modernization and its accompanying phenomena of industrialization, technological advances, and scientific progress as necessary for the economic and political development of their fledgling nations, or they critiqued it, viewing those same characteristics of modernization as dehumanizing and alienating practices. Thus members of the first group, for example, enthusiastically adapted Auguste Comte's positivism to the Latin American stage. Positivists in Latin America focused on the educational system, as we will see in greater detail in chapter 4, and sought to implement a pedagogical program that focused on the scientific and the practical and that was secular and controlled by the state rather than the Catholic Church.[4] Meanwhile, those who rejected the rhetoric of modernity as ultimately resulting in fragmentation and alienation sought to create a Latin American intellectual life outside of the modernizing milieu.[5]

My argument is that both those intellectuals who welcomed what they believed modernity represented and those who rejected it, in part or in whole, were able to do so precisely because modernity was predominantly a rhetorical phenomenon. Because the discursive practices of modernity entered Latin American society prior to the material conditions that would authorize its existence, writers deployed discourses of modernity in order to argue for material changes and used the arguments of modernity to advocate modernization. Writers put the rhetoric of modernity to work as they advanced their own modernizing agendas, frequently contending that such "women's issues" as access to higher education and participation in the political process were part and parcel of the progress and social advancement that true modernization entailed. Finally, because in Latin America modernization came after modernity, men and women writers alike shaped the rhetoric of modernity as a utopian projection of the national future rather than as an objective reflection of the present.

Especially later in the nineteenth century, numerous female writers tended to respond more positively to the rhetoric of modernity than did their male counterparts in large part because women had much more to gain, while many men saw modernity as a potential threat to their status. Industrialization and mechanization dismantled the aristocratic culture that sustained writers under a system of patronage. Earlier writers had often combined their writing with paid positions, typically in the government, and this phenomenon continued throughout the nineteenth and twentieth centuries. Ignacio Altamirano was a judge and diplomat; Alberto Blest Gana served in the Chilean diplomatic corps; and, most famously, Domingo Faustino Sarmiento was president of Argentina. Increasingly, however, venues appeared in which writers could publish their work for pay. José Martí, Manuel Gutiérrez Nájera, and Clorinda Matto de Turner, to name but a few, earned their living as writers and editors. Paradoxically, however, a system that allowed for the possibility of making one's living by the pen marginalized both those who were successful and those who were unsuccessful. Writers who failed to sell their work were now viewed as having failed in the market system, whereas earlier in the century authorial success had depended more on critical reception than on numbers of copies sold. Meanwhile, writers in the new economies who managed to make a living by publishing suffered from the implication that their art was nothing more than a commodity. It is no accident, as Cathy Jrade has pointed out, that one of *modernismo*'s guiding principles was that of art for art's sake, rather than art for commerce's sake. As writers had the chance to engage with the public sphere, one of the responses of some writers was to turn away and to re-envision reading and writing as private, not public, activities.

Yet few female writers, like Afro-Hispanic and indigenous writers, had been able to participate in the patronage system; early in the nineteenth century, women who wrote and participated in intellectual life had the luxury of doing so because they enjoyed financial support from their families. Modernity offered many women more acceptable options than it did some of their male counterparts. With increased access to education and a growth in venues for publication in the form of greater numbers of periodicals that catered to a female reading public, such writers saw the potential for circulating their works and gaining access to economic freedom. In some cases, indeed, women had no choice but to support themselves by writing, as the traditional support systems that should have taken care of them failed. Juana Manuela Gorriti ran a children's school and published prolifically after the collapse of her marriage to Manuel Isidoro Belzú in the late 1840s. Clorinda Matto de Turner, widowed and impoverished, likewise turned her writing into a source of income. Other women supplemented meager family income through their writing, which formed a socially acceptable means by which middle- and upper-class women could work for pay.

Such Latin American women took advantage of modernity's emphasis on progress to define the terms of that progress. Because modernity was primarily a rhetorical phenomenon, as I have stated, it was in certain crucial ways more malleable. Writers could deploy its rhetoric strategically, emphasizing the elements of modernity that suited their purposes. In the case of many female writers, this meant defining national progress as inclusive of women and the modern society as one that encouraged women's education and participation in the workforce. At the same time, discourses of modernity did not supplant other elements commonly seen in writing by women but rather augmented them. In this way, for example, writers often strategically deployed domestic ideology and the image of the angel in the home to argue for education for women. The very rhetoricity of modernity allows for the use of the trope of the domestic angel alongside discourse advocating progress for women. The separation of the public and private spheres with which the appearance of the household angel is linked is another rhetorical occurrence that has been associated with industrialization. Under industrialization, work that had traditionally been carried out in households or in small workshops attached to homes was shifted to factories, thus decisively severing industrial labor from household labor and the public from the private sphere. These conditions helped give rise to the enshrinement of the domestic angel. Yet again, however, when the rhetorical phenomenon of domestic ideology appears in the Latin American situation, it is detached from the material conditions that produced it elsewhere and is in this way available for use in what might in other contexts be considered contradictory ways, that is, alongside the other central idea taken from the discourse of modernity, the educational advancement of women as a necessary element of national progress.

This book focuses primarily on the period from 1850 to 1910 because narrative production in Spanish America grew exponentially in the second half of the nineteenth century, as did the publication of newspapers and journals, which allowed for the greater circulation of the discourses of modernity. As the nineteenth century wore on and as the material phenomena of modernization such as industrialization and urbanization increased, there was growing resistance to the ideologies associated with modernization. At the beginning of the twentieth century, the material conditions of modernization in Latin America, at least partially, began to reflect those of the imitated countries, and continuing my study through that time allows me to analyze reactions to the concrete effects of industrialization and urbanization in Spanish America.

Throughout this book the scope of analysis includes fictional narratives, journalistic essays and reporting, and poetry, as well as visual texts such as paintings, engravings, and photographs. Chapter 2 analyzes the representation and use of spaces typically codified as public and private in four novels, Jorge Isaacs's *María*, Clorinda Matto de Turner's *Aves sin nido*, Alberto Blest Gana's *Martín Rivas*, and Eligio Ancona's *La mestiza*.

Chapter 3 focuses on the ways in which writers deployed ideas about domesticity in nineteenth-century texts, with readings from periodicals such as *Semana de las Señoritas Mexicanas* (1850–52), *El Eco de Ambos Mundos: periódico literario dedicado a las señoritas mexicanas* (Mexico, 1873), and the general interest publication *Repertorio Salvadoreño* (1888–94), as well as articles from Colombia and Peru. Fictional works analyzed here include Juana Manuela Gorriti's short stories "El guante negro" and "La hija del mazorquero" (Peru/Argentina, 1865) and the introduction to her 1892 cookbook, *Cocina ecléctica*. I offer a reading of the Mexican author Ignacio Altamirano's *El Zarco* (written in the mid-1880s but not published until 1901, eight years after Altamirano's death), using the context provided by the Mexican journals mentioned above. I also discuss the interrelated stories in *El corazón de la mujer* (1869), by the Colombian writer Soledad Acosta de Samper, and her novels *Laura*, which appeared as a serial in the pages of *El Bien Público* in 1870, and *Una holandesa en América*, serialized in *La Ley* in 1876.

In chapter 4, I explore attitudes toward education for women in Miguel Riofrío's novel *La emancipada* (Ecuador, 1863), the women's magazines *La Camelia* (Argentina, 1852) and *Violetas del Anáhuac* (Mexico, 1887–89), and the general interest literary journal *El Museo Literario* (Colombia, 1871). I go on to discuss talks given by men and women on education at Juana Manuela Gorriti's literary salons in Lima in 1876 and 1877, which were reprinted in Peruvian newspapers of the day and in a collected volume of the salon's selected proceedings in Buenos Aires in 1892, and an important essay on women's education by the Mexican author Laureana Wright de Kleinhans (1891).

Chapter 5 moves forward chronologically and thematically by examining the representations of technology, industrialization, and the increasing access of women to the job market; the majority of the texts to be analyzed here will be from the period 1880 to 1910. I examine representations of modern forms of transportation in Matto de Turner's *Aves sin nido*, a poem by the Mexican writer Rosa Navarrio (1888), writings by Manuel Gutiérrez Nájera, and articles in *La Ilustración Guatemalteca* (1896–97). I continue with an analysis of the ways in which certain technologies facilitated women's access to new forms of work, referencing the Chilean magazines *Zig-Zag* and *Familia* in particular. To trace the shift as writers continued to press for increased female involvement in the modernizing project, I discuss Juana Manuela Gorriti's *Oasis en la vida* (1888) and César Duáyen's *Mecha Iturbe* (Argentina, 1906). This chapter concludes with a novel that epitomizes growing anxiety about the effects of modernization in changing gender roles, Federico Gamboa's *Santa* (Mexico, 1903). This chapter argues that as the physical conditions of modernization spread in Spanish America, intellectuals saw the realization of both their hopes and their fears about the consequences of modernization and continued to project those hopes and fears specifically onto the status of women. In all chapters the texts to be analyzed include novels, essays, and journalistic publications, placed into their sociocultural contexts. The aim is to give a complete picture of the ways in which writers thought about gender roles, modernization, and national identity.

To illustrate some of the varied responses to ideas about modernity and gender, I turn now to several texts and images that represent some points on the spectrum of discourses about nation, identity, femininity, and masculinity. In 1830, Petrona Rosende de Sierra published *La Aljaba* in Buenos Aires, one of the first Latin American periodicals explicitly dedicated to women and published by a woman. An early issue contained a prospectus that carefully announced that the magazine's intentions "no llevan más objeto que formar hijas obedientes, madres respetables y dignas esposas" (have as their sole purpose that of forming obedient daughters, respectable matrons, and worthy wives; 1). Rosende de Sierra emphasizes women's roles within the family, as dependents of and connected to men; indeed, women were defined legally via their relationship to men, as well as being economically dependent on them.[6] Rosende de Sierra's affirmation of women as daughters, mothers, and wives underscored her support of that system. Throughout the three-month run of the periodical, she repeated the idea that women's role in the nation was that of a moral arbiter who exercised her influence from within the domestic sphere. In the November 19, 1830, issue she wrote that women

> son columnas de los estados cuando, además de desempeñar debidamente los principales fines para que fueron creadas, cooperan, dentro de esa misma esfera, con sus virtudes morales y religiosas, a la conservación, honor, y crédito de ellas.

> are pillars of their nations when, besides carrying out the principal ends for which they were created, they cooperate, within that same sphere, with moral and religious virtues, to the conservation, honor, and credit of those same virtues. (1)

While she also affirmed women's right to a secular, advanced education, Rosende de Sierra situated that argument in a context that presented women as supporting a more important project directed by men. Women do not initiate activity in the public sphere; rather, as she tells her readers in "Deber de las damas argentinas con respecto a la sagrada causa y engrandecimiento de su patria" (Duty of the Argentine ladies with respect to the sacred cause and ennobling of their nation; December 28, 1830), in order to resolve the civil conflict racking the new nation, women need to "manifestar lo que podeis sobre el corazón de los hombres" (demonstrate all that you can to the hearts of men; 1–2). Women have a role in the issues affecting their country, but that role should be played in the private sphere. Women's work is not cerebral but emotional and sentimental. She glosses this idea a few more times in the same issue when she avers,

> El influjo de las mujeres es mayor de lo que algunos lo reputan: una mujer puede formar con su conducta doméstica la desgracia eterna de generaciones enteras; y por el contrario con la misma, fundada en virtud, hará la dicha de otras tantas.

> The influence of women is greater than some would credit: a woman can precipitate with her domestic conduct the eternal disgrace of entire generations; and on the contrary, with that same conduct, now grounded in virtue, she can create good fortune for just as many others. (3)

Women's power is limited to their familial roles and identities as adjuncts to their fathers, husbands, and children and to their behavior in the domestic realm. In these ways, while Rosende de Sierra works to affirm women's importance to their nation, she does not advocate for women's active participation in political, economic, or educational processes outside the home. Understandably, given that she was writing at a time when the boundaries of the Southern Cone countries were still very much in question, and when Argentina's government was fractured and fragmented, her emphasis falls on the ways in which women can support the stability of their fragile new country and aid it on its progress toward modernity. Her careful and heavily mediated approach constitutes an important and telling early intervention in the cultural conversations about gendered identities and the involvement and roles of men and women alike in the national and social issues that became ever more urgent throughout the nineteenth century and into the twentieth.

Over the course of the century, Latin American intellectuals were increasingly preoccupied with the question of gender roles and appropriate behaviors and beliefs for both men and women. As national identities continued to be interrogated, men and women writers often appealed to the concept of women as mothers of the nation who needed to have access to a greater understanding of political and social functions in order to adequately raise their countries' next generation of citizens. Intellectuals also called into question the categories of the private and the public spheres with greater frequency, and numerous works show the blurring of the boundaries between those literal and metaphorical spaces as well as increasingly desperate attempts to limit gendered activities to one space or the other. Men and women worked to construct particular notions of the domestic realm, both empowering and disempowering women as, like Rosende de Sierra, they presented women as exemplars of virtue and guardians of the near-sacred space of the home, a refuge from the vice-ridden public sphere. In this vision women held sway as long as they did not attempt a real or imagined escape from the home. Yet as the century progressed, writers openly presented other possibilities for women, mirroring and predicting the potential for change in their material conditions. Women could leave the home without censure to work as independent wage earners with increased ease of access to the labor market. Lower-class women had always had to do so, of course, but now middle-class women were empowered to seek paid employment as well. The tensions related to these changes, and other cultural phenomena such as the increased influence of the marketplace on writers, as mentioned previously, continued to play out in the pages of periodicals, novels, and stories.

Manuel Gutiérrez Nájera's story "En el Hipódromo" offers a compelling instance of gendered responses to modernity and modernization. In his account, the Hippodrome is a space specifically visited by and inhabited by women as well as men, but used differently according to gender. Men and women occupy the space of the Hippodrome and understand its spectacles differently: "Yo sé de muchas damas que han reñido con sus novios, porque éstos, en vez de verlas preferentemente y admirarlas, fijaban su atención en los ardides de los jockeys, y en la traza de los caballos" (I know of many ladies who have quarreled with their suitors, because the men, instead of preferring and admiring them, paid attention to strategies of the jockeys, and the appearance of the horses; 17). On the one hand, the women believe that they themselves are the spectacle; from the female point of view, the men misread the spectacle and fail to understand what is on display. The "novios," on the other hand, argue that it is the women who misunderstand the space. Gutiérrez Nájera points to the contingent and shifting nature of this modern place—modern because it offers secular entertainment for a mixed group of men and women, members of the newly emerging middle class with the money and leisure time necessary to partake in such events. Gender conditions the ways in which the space's users understand and employ its functions; yet at the same time, women use the space in the same way as the men do. "[L]as damas [. . .] apuestan como nosotros apostamos y emplean en su conversación los agrios vocablos del idioma hípico, erizado de puntas y consonantes agudísimas" (The ladies [. . .] bet as we bet and employ in their conversation the bitter words of the hippic language, spiked with points and extraordinarily sharp consonants; 17). Lest the reader think this makes them unfeminine, the narrator then explains that men and women bet with each other for tokens, the men offering new gloves or perfume in exchange for a flower or hairband. Because the items offered by the men are more costly, the unequal exchange emphasizes their capitalist value and places men above women in a hierarchy based on economic power; because the items offered by the women are more personal, the women's symbolic place in the emotional realm is underscored. "En el Hipódromo" cogently offers an example of the complex reactions that the confluence of modernity and gender aroused.

The story is also about the threat posed by women and the dangers of sex and eroticism; as the narrator informs us, "todo amor da la muerte" (all love brings death; 17). The horse and the woman are equated semantically through an interjection, "—¡oh caballo!—"; "—¡oh mujer!—" (oh, horse! oh, woman! 17), and by being addressed in the informal second person by the narrator. Like the horse, whose breakneck pace can endanger its rider, the woman addressed by the narrator can be fatal to the man who adores her. This comparison animalizes women and emphasizes once more their inferiority in the intellectual realm; while they may dominate in the world of emotions, sentiment, seduction, and carnal pleasures, men control the space of logic, the exchange of goods and money, and literacy. It is a male narrator, after all, who conveys his version of the woman's feelings and life.

Gutiérrez Nájera's text encapsulates the mixed emotions of excitement and trepidation with which modernity and its associated phenomena were received. In the Hippodrome women have at least some measure of autonomy and control, but when they overstep the boundaries created and imposed by men, women are also perceived by their male counterparts as threatening. The problem that Gutiérrez Nájera's readers faced, however, especially his female readers, was that those boundaries were constantly in flux. Due to the instability of the preconditions determining functions such as women's entry into the public sphere of commerce, capitalism, and the open display and exchange of erotic properties, women regularly ran the risk of violating those boundaries even when they did not wish or intend to do so. "En el Hipódromo" serves as a telling commentary on the ambivalent reactions of some intellectuals, even those closely associated with discourses of modernity, to the possible reconfiguration of the public sphere to allow for active female participation.

Elsewhere, the journal *Lectura y Arte*, published in Medellín, Colombia, from 1903 to 1906, engaged its male writers and illustrators explicitly with the modernizing project and sometimes used portrayals of women's degradation to argue for modernization.[7] In the second issue (August 1903), Antonio José Montoya published a supposedly true story in which the male narrator, traveling through rural Colombia, stumbles across, or into, a scene in which a man is dragging a woman along the ground. The woman has been accused of fornication, although her only "crime" is that of resisting the advances of the mayor, and she is being taken to the local jail, a reaction that the narrator considers backward almost beyond belief. As he says, "No me explico que en un pueblo educado bajo el régimen republicano y formado de hombres valerosos y altivos dejen maltratar a un ser débil e inocente" (I do not understand how, among people educated under a republican regime and composed of brave, proud men, a weak and innocent being could be mistreated; 51). Here, the republican project is masculine; women, defined as weak and innocent, cannot participate actively in it. Their political role and legal status have not changed, at least in Montoya's approving rendering, since the days of independence. He advocates not for female emancipation but for more enlightened treatment of a group of people whom he defines as weak and incompetent. The accompanying illustration to the story shows the woman being pulled, literally manhandled. Worse, however, the next morning the narrator learns that the woman was killed in jail by corrupt guards. As a sympathetic local tells him, "Señor forastero: se ha cometido esta noche el mayor atentado contra el derecho humano que han visto los siglos" (Mr. Stranger: the worst attack against human rights seen in centuries has been committed this evening; 51).

The treatment suffered by the woman in this isolated village is clearly associated with a barbarous past, not with the progressive present the narrator is used to in the urbanized areas of Colombia. Montoya uses the story to critique a political system in which power accretes to a strong man, or *caudillo*, who then uses that power and his personal charisma to force others to do his bidding and to perpetuate his control. Moreover, by linking the murder of the woman to the issue of human rights, not just women's rights, Montoya connects the advancement of women, limited though it may be due to his own inability to imagine women as political citizens, with that of the nation—and their lack of progress with the nation's inability to move forward into the twentieth century. His commentary is all the more pointed for appearing in a journal published in a provincial city rather than in the political and cultural capital of Bogotá.

Lectura y Arte also reflected on its own function as a harbinger or stimulus of the progress the editors hoped to support in their country. Two cover illustrations that deal with reading as a collective or shared activity also comment on the relationship between the activity of reading and gender. On the cover of the April 1905 issue, a man and a woman read a journal, probably *Lectura y Arte* itself (fig. 1). The woman is seated at a table, the man standing on the other side of the table, leaning over. The woman's body is turned toward the viewer, inviting the viewer into the scene to share the pleasure of reading; her pose is much more open and inviting than that of the man, whose arms are crossed on the table behind which much of his body is hidden. In this way the magazine uses the female body to seduce the viewer into the scene of reading. In addition, the couple seems to be in the private space of the home; both are hatless, and the vase of flowers on the floor indicates a domestic decoration. In the second image, from February 1906, two men similarly share the experience of reading, but this time in a public space, as one leans on the shoulder of the other to look at the journal that the man on the left is holding (fig. 2). In this second image, both men have their backs turned to the viewer; seduction (of the viewer, at

Figure 1. Cover to *Lectura y Arte*, Medellín, Colombia, nos. 9–10 (April 1905)

Figure 2. Cover to *Lectura y Arte*, Medellín, Colombia, no. 12 (February 1906)

least) is not an issue. Even the man who is slightly turned toward the viewer is closed off to the viewer's gaze by having his arm resting on the other man's shoulder. Male homosociality, to use Eve Kosofsky Sedgwick's term, excludes those who could not imagine themselves in the easy intimacy of this scene—the female readers of the journal, I would suggest. The contrast between the two images also demonstrates that women's reading was mediated through men, while men did not depend upon women's presence for social interactions or for access to literate culture.

The analysis of these images, which appeared in a magazine written and published by men but with a significant female readership (as indicated by the advertisements in the journal and by the fashion column), places readers and writers in the nineteenth century in yet another cultural context—to show, in Pierre Bourdieu's term, another one of the forces acting in the cultural field. In *Lectura y Arte*, at least, women did not make it into the public sphere; the magazine presents its female readers in their traditional roles as consumers of fashion and beauty products and as seductive, decorative objects in the private space of the home. Nonetheless, the magazine's depiction of a woman engaged in accessing a cultural product—most likely the very magazine whose cover the image graced—as well as the previous, negative depiction of a woman murdered by barbarism, like Gutiérrez Nájera's work, demonstrates that male intellectuals, like their female counterparts, clearly saw and made use of the connection between women and modernity to further their own cultural and political agendas. The impact on the cultural field of the insistence on the link between women and modernity was widespread, and it is plain that the question of women and their relation to national progress and the modernizing project was an important one, albeit one whose apparent contradictions continued to surface in many venues.

2

Public Space/Private Discourse

Discourses about public and private spaces and the separation of masculine and feminine activities circulated throughout nineteenth-century Spanish America. In fictional and nonfictional texts alike, writers addressed questions about male and female roles, the nature of domesticity, codes of conduct in the private and public spheres, and the connection between morality, gender, and the family. Recently work by cultural geographers has called attention to the specificity of place and its relationship to gender.[1] As Doreen Massey writes,

> From the symbolic meaning of spaces/places and the clearly gendered messages which they transmit, to straightforward exclusion by violence, spaces and places are not only themselves gendered but, in their being so, they both reflect and affect the ways in which gender is constructed and understood. The limitation of women's mobility, in terms of both identity and space, has been in some cultural contexts a crucial means of subordination. Moreover the two things—the limitation on mobility in space, the attempted consignment/confinement to particular places on the one hand, and the limitation on identity on the other, have been crucially related [...].
>
> One of the most evident aspects of this joint control of spatiality and identity has been in the West related to the culturally specific distinction between public and private. The attempt to confine women to the domestic sphere was both a specifically spatial control and, through that, a social control on identity. (188)

The emphasis on the physicality of what has often been envisioned in rather more abstract terms as the public and private spheres illuminates the textual depictions of the spaces in which activities coded as "public" or "private" occur. Such representations may be read as enactments, enforcements, or subversions of accepted spatial practices. Specifically, I propose that in nineteenth-century Spanish America, the notions of public and private, while mapped onto exterior and interior spaces, respectively—the street and public institutions such as Congress, city hall, churches, and courts vs. the home in general and living rooms, kitchens, and bedrooms in particular—are, in fact, slippery and uncontainable within those supposedly set parameters. The abstract concepts of public and private may be plotted onto exterior and interior, but the permeability of the barriers between exterior and interior means that private and public become enmeshed in ways represented as both positive and negative, sometimes simultaneously. Men may be free to roam outside, but private activities seep into that exterior landscape; women may be confined to the home (if indeed they are), but they bring public activities into it. Even the notion that one sex is empowered to occupy one type of space while the other is limited to a different type of space unravels in numerous texts; women occupy outside spaces and traverse streets and landscapes and men mark out locations within homes where they transact business and tend to personal affairs. In novels, journalistic essays, and other representations of the (en)gendering of space, authors explore, test, and question the ways in which social norms are mapped onto physical and psychic spaces. As these representations enforce or subvert particular behavioral codes, they also draw attention to the constructed nature of the ways in which human beings possess and use the spaces around them.

The division between the private and the public spheres has traditionally been seen as a product of the Industrial Revolution, as discussed in chapter 1. Many historians have viewed the Industrial Revolution in Great Britain, Europe, and North America as "the cause of the rift between public and private, since men's work took them outside the home and left middle-class women alone, stranded with housework and child-rearing duties, and eventually, later in the [nineteenth] century, with increasingly more leisure time" (Elbert 9). In Great Britain and Europe, one of the concrete results of the Industrial Revolution was a stricter delineation between work and home spaces. In preindustrial economies based predominantly on agriculture, families lived on the land where they labored. The small class of artisans and craftspeople also worked from their homes, and entire families were involved in the productive work of the home space. The Industrial Revolution drew workers away from the countryside into cities, centralized work in factories, and ended much artisanal, home-based production. While many lower-class women participated in this movement, public discourse often viewed these women and their departure for the factories as a moral and social problem. By leaving the home and abandoning traditional feminine pursuits, these women threatened family stability. Numerous politicians, religious leaders, and other social arbiters attempted to counteract this perceived problem by exploiting the growing division between home and work and assigning gender-dependent meanings to those spaces: women were associated with the home and family work, while the workplace was figured as masculine. As Griselda Pollock succinctly summarizes, "The public sphere, defined as the world of productive labour, political decision, government, education, the law, and public service, increasingly became exclusive to men. The private sphere was the world [of] home, wives, children, and servants" (94–95).

As we saw in the first chapter, the connection between physical conditions and ideological phenomena is not always exact. Indeed, there is hardly ever the perfect correlation supposed in such assumptions, even in Great Britain and North America, which experienced the most thorough effects of industrialization, and similarly the development of social attitudes about men's and women's respective places should not be attributed solely to the Industrial Revolution. Assigning gendered norms to the private and public spheres had gone on for centuries if not millennia, but with the advent of industrialization, the connection between gender and space acquired another layer of meaning and social force.

In Spanish America, the processes of modernization occurred very differently than in Europe and North America. Industrialization and its accompanying phenomena of mass migration to cities, the redistribution of productive work from home-based workshops to large-scale factories, and the rise of a middle class with sufficient money and free time to pursue leisure activities did not take place at the same time or in the same way as in Europe and North America. Yet the rhetoric of separate spheres appears consistently in Spanish American fiction and essays of the nineteenth century, as it did in European and North American writings. These writings by Spanish Americans reveal that similar, if not identical, ideas about the proper domains of men and women, the sanctity of the home, and the dangers posed by—and to—women who left their homes prevailed in discourse about the public and private spheres as they did in the European context. These constructions of the separation of spheres and the appropriate roles for men and women did not arrive in a vacuum but mapped onto already existing social norms governing gender roles in Spanish America. Colonial Spanish American society's emphasis on the honor code and female chastity privileged the enclosure of women in the private world, although "private" and "public" were understood differently before the nineteenth century. Ann Twinam, writing of colonial New Spain, notes that the private sphere in the Spanish colonies consisted of the family, both nuclear and extended, close friends, and family servants, while the public sphere was everyone else (257). Women were closely associated with the family and the space of the home, but their status as bearers of family honor meant that they also had public roles, since they were responsible for maintaining and imparting family status and legitimacy.

> Para las elites, estas distinciones conscientes entre lo privado y lo público estaban integradas en las negociaciones relativas al honor, un complejo y cambiante concepto que incluía la exclusividad de la elite, la *limpieza de sangre*, y la descendencia legítima de muchas generaciones de ancestros legítimos. Las mujeres de la elite poseían personalidades y posiciones públicas en la esfera civil precisamente porque tenían un honor que mantener y transmitir a la siguiente generación.

> For the elites, these conscious distinctions between private and public were embedded in negotiations having to do with honor, a complex and changing concept that included the exclusivity of the elite, the "cleanness of blood," and the legitimate descent from many generations of legitimate ancestors. Elite women possessed public personas and positions in the civil sphere precisely because they had honor to maintain and transmit to the next generation. (262)

The fact that such precepts about women's subordination to family and home dominated in the colonial era meant that the rhetoric of the separation of spheres associated with the modernizing effects of the Industrial

Revolution mapped conveniently, if not exactly, onto preexisting gender norms despite arriving in a continent that would not fully experience the Industrial Revolution until the twentieth century.

This chapter focuses on four novels to elucidate some of the ideas in circulation in mid-nineteenth-century Latin America about gender roles and their connection to the private and public realms. I argue that the representations of the ways in which gender determines the occupation and use of various types of physical space in these works demonstrate that the collisions between the modern and the premodern, public and private, were conditioned by and in turn conditioned contemporary understandings and projected imaginings of gendered identities and gender roles. The novels in question are dispersed over a geographical range in more ways than one: Jorge Isaacs's *María* (Colombia, 1867) takes place in the rural environment of the Valle de la Cauca. In Clorinda Matto de Turner's *Aves sin nido* (Peru, 1887), the fictional village of Kíllac forms the setting for the novel's plot of clerical abuse, and Alberto Blest Gana's *Martín Rivas* (Chile, 1862) is an eminently, and preeminently, urban text.[2] While those novels fall within the current canon of Latin American nineteenth-century literature, Eligio Ancona's *La mestiza* (Mexico, 1861), set on the outskirts of Mérida, Yucatán, is a lesser-known text.[3] Yet in all four novels the uses of space are continually negotiated and shifting; the understanding, creation, and representation of public and private spaces are contingent upon those who use them rather than objective, externally determined forces. In Massey's words, places "are not so much bounded areas as open and porous networks of social relations" (130). Places accumulate meaning according to the uses to which they are put, and their inhabitants both give and acquire meaning and identity through their relationship to those places.

The configuration and use of spaces in Isaacs's *María* on the surface seem to follow gendered norms, in which women occupy the interior and engage in domestic tasks while men carry out public duties outside the home. However, throughout the novel, supposedly standard spatial configurations are subverted and undermined.[4] The space of the house is repeatedly the *locus* of transactions that by rights belong to the public sphere, and private business and emotions are displayed outside the home. In addition to the slippages between the public and the private realms, nature and civilization, or the wild and the constructed realms, also suffer from a

problematic collapse of barriers. Definitions and limits that should separate those two areas and define their domains are too easily crossed and
even ignored. In these ways the porosity of spheres in *María* is contingent
upon the permeability of nature and the characters' interactions with nature. One of the novel's deep contradictions has to do with the way that
Isaacs consciously employs the modernizing rhetoric of the separation of
spheres and the construct of the domestic angel of the house at the same
time as he sets the novel up as an idyllic evocation of the preindustrial state
described by many theorists as the "before" of the public/private divide.
Both strategies allow him to place the house itself as the epicenter of a
vanished happiness, yet the disconnect between them reveals fissures in the
construction of gendered social norms and disrupts what is intended to be
an unproblematic description of a vanished, and perfect, past.

The novel famously begins with a scene of (male) departure from the
home: "Era yo niño aún cuando me alejaron de la casa paterna" (I was still a
boy when they removed me from my paternal home; 5). The opening scene
figures the family home not only as a paradise from which Efraín is exiled
but also as a bastion of patriarchal power (la casa paterna). Throughout the
novel, however, Isaacs also constructs the space of the house as essentially
female. In the first scene the house almost literally encloses María: "María
estaba bajo las enredaderas que adornaban las ventanas del aposento de mi
madre" (María was under the falling vines that adorned the windows of my
mother's bedchamber; 5). The vines drape over and around María, attaching her figuratively to the house and specifically to the mother's space. This
description, too, is an immediate prefiguration of the ways in which the
novel blurs the nature/culture divide and the premodern and modernizing
discourses that it manipulates. The vines (nature) come from the house
(culture) and are a part of it; María is connected to the house, which at
first is characterized as an element of patriarchal power (premodern), but
then more specifically as a bastion of femininity and ideal motherhood, a
concept related to the discourses of modernity.

María's connection to maternal space is repeated throughout the novel,
with frequent references to her use of the mother's sewing room (8, 15, 58,
87). Sewing, as Bonnie Frederick points out, occupied hours each day in
the lives of women in the nineteenth century; until late in the century it
was one of the few socially acceptable means by which women could earn

a wage, but until the sewing machine was invented and became affordable, the literally laborious task of hand-sewing a family's clothes and linens was a hugely time-intensive job. Sewing also acquired a social significance above and beyond the investment of time and labor it required: "Sewing in all its myriad manifestations was far more than simple necessity; it became a resonant symbol of traditional roles for women and the cult of ultradomesticity" (67–68). The repeated comments about María's involvement in sewing, by herself or in the company of other women, invoke this image of conventional gender-normed activity and insert María in the domestic economy. Isaacs insistently connects his heroine to the house-based, female-associated work of sewing.

The constant association of María in particular with the domestic space of the Cauca house means that Efraín's longing for his home when he travels first to Bogotá and then to London is a longing for María. The two desires are inseparable. As Massey comments on domestic space generally,

> the construction of "home" as a woman's place has [. . .] carried through into those views of place itself as a source of stability, reliability, and authenticity. Such views of place, which reverberate with nostalgia for something lost, are coded female. Home is where the heart is (if you happen to have the spatial mobility to have left) and where the woman (mother, lover-to-whom-you-will-one-day-return) is also. (189)

The home in Cauca, seen and remembered through the overlay of Efraín's nostalgia, is edenic because it contains—or contained—the intact family, to which Efraín attempts and fails to return, and because it both metaphorically and literally contains María herself. On the one hand, the hacienda has strong paternal associations; it is, as we shall see, the space from which Efraín's father conducts his business, and it is the collapse of the father's finances that leads to the family's loss of this land and home.[5] On the other hand, it is inhabited and made habitable, and hospitable, by the female members of the family. House space thus takes on an almost overwhelming significance, as it is overdetermined as both male and female, paternal and maternal, parental and amorous.

The competing interests of gendered and family roles intersect in the house, the very place that, according to the rhetoric of modernity, should constitute a carefully delineated area limited to, and limiting, certain feminine activities. Yet in *María*, the convergence of masculine and feminine roles in all capacities makes the space of the house a place where gender meanings proliferate and gender norms are both reinforced and undermined.

One of the crucial contradictions related to and taking place in the house that is brought to light in the novel is the blurring between nature and culture, which continues to reinforce house space as the holder of rapidly multiplying signifiers. Natural elements frequently invade or are voluntarily brought into the cultivated, controlled space of the house, while the rural setting of the novel means that the landscape itself is predominantly natural, holding only the occasional building, positioned so far from another house that visiting one's neighbor is a daylong event.[6] This means that what would seem to be the logical division between public (outside) and private (inside) space that Isaacs attempts to enact in his text in order to support the separation of gender roles completely collapses. In *María*'s rural environment there are no streets, simply a permeable "outside" that is defined only in opposition to the enclosed space of the home. Yet the novel creates a rhetorical division between the public and the private and insistently works to associate those spheres with stringently defined gender roles.[7]

Isaacs appears to maintain this divide through representations of the varying levels of access of male and female characters to the outdoors, the literally out-of-doors, unconfined area that is everything not-house. When Efraín returns after six years in Bogotá, María and other female family members venture only as far as the patio to greet him. The patio is a liminal space between the house and the outdoors, a construct that extends the footprint of the house out beyond the roof and walls of the house. Yet it is also so much a part of the outdoors that Efraín can ride his horse onto it. "Las herraduras de mi caballo chispearon sobre el empedrado del patio. Oí un grito indefinible, era la voz de mi madre" (My horse's shod feet struck sparks on the stones of the patio. I heard an indefinable shriek; it was my mother's voice; 6). Outside the home, Efraín's mother does not produce coherent speech, but rather emits an incomprehensible noise similar to that of the striking of the horse's hooves on the stone patio, thereby underscoring her association with natural phenomena. The mother has no access to language and the symbolic higher order; she can express herself only through unformed sounds. To put it in Julia Kristeva's term, the mother is abject, horrifyingly other to the rational realm, which draws the speaking subject "toward the place where meaning collapses" (*The Powers of Horror*). While the domestic(ated) women venture outside into nature, María herself brings natural elements into domestic, cultivated space by placing flowers in Efraín's bedroom. Notably, she obtains these flowers not from the wilderness but from the family garden, another liminal space that combines wild and cultivated aspects; much like María herself, it is nature supposedly under human control.

Such associations between women and nature are by no means unique to Isaacs. Several years later, C. Domínguez S. wrote of the ideal woman in the pages of the Colombian journal *Museo Literario*:

> Ella es la delicia del hogar paterno: tímida como una alondra, pura como un querube, tierna y amante como una virgen. [. . .] Convierte su casita blanca en un pequeño edén, donde las hermosas flores brindan su grato perfume y ostentan sus alegres colores, y donde las aves canoras levantan sus melodiosos trinos que unidos a su voz hechicera forman un concierto celestial . . . ¡y todo, todo para agradar al ser que idolatra su alma!

> She is the delight of the paternal home: timid as a lark, pure as a cherub, tender and loving as a virgin. [. . .] She turns her little white house into a small Eden, where beautiful flowers spread their pleasing perfume and display their happy colors, and where songbirds share their melodious trills which, joined with her bewitching voice, form a heavenly choir . . . and all, all to please the being whom her soul adores! (185)

Like Isaacs, Domínguez inscribes a representation of the ideal woman as associated with nature and using those natural associations for the benefit of the private space of the home and the family members who occupy such space. His perfect woman tends a visually pleasing garden and sings like, and with, birds as she carries out her duties as resident angel of the house, actions which embed her in nature and embed the natural in the constructed space that is the house. Furthermore, the house is character-ized as "paternal" in the same way that the father in *María* dominates the physical and metaphorical spaces of the novel. Characterizations of the home under patriarchal control continue to subordinate women to mascu-line power. Isaacs's representations of María's flower arranging and decora-tive habits invoke and enforce the gender norms that dictated that upper-class women should exist to serve the men around them. That would seem, at least, to be the explicit purpose of the associations with and references to women as purveyors of beauty. Yet those characterizations unravel the tidy web of associations that subordinate women/nature/domesticity to men/civilization/commerce, because of the previously mentioned overde-termination of the house as the place that ought to contain a plethora of contradictory interpretations.

In this way, in the novel "wild" and "civilized" spaces overlap and cross-contaminate each other, breaching the supposed impermeability of the spheres of influence. María wears the flowers that Efraín collects during his walks in the mountains, making these wild elements serve her as adorn-ments. Natural elements penetrate Efraín's room as branches of the rose-bush outside the house poke in through his open window (7). Most strik-ingly, nature literally invades the family home when a deer runs into the house: "El animal entró al corredor desatentado y tembloroso, y se acostó casi ahogado debajo de uno de los sofás [. . .]. Emma y María se aproxi-maron tímidamente a tocar el venadito, suplicando que no lo matásemos" (The animal entered the hallway impetuous and trembling, and lay down, almost suffocated, under one of the sofas. . . . Emma and María timidly went to touch the fawn, begging us not to kill it; 56–57). What should have been a primal hunting scene in which men show their domination of nature by slaughtering the deer turns into a half-comic, half-pathetic interlude in which the women and children plead for the fawn's life as it thrashes around the interior of the house. The fawn becomes a pet or even another child and, crucially, is assimilated to the women's sphere of influ-ence. Because of the connections between women, the house, and nature, the fawn's entrance is both a rupture in the rhetorical divide that Isaacs works to establish and a normalized extension of the private activities that also take place outside. When Efraín's friend Carlos visits in order to propose marriage to María, he does so during a stroll to the river, an outing expressly arranged for this purpose. In this, the first instance in which the women leave the house or garden, each woman is accompanied by a man upon whose arm she leans, supported—or restrained—by male strength as she ventures outside the domestic sphere. The scene marks an apparent turning point in the novel; after this first (ad)venture outdoors, there are several other prominent scenes in which women leave the house for extended periods of time.[8] In these instances, when the mother, Emma, and María journey outside their home, they operate under certain restrictions. Their trips are theoretically related to private events, such as a wedding, and their travels expand the scope of family life outside the home. Male relatives always accompany the women. Such conditions permit women's departure from the home. At the same time, the private space of the home includes activities typically assigned to the public sphere; most business is conducted within the house. The fact that Efraín serves as his father's secretary emphasizes the incorporation of supposedly public activities into the private space of the home. In one especially telling scene, the father has María cut his hair while he dictates a letter to Efraín, completely erasing the division between private and public.[9] Hence even the space theoretically allocated within the home for public work-related activities—in itself a boundary-crossing maneuver—is used for private family interactions.

In general throughout *María*, Isaacs represents very little of women's domestic duties, the sort of work within the house that maintained and nurtured the household members directly and that formed the supposed justification for confining women to the private sphere; the exception is María's sewing, whose representation has the effects described earlier in this chapter. Black female domestic servants and slaves, who are most conspicuous in the novel by their absence, would have performed the overwhelming majority of household work. Even later in the century it was still the case that most women working in the homes of others were women of color employed to clean, cook, sew, and tend children for their employers (Ortiz Mesa 184). The limits imposed on women's movements as represented in the novel did not apply to black women, be they free or slaves, who had to work in the fields and at the sugarcane mill as well as in the house. Nina S. de Friedemann and Mónica Espinosa Arango list some of the tasks and workplaces of female slaves:

Las esclavas negras laboraron hombro a hombro en las cuadrillas mineras y en las plantaciones y haciendas. Estuvieron vinculadas al comercio callejero de comestibles o se convirtieron en parteras. Se desempeñaron como cocineras, ayas de los niños, amas de compañía y lavanderas. Algunas llegaron a ocupar importantes papeles en el campo de la religiosidad y la medicina popular [...]. A otras se les obligó a trabajar en la prostitución, en ventas callejeras, en negocios ilícitos y en contrabando.

Female slaves worked side by side in the mines and on plantations and haciendas. They were food vendors on the streets or became midwives. They worked as cooks, cared for children, were companions and laundresses. Some came to play important parts in popular religion and medicine [...]. Others were forced to work as prostitutes, on the black market, and as smugglers. (53)

None of these tasks, and very few of these women, are visible in *María*, nor are the spaces where such work was carried out made evident. The exception is the reference to the childcare performed by Feliciana (Nay), the doomed African princess whose story is meant to parallel that of Efraín and María. But aside from the violence that she experiences during her journey to in the New World, Feliciana does not represent other slaves. Her work is not dangerous, and the conditions under which she labors are not physically oppressive. Nor is she forced to marry, as Friedemann and Espinosa Arango indicate was typically the case for enslaved women. In short, "la situación de Feliciana [...] no era tan común entre las esclavas de haciendas" (Feliciana's situation ... was not so common among hacienda slave women; 61). By erasing black domestic labor from the novel, Isaacs strives to maintain the distinction between men's work and women's work and between the public and the private, yet those distinctions have already been lost due to the novel's nostalgic evocation of a long-lost or never-existing rural paradise.

In short, the novel's rural setting means that "outdoors" is not synonymous with "public." The public sphere of *María* is not a specific physical space but an area that should be defined by the activities that take place there, as it also is in the other novels discussed in this chapter. As Jürgen Habermas argues, it is possible to conceive of the private and public realms within the scheme of a three-part rather than two-part distinction. For Habermas, there are two types of public spheres. One, coextensive with public authority, is the place of government and civic authority; this is the domain of the state. The other public sphere, which Habermas characterizes as bourgeois, consists of private individuals carrying out acts regulated at least in part by an authority emanating from the public civic sphere. Latin American intellectuals invoking the rhetoric of modernity generally favored the bipartite division between public and private that their European counterparts envisioned, but Habermas's nuanced view of the public realm helps to make sense of the chaotic spaces of *María*. Habermas places the second public sphere at least partially in the private realm, because it involves private individuals who work in public venues. "Within the realm that was the preserve of private people we therefore distinguish again between private and public spheres. The private sphere comprised civil society in the narrower sense, that is to say, the realm of commodity exchange and of social labor; imbedded in it was the family with its interior domain" (30). This public sphere populated by individuals working in a private capacity includes commerce, markets, and intellectual activities such as publishing, journalism, literary salons, and academic institutions, this last category indicating the commodification of culture. While at other times and in other texts the public sphere would be more closely associated with physical spaces outside the home (governmental buildings, banks, courthouses, office buildings), in *María* actions rather than physical space define "public" as they do for Habermas. The family lives at the father's place of business, the hacienda, and the father's office, situated in the family home, is sometimes even occupied by family members carrying out private errands and chores, as in the scene of the haircut. María Fernanda Lander asserts, "En Latinoamérica, no se da un divorcio entre el hogar y el espacio de la sociedad civil" (In Latin America, there is no divorce between the home and the space of civil society; 163) and claims that the space of the home in nineteenth-century Latin America was generally premodern inasmuch as the division between the private and the public was not strictly drawn or observed. Yet if in practice these divisions were not observed, rhetorically they did form the discursive ideal to which authors like Isaacs were responding in one way or another. The commercialization of home space was not a continuation of a premodern mode as much as the expansion of the public sphere to include activities previously marked as private.

The blurring of public and private space has much to do with the way the novel nostalgically harks back to the narrator's lost youth. Isaacs is imagining a simpler, happier time—but also a time that is safely and decisively over. I would also point out that this "lost paradise" turns out never to have been so delightful after all. The father's total control over his family and his finances becomes dangerous rather than protective, as he forces Efraín to attend medical school in London.[10] This plan is meant to restore the family fortunes imperiled by the father's unwise choice of business associates, but Efraín's prolonged absence results in María's death and the loss of her rich dowry. Private and public commingle with disastrous results for the family. Indeed, the inability to complete the separation of public and private may be the decisive factor in the family's fall from paradise. At the novel's end the family has abandoned their rural home in the Cauca for life in Cali, where city existence means a more strictly regimented division between public and private. Such a division cannot be represented within the novel itself, which depends on the disjunction in order to maintain conventional gender roles but cannot support it, as we have seen, because of the consistent effort to inscribe a rural idyll made possible only by the collapse of the public and private realms. This tension serves as one of the factors, perhaps even the primary factor, in the family's failure to negotiate a successful move into the world of modernity and progress that Efraín's professionalization was meant to enable. If the family were to manage the transition into modern urban life without loss (the loss of María, the loss of the hacienda), then the nostalgizing drive that structures the book would vanish; yet if the novel rejected the discourses of modernity that structure it, Efraín would have little or nothing for which to feel nostalgic. Thus Isaacs must invoke a rhetorical modernity that both structures and undermines his nostalgic project of evoking a past before modernity and before modernization.

If in *María* private activities are conducted outside the space of the home and public activities within it, in Clorinda Matto de Turner's *Aves sin nido*, houses serve as sites of public acts both appropriate and inappropriate.[11] In the novel a young couple from Lima, Lucía and Fernando Marín, struggle against the entrenched racism and systemic corruption of the local clergy and government in the fictional Andean town of Kíllac. The conflict plays out against a backdrop of should-be public spaces such as the church, courthouse, and other government buildings as well as the homes of the Maríns, the indigenous Yupanquis, the priest, and the governor. Such specificity of space allows public and private activities to be more closely, even "traditionally," aligned with physical locations. *Aves sin nido* opens with a lengthy description of the town, mapping out significant landmarks and buildings and commenting on the town plaza and on the class divisions evidenced by the different types of houses:

> La plaza única del pueblo de Kíllac mide trescientos catorce metros cuadrados, y el caserío se destaca confundiendo la techumbre de teja colorada, cocida al horno, y la simplemente de paja con alares de palo sin labrar, marcando el distintivo de los habitantes y particularizando el nombre de casa para los notables y choza para los naturales.

> The only plaza in the town of Kíllac measures 340 square meters, and the houses are noted for the confusion of terracotta roofs and those simply made of straw with eaves roughly made of wood, marking the status of the dwellers and specifying the word "house" for notable citizens and "hut" for natives. (53)

This description emphasizes both the plaza and the types of private residences available in the town, assigning them values of class and race. Despite the apparent centrality accorded to the plaza by this opening description, however, the plaza is a geographical element largely ignored by the narrator and the characters alike. It is an obstacle, an open area that threatens to give away its occupants' identities if they cross it carelessly, as when Marcela Yupanqui ventures out to Lucía Marín's house (54). The plaza does not appear again in the novel as the site of any significant action, thus discounting the potential importance of the most public place in the text. The fact that the second half of the introductory sentence, detailing the types of houses in the locale, is much longer than the section describing the plaza also de-emphasizes the public space of the plaza in explicit favor of the private space of the home. Characters are rarely described in transit, and there are no other major scenes that take place outdoors. The only explicit reference to the town's streets later in the novel is a comment about "las lóbregas calles de Kíllac" (the gloomy streets of Kíllac; 133). Moreover, while we see men entering houses and other interior spaces from the street, there are no depictions of women on the street aside from this reference to Marcela. The only other women who explicitly walk the streets of Kíllac are Petronila Pancorbo, the wife of the governor, and Melitona, the priest's mistress, but their journeys through the town are not detailed. Nor does Lucía appear outside the house except when she leaves Kíllac with her family en route to the train station, a multiday journey that is greatly compressed in the narrative. The omissions of descriptions of women physically located within and using public spaces serve to minimize, even erase, their presence in public spaces and in the activities typically assigned to the public sphere.

Marcela approaches but does not enter the Maríns' house: "se dirigió a una casita blanquecina cubierta de tejados, en cuya puerta se encontraba una joven" (she went toward a little white house roofed with tiles, in whose doorway a young woman was standing; 55). She and Lucía speak on the very threshold of the house, occupying a liminal space that is neither inside nor outside. The threshold marks the border and constitutes it at the same time, which makes it a contact zone, to use Mary Louise Pratt's term. They conclude their conversation in the garden, also a liminal, outdoor space controlled by the activity of the house, nature under human control. Marcela and Lucía are able to cross class and racial boundaries to interact precisely because they meet in these transitional spaces. On the threshold and in the garden, they are neither limited by the domestic space and its expectations of correct female comportment nor are they dangerously threatened by the openness of public exterior space.[12]

Domestic space is represented in both the Yupanquis' humble hut and the Maríns' more luxurious house, showing that the indigenous family, just like whites, can participate in the domestic ideology being advanced by Peru's intelligentsia at the time.[13] If such domestic ideology centered on the middle-class white family, however, Matto de Turner presents explicit imagery which furthers her argument that indigenous families create house space similar to that of their white counterparts and thus that indigenous people are as complicit in and important to the project of modernity as the white elites. Indigenous domesticity includes the traditional Andean activity of weaving: "Marcela tomó con afán los tocarpus donde se coloca el telara portátil, que, ayudada por su hija mayor, armó en el centro de la habitación"

(Marcela happily picked up the poles of the portable loom which, helped by her older daughter, she set up in the center of the room; 64). Pre-conquest Andean women produced textiles for the Inca government, labor that granted them social status: Women "produced the goods necessary for rituals. In Inca culture women spun and wove the textiles that were the material expression and the tool of social life and politics" (Bruhns and Stothert 240). In *Aves sin nido*, Marcela's multivalent weaving signifies her indigenous, domestic, female identities. Her status is doubly underscored when she performs a typical domestic, feminine task on a specifically Quechua loom, to describe which Matto de Turner even employs a Quechua word, "tocarpus." While Marcela's weavings are sold to earn money for the family, here her work is socially acceptable for several reasons. In addition to being marked as "women's work" both by Creole and Quechua societies, it is artisanal activity, work that in a preindustrial society is sited within the home. Finally, her daughter helps her, signaling the traditional, intergenerational nature of weaving and marking it as a feminine skill passed on from mother to daughter.

In the Marín home, Manuel comes upon a second domestic scene that counterpoints Marcela's industrious and pleasant weaving: "Al entrar al salón de recibo, encontró a Lucía dando las últimas puntadas a una relojera de razo celeste, en que había bordado con sedas matizadas de colores una flor de nomeolvides con las iniciales de su esposo al extremo" (Upon entering the receiving parlor, he found Lucía putting the finishing touches on a sky blue watch pocket, on which she had embroidered in colorful silks a forget-me-not with her husband's monogram; 127). Nearby Margarita studies the alphabet and Rosalía plays with a friend. Here Lucía's elite status is notable in the fact that she is not weaving cloth to be sold but embroidering a decorative object; her "work" is purely ornamental, and the detailed description of the watchguard emphasizes the decided uselessness of her embroidery and of the object itself. Instead of helping her, the girls have the luxury of studying or playing. In both the Yupanqui and Marín homes, however, the same key elements are present: safely ensconced in the domestic interior, a doting mother creates a textile item while accompanied by her children. For Matto de Turner the house is an intensely female space, one of productivity both literal—the production of clothing—and metaphorical—the production and raising of children. Yet conflating Marcela's economically productive work with Lucía's extraneous decorations incurs the risk of minimizing the significant differences in class and racial identity that those scenes also highlight. While Matto de Turner's narrative creates solidarities and commonalities across spatial interiors, by silencing difference it can also reenact the very systems of oppression that she seeks to critique.

Although *Aves sin nido* painstakingly creates an idealized domesticity, "private" and "public" are radically confused. Despite the presence of spaces clearly marked as having public functions separate from the private sphere, which should alleviate the pressure on the private sphere to absorb the work of the public sphere, private spaces are misused for public activities. These transgressions are constructed as such because of the ways that Matto de Turner invokes the discourse of modernity about the sanctity of the home. As Habermas explains, with the advent of the bourgeois family and the creation of private interiors of houses came the delineation of public and private space, and the "privatized individuals" who entered public society "only entered into it [. . .] out of a private life that had assumed institutional form in the enclosed space of the patriarch conjugal family" (46). Matto de Turner evokes this modern norm in her depiction of the Yupanquis' and Maríns' homes in order to construct valid grounds for a critique of public corruption and social injustice. In her scheme, the fact that family space is continually under attack, often literally, by public interests is in itself a negative factor associated with the lawlessness and backwardness of the Andes under local control.

Many kinds of supposedly public business are transacted within domestic space; for example, Fernando Marín runs his mining business from his home office, and Sebastián Pancorbo's house is the site of local government.[14] When Manuel and his stepfather visit Fernando to discuss making reparations to the Maríns for the attack on their house, they do so in Fernando's office (113–15). The fact that the office is in the Maríns' home permits the presence and active participation of Lucía in the meeting, which otherwise would have been impossible to negotiate. Some uses of private space for public purposes are coded as "right" and have positive effects, or at least positive intentions, while others are coded as "wrong" and are intended maliciously. The "right" uses include such scenes as Lucía Marín inviting the governor and the priest to her home to curtail their abuse of the Yupanquis, an appropriate use because she employs her control over private space to enact a public good. In a flirtatious, sexually charged scene set in their bedroom, she also persuades her husband to give her money to help the Yupanquis (66–67).[15] While at home, Petronila Pancorbo persuades her husband to cease his unjust activities and to leave his post; again, she works for the public benefit, and her efforts, undertaken in the private sphere, have effects in the public sphere. Indeed, Matto de Turner suggests that women are the only moral arbiters in Kíllac; when Fernando Marín complains, "aquí abusan y nadie corrige el mal ni estimula el bien," his wife replies, "¡Si también las mujeres fuesen malas, esto ya sería un infierno, Jesús!" (Here they abuse and no one corrects the bad or promotes the good. If the women were also bad, this place would be hell. Jesus! 175). The women of the novel have a moral duty to act in the public sphere. Right uses of private spaces are always associated with women and wrong uses with men. Writing of this dynamic in the novel, Davies notes that Matto de Turner marks interior private space as associated with "the course of modernity" ("Spanish-American Interiors" 35).[16] Women's traditional roles as moral guardians, confined to the domestic interior, become in *Aves sin nido* important elements of modernity as Matto de Turner reinscribes the codes of public vs. private spheres.

In other cases, however, public and private commingle in ways that have negative results, facilitating the oppression of the indigenous population. As we have previously noted, the "casa de gobierno" (house of government) is the governor's residence. His public reception room is another liminal space allowing for the regulated entrance of the public to the private house. It mixes Peruvian and imported décor:

> El menaje de la sala, típico del lugar, estaba compuesto de dos escaños sofá forrados en hule negro, claveteados con tachuales amarillas de cabeza redonda; algunas silletas de madera de Paucartambo con pinturas en el espaldar, figurando ramos de flores y racimos de frutas; al centro, una mesa redonda con su tapete largo y felpado de castilla verde claro y sobre ella, bizarreando con aires de civilización, una salvilla de hoja de lata con tintero, pluma y arenillador de peltre. Las paredes, empapeladas con diversos periódicos ilustrados, ofrecían un raro conjunto de personajes, animales y paisajes de campiñas europeas.

The room's décor, typical of the area, was made up of two sofas up-
holstered in black oilcloth, fastened with round yellow pins; some
chairs of Paucartambo wood with pictures on their backs, depicting
fruit and flowers; in the center of the room, a round table with a long
green felted tablecloth and on it, showing off with civilized airs, a tin
tray with an inkwell, pen, and blotter. The walls, papered with different illustrated magazines, offered an unusual conglomeration of
characters, animals, and European landscapes. (69)

The majority of the furnishings have been made in Peru; Matto de Turner
even specifies that the wood for the chairs is sourced locally. While Francesca Denegri argues that the interior decoration of the homes in *Aves sin
nido* contributes to a positive view of *mestizaje* (*El abanico* 185), it seems
rather that in this case the exactitude with which the particularly Peruvian
attributes of the room are described contribute to the idea that the room
and those who work within it are mired in the premodern. The room is
both an office and a parlor; in lieu of a desk Pancorbo uses a table upon
which the writing implements seem strange and out of place with their
"civilized airs." The furniture and decorations are not just Peruvian but local and traditional; only the pages cut out of periodicals indicate a nod
toward the print culture and mass media associated with modernity. The
pictures on the walls demonstrate the hybridity of this room (modern and
traditional, public and private) as they depict a mixture of Peruvian and
European images sliced out of their original contexts—illustrated journals doubtless much like *El Perú Ilustrado*, which Matto de Turner herself
edited for several years (Berg, "Prólogo" xiii–xiv)—and rearranged for the
viewing pleasure of the house's inhabitants and visitors. If the ideal separation of private and public were to be enacted, this room would function as
an upper-class home's drawing room where guests are entertained. In *Aves
sin nido*, however, just as its hybrid furnishings suggest, the parlor cum
hearing room serves as the setting for several scenes in which Killac's local
officials, sometimes in connivance with the town priest, conspire to cheat
and oppress the local indigenous populations, inappropriately inserting the
public into what should be a private space.

When Rosalía, the Yupanquis' younger daughter, is taken as hostage
to the family debt, she is removed to Pancorbo's house. Fernando Marín

and Juan Yupanqui go there to ransom her: "Don Fernando se presentó en compañía de Juan en casa del gobernador, quien se encontraba rodeado de gente, despechando asuntos que él llama de alta importancia; gente que fue desfilando sin etiqueta, hasta dejar solos a Pancorbo y el señor Marín. Casi a la entrada de la casa estaba en cuclillas una chiquilla de cuatro años de edad" (Don Fernando appeared, accompanied by Juan Yupanqui, in the house of the governor, who was surrounded by people, dealing with matters that he deemed of great import, people who straggled out mannerlessly until Pancorbo and Mr. Marín were alone. Almost at the entrance to the house a four-year-old girl was squatting; 75). The adults using the space do not conduct themselves correctly, according to Fernando's urbanized standards. Pancorbo fails to distinguish adequately between important topics and minor details. Lastly, Rosalía, squatting in a typically indigenous pose, is an anomaly for several reasons. She is a female and indigenous in a quintessentially male, white space, albeit one marked by signs of *mestizaje* in its décor and furnishings. Her status as a child assigns her definitively to the domestic realm, under her mother's care. Yet her removal from her home to the governor's office is clearly standard operating procedure for the abusive merchants and clerks of the town, and the anomaly in Kíllac's skewed internal logic is Fernando's arrival and his plan to return her to what his modern perspective understands to be her "correct" place.

Matto de Turner consistently represents Kíllac as a site of confusion about the boundaries between the public and private realms, or more aptly, about the *lack* of boundaries separating the two spheres. The local officials plotting against the Maríns meet first in Pancorbo's parlor-office and later in the priest's house. The narrative never depicts Father Pascual in church or carrying out priestly functions, an indicator of the ways that decades, even centuries, of priestly abuse have devalued the church as a public gathering place. In many cases, the private sphere guards against public disclosure, keeping secret things that should be shared. For this reason the conspirators meet in houses, over drinks and meals, feigning domestic normality, and when the new subprefect arranges to return Pancorbo to power, these machinations take place in Pancorbo's house. Although Petronila is present, she does not appear during this meeting. Her decision not to intervene is in stark contrast to her earlier scolding of her husband, when "tomándole el brazo con cierta dureza le dijo:—¡Si no puedo ya contigo

Sebastián!" (taking his arm a little roughly she said, "I can't do anything with you, Sebastián!" 76–77). In the earlier episode, Petronila bursts into the governor's receiving room immediately after Fernando and Juan Yupanqui have retrieved Rosalía. The difference seems to be that Petronila intervenes in the first scene because of the child, just as later she will shelter Teodora, an adolescent girl threatened with rape by a government official. By rebuking her husband for his treatment of Rosalía, she takes advantage of her maternal role to advocate for the reunion of parents and child; her domestic role is a bridge for her to enter the public sphere, which in turn has invaded the domestic space of her house. Pancorbo responds to her scolding by retorting, "Francamente, las mujeres no deben mezclarse nunca en cosas de hombres, sino estar con el agua, las calcetas y los tamalitos, eh?" (Frankly, women shouldn't ever get mixed up with men's affairs. They should just stick with the laundry, darning socks, and making tamales, eh? 77) He describes women's traditional duties in an effort to evict his wife from the "cosas de hombres" that are taking place in what should be Petronila's domain, her house. Yet Petronila intercedes precisely because the men are interfering with "cosas de mujeres," conducting government business in the private space of the house and disrupting normal family relations. Thus, like Lucía, Petronila has recourse to the idea that women are morally superior: "Sí, eso dicen los que para acallar la voz del corazón y del buen consejo, echan a un diantre nuestras sanas prevenciones" (Yes, that's what they tell us. To shut up the voice of compassion and good advice. They send our wise counsel to the devil; 77).

The novel makes the corruption of male public spaces explicit when, after the attack on his house, Fernando Marín takes part in a judicial process supposedly meant to establish the identities of the attackers. This takes place in the ironically named "juzgado de paz" (court of peace), where Marín encounters the judge: "El juez de paz estaba gravamente sentado en el despacho ante una mesa de pino, en un sillón de vaqueta y madera, de los que se fabricaban en Cochabamba (Bolivia) hace cuarenta años, y que hoy son, en las ciudades del Perú, una rareza de museo" (The judge was solemnly seated in the office before a pine table, in a wooden and leather chair, the kind they made in Cochabamba forty years ago, and that are now, in Peru's cities, museum pieces; 123–24). Like Pancorbo's public/private "sala de recibo," the judge's office is furnished with (stereo)typically Peruvian articles; more, in Fernando's presence the chair—and the man sitting in it—are suddenly seen as old-fashioned, underlining Fernando's status as a harbinger of modernity and the civil authority's status as holdovers from a traditional, less progressive era.

The judge and his clerk, members of the group that conspired to attack the Maríns' house, suppress Fernando's testimony and lead him to "abandon[ar] el santuario de la ley" (abandon the sanctuary of the law; 125). Matto de Turner's sarcastic use of the word "santuario" emphasizes the idea that the public functionaries have betrayed their moral and legal duties, making the courthouse the very opposite of a "sanctuary"—just as the sanctity of the Maríns' house was destroyed in the attack. Tellingly, the attackers broke down the front door to the house, removing the boundary between public and private and enabling one character to access private conversations simply by standing outside the ruined door and eavesdropping (101). The malicious erasure of the distinction between public and private can never fully be overcome. Even Lucía's efforts to bring the corrupt male officials into the morally upright domestic sphere in order to correct their behavior ultimately fail, and the Maríns leave Killac with their adopted daughters.[17]

Although the women of *Aves sin nido* do not leave their homes with the ease of the women in *María*, their ability to participate in public sphere activities is greater precisely because the men fail to maintain the boundaries between public and private. Given that men are responsible for transforming house space into public space, women are justified in their public interventions. Matto de Turner manipulates the accepted codes governing the separation of spheres and the gender norms that are mapped onto physical spaces in ways that grant her female characters greater autonomy and that demonstrate female capability for taking on public decision-making roles. At the same time that she empowers female characters to take advantage of masculine insufficiency in maintaining the private/public distinction, however, she undermines her own push for modernity as a phenomenon that should depend on female commitment. Her female characters intervene in public sector affairs not because the public/private divide is successful but because it fails. These textual fissures cannot be resolved in the space of the novel, leading the Maríns to abandon the chaotic spaces of Killac and return to the capital where, in *Herencia*, Lucía notably does not engage in any public sphere activities.

If in *María* and *Aves sin nido* the delineation of public and private spaces is honored more in the breach than in the observance, in Alberto Blest Gana's *Martín Rivas* (1862), the narrative carefully alternates among scenes in various houses, in public spaces such as the university that the title character attends and, in the novel's climactic scenes depicting a failed revolution, the streets.[18] In this sense *Martín Rivas* more closely hews to the idealized model proffered by the images of modernity emanating from Europe and the United States and enacts gender-based codes of behavior associated with and mapped onto the public/private space divide. Blest Gana (1830–1920) was writing about and during a period in Chilean history when the elites experienced an unprecedented series of cultural exchanges with Europe and North America. As John Rector notes, "French acculturation became a rite of passage for upper-class youth" (91) such as Agustín Encina, who is described throughout the novel as "afrancesado" or Frenchified. European intellectuals who migrated to Chile and articles reprinted from European periodicals in Chile's newspapers helped bring ideas about modernity to the country as well. This eminently urban novel carefully marks out appropriate and inappropriate behaviors in private spaces and the acceptable modes for crossing from one to the other. Blest Gana, the son of an Irish doctor, joined the Chilean military and spent four years in France as a young man. Upon his return to Chile in 1851 he began publishing a series of novels, thirteen in all, including *Martín Rivas*. The novel's setting most clearly echoes that of contemporaneous European and North American texts. Blest Gana acknowledged that he found inspiration in Balzac's work, and critics have also identified resemblances to Stendhal's *Le Rouge et le noir*.[19] Such echoes may explain in part *Martín Rivas*'s apparent adherence to gender norms related to the occupation of particular spaces; Blest Gana not only makes use of European ideas about progress, modernity, urbanization, and spatial divisions, but he also has recourse to specific literary models in which those ideas have already been enacted in fictional form.

While *Martín Rivas* is concerned with the ways in which public and private spaces are and should be used by men and women, the novel also represents appropriate movement between those spaces by both genders. In the very first sentence of the novel, Blest Gana explores the idea of the transition between spaces: "A principios del mes de julio de 1850 atravesaba la puerta de calle de una hermosa casa de Santiago un joven de veintidós a veintitrés años" (At the beginning of July 1850, a young man in his early twenties was passing through the door of a beautiful house in Santiago; 9). By initiating the text with Martín's act of going through the door—not yet in the house, not wholly on the street—Blest Gana introduces liminality immediately; also, the use of the imperfect ("atravesaba") emphasizes the ongoing nature of the action of crossing. Transitions are not instantaneous but processes to be explored. This preoccupation with the ways in which characters traverse spaces runs throughout the novel, a counterpoint to the scenes in which public and private spaces are fully and correctly occupied.

While Martín frequently travels around Santiago and is depicted in multiple interior and exterior scenes, all of which he inhabits with ease, his female counterpart, Leonor Encina, is represented as ideally suited to her domestic interior.

> Magnífico cuadro formaba aquel lujo a la belleza de Leonor [. . . A]l verla reclinada sobre un magnífico sofá forrado en brocatel celeste, al mirar reproducida su imagen en un lindo espejo al estilo de la Edad Media [. . . el] observador habría admirado la prodigalidad de la naturaleza en tal feliz acuerdo con los favores del destino. Leonor resplandecía rodeada de ese lujo como un brillante entre el oro y pedrerías de un rico aderezo.

> Such luxury formed a magnificent backdrop to Leonor's beauty. Seeing her posed on a magnificent sofa upholstered in sky blue brocade, seeing her image reproduced in a beautiful medieval-style mirror, [. . .] an observer would have admired nature's prodigality in such happy accord with destiny's favors. Leonor shone, surrounded by that luxury like a diamond among the gold and precious stones of a rich parure. (15)

Leonor is a jewel among other jewels, a decorative element in the perfect, highly ornamented domestic setting. Indeed, the house's luxurious interior forms a frame that both sets off and encloses Leonor, sealing her inside. She is doubly commodified by her reflection in the mirror, a detail that confirms her status as an object to be observed for visual pleasure. Finally, whereas Martín is in motion when first seen, crossing the threshold of the Encina house, Leonor is still, seated on the sofa. The initial descriptions of both characters highlight gender norms. Men are exterior and active, women are interior and passive; men move and talk, women sit and are viewed by others. These binarisms are closely and insistently associated with the duality of public versus private spaces.

The first half of the novel takes place in interior scenes in the houses of the upper-class Encinas and lower-class Molinas, whose stories Blest Gana compares and weaves together. The Molina daughters, particularly Adelaida, offer sexual opportunities for upper-class men, who in their turn are economically exploited by the Molinas. The private activity of sex and the public activity of finance intersect in the chaotic space of the Molina house.[20] Blest Gana deploys descriptions of these two families and their festivities—the *tertulias* of the Encinas and the *picholeos* of the Molinas—to highlight class and gender differences in midcentury Santiago, and such differences are enacted through and mapped onto private and public spaces.[21] During the Encinas' *tertulias*, or salons, gender distinctions are carefully observed even in conversation; men analyze politics and women discuss domestic topics such as romance and clothing. Only the middle-aged Francisca Encina breaks with this division. As the omniscient narrator comments, "Había leído algunos libros y pretendía pensar por sí sola" (She had read some books and tried to think for herself; 31). Yet her engagement with reading is mocked by the use of the word "pretendía"; she is only trying, and failing, to think. Nonetheless, Francisca repeatedly intervenes in the men's conversations about politics and is told by her husband, "Las mujeres no deben hablar de política" (Women shouldn't talk about politics; 32). Francisca lacks the basis of knowledge that would allow her to make meaningful contributions to the conversation; a George Sand fan, she is reflexively and ignorantly liberal.[22] Later references to her reading reduce her understanding of Sand's work to an enthusiasm for plots about young love, further diminishing any claims Francisca might have had to legitimate participation in political discourse. Throughout the novel Blest Gana represents her efforts to penetrate the public sphere by taking part in male conversations about topics of public interest as comical and undermines any reading of her political commentary as meaningful.

The orderly, decorous scenes of the Encinas' *tertulias* are countered by the carnivalesque chaos of the Molinas' *picholeos*, with their excessive drinking and riotous dancing. The Molinas' parties allow, even encourage, the disorderly interactions and exchanges of genders and social classes. This disorder only worsens when

> en la segunda [cuadrilla], la niña de catorce años quiso hacer lo mismo que en la primera, turbando también al que bailaba a su frente e introduciendo general confusión [...]. Este desorden, que desesperaba a los jóvenes y a las niñas que pretendían dar a la reunión el aspecto de una tertulia de buen tono, regocijaba en extremo a doña Bernarda.
>
> in the second dance, the fourteen-year-old girl wanted to do the same movements as in the first, throwing off the man who was dancing in front of her and introducing general confusion. . . . This disorder, which sent the young men and women who were trying to give the party the tone of an upscale salon into a state of despair, made doña Bernarda very happy. (64)

In the Encina house, efforts to effect the move of women into the public sphere are rejected, but in the Molina home, the head of the household welcomes the chaotic mingling of the sexes and spheres. Bernarda, a widow, actively encourages dissipation and debauchery in her home, creating scenes that explicitly transgress the *tertulia* norm established in upper-class houses. The Molina house is not a safe space for Adelaida and Edelmira, the unmarried daughters, a fact that contradicts the convention that young, unmarried women in particular would be best protected within the secure confines of the home. The laxity of moral standards within the private spaces of the Molina house enables Rafael San Luis to seduce and impregnate Adelaida, while Edelmira flees her home to avoid an unwanted marriage. The narrative attributes this to Bernarda's maternal failings; in the absence of a husband and father, Bernarda is responsible for maintaining standards of gender-appropriate behavior, which she fails spectacularly to do. In the Molina house, unlike the Encina mansion, societal norms associated with private spaces are routinely violated from the beginning of the novel because of Bernarda's incapacity to fulfill her maternal duties. In short, she does not create a home for her children as the republican ideal of motherhood demands.[23] Yet these problems are attributed to Bernarda's lack of oversight; the problem is not with the absence of boundaries between public and private or between men and women but with a failure of individual enforcement. Blest Gana thus supports the modernizing ideal of the separate spheres of influence in a way that critiques the lower classes for failing to enact that ideal.

In the Encina house, norms governing the appropriate behavior of men and women in the private sphere are strictly observed. While Dámaso Encina has an office in his home, work and family are separated once Martín and Encina go into the office. The door is firmly shut, and neither man ever brings work out of the office into the rest of the house. Nor do women enter the office, as María and Lucía do in the other novels. Indeed, Blest Gana rarely even describes the business conducted in Encina's office. Family conversations at the dinner table revolve around personal and intimate topics, not around Dámaso's business dealings or financial machinations. When economic concerns appear in the home, it is within the context of domestic or romantic entanglements. Just as during the *tertulias* men and women remain separated to speak of their own gender-based concerns, in the Encinas' domestic space public and private are carefully isolated from one another.

The novel moves from a focus on interior spaces to exterior spaces in its second half. The outdoors scenes often feature the *paseo*, a formalized version of a leisurely stroll, during which unmarried men and women may speak with one another relatively unchaperoned, albeit still under the nominal supervision of the group; these outings, controlled and permitted by social norms, offer opportunities for unmarried men and women to interact out of the sight and control of their parents. Ironically, this use of public space creates the privacy that potential lovers lack in the domestic realm; only in the street can Matilde Elías and Rafael converse freely (124–26). Later, a mass outing to the Campo de Marte during the national holidays of September 18 and 19 permits the narrator to expound on the differences between men's and women's approaches to the *paseo*: for women, it is "una ocasión de mostrarse cada cual los progresos de la moda y el poder del bolsillo del padre o del marido para costear los magníficos vestidos que las adornan en estas ocasiones" (an occasion for each woman to show off the latest fashion and the power of her father's or husband's wallet to pay for the magnificent dresses that adorned her on these occasions; 149). The Campo de Marte, which later became the Parque Cousiño, was located in one of mid-nineteenth-century Santiago's elite neighborhoods. In addition to bourgeois *paseos*, civic celebrations that had their roots in colonial popular gatherings called *ramadas* were held there. Such gatherings brought together different social classes in celebrations of patriotism and nationalist sentiment ("El Barrio Dieciocho"). During the September 18 and 19 festivals, the correct display of patriotic fervor as represented in *Martín Rivas* permits, even requires, the presence in the public sphere of women and the occupation of public spaces by different socioeconomic classes. Public "appearance" in the novel is twofold: women appear in public, and their physical appearances and their apparel are made public. Their elegant dresses, objects purchased and enjoyed thanks to male economic power, are objects of visual consumption just like the women themselves and, in fact, heighten the objectification of the women wearing them. Via the *paseo* women move into a public space where further objectification occurs, as they are on display for a wider variety of gazes.

The same is true when the Encina family attends the theater, another acceptable public space for female occupancy and an extension of the patriotic celebrations that begin in the Campo del Marte. Elite women travel to and stay in the theater in the company of men, and the theater, itself an enclosed space, also contains further enclosures, the boxes that wealthy families occupy. There Leonor is the cynosure of all eyes: "Casi todos los anteojos se dirigían al palco en que la niña ostentaba su admirable hermosura" (Almost all the opera glasses turned toward the box in which the girl displayed her admirable beauty; 197). "Ostentar" here emphasizes that, just as in the scene that first introduces her, Leonor is on display, and flamboyantly so, an idea underlined by the further use of the word "admirable" to describe her physical appearance. She is indeed to be admired. Moreover, she is framed within the theater box, just as she was framed within the *cuadro* of her living room earlier, and viewed through opera glasses, distancing her from interactions with others and turning her into a passive object for visual consumption and male viewing pleasure.

At the same time that the *paseo* and similar excursions commodify women by serving as a means for a greater viewing audience to access their physical appearance, including the clothing and accessories purchased by men to decorate female bodies, these trips out of the house permit female agency in specific cases. While the discursive strictures of the novel define the general category of "women" as those who attend public celebrations solely to wear new clothes and to be admired, in individual cases certain women can exercise more autonomy. Tellingly, Leonor becomes more natural and authentic when she rides on horseback: "No era en aquel instante la niña orgullosa de los salones, la altiva belleza en cuya presencia perdía Rivas toda la energía de su pecho; era una niña que se abandonaba sin afectación a la alegría de un paseo" (She was not in that moment the proud girl of the salons, the haughty beauty in whose presence Riva couldn't breathe; she was a girl who abandoned herself to the pleasure of an outing; 151). Outside the constricting space of the house, in an environment that the novel represents as literally and emotionally freer, the restrictions placed on female behavior loosen and Leonor acts and speaks in ways which the novel constructs as more authentic than her comportment in the controlled and monitored atmosphere of the salons. She and Martín are outside on horseback when she first encourages Martín's romantic attentions. The narrator singles out "la naturalidad de sus palabras" and her "voz [. . .] afectuosa y confidencial" (the naturalness of her words, her warm and confiding voice; 154), phrases that underscore the freedom Leonor has to express her real emotions in the more natural setting of the Campo del Marte. The narrative implies that love and other pure sentiments can only be displayed in a natural setting, away from the artifice of both the domestic space and the interior yet paradoxically public space of the theater. Habermas argues that the privatization of the bourgeois family depends on the changes in the way the house is conceived, from a building where elites conduct family life as a spectacle to a home of interiors for family intimacy. This change in turn permits what Habermas calls a "private autonomy" of the family "that provide[s] the bourgeois family with its consciousness of itself" (46) and that enables the fiction of romantic love, disassociated from economic concerns.

When the novel constructs Leonor on horseback as more "real," more open and revealing of the true self that the world of parlors, carriage rides,

and outings to the theater forces her to conceal, it is because the privatization of the family allows for the privileging of intimate sentiments and the
development of personal autonomy. That is, only because of the careful delineation of private and public spaces can Leonor in turn be constructed as
"natural" when she is outside either of those realms. Blest Gana also implies
that interior spaces unduly restrict female emotional behavior and speech.
Yet in his text, those restrictions are necessary for normalizing gender-
based behaviors in which women remain in the private space of the home,
engaged in domestic pursuits and serving as objects of visual pleasure, and
men take action in the public space.

In the climactic scenes of the novel, Martín and Rafael San Luis take
part in the liberal uprising of 1851. Blest Gana puts into play the possibility of the imminent collapse of public and private distinctions, beginning with Rafael's statement, "Mi nueva querida [. . .] es la política" (My
new love [. . .] is politics; 291), an affirmation that moves politics to the
domestic sphere of romance and transfers private emotions to the public
sphere. By using the intimate language of relationships to characterize his
political involvement, Rafael dangerously conflates the two domains. Such
contamination must be contained and reversed. The rebellion culminates
in a ferocious battle waged in the streets of Santiago. Blest Gana describes
the locations where the fighting occurs with map-like precision, specifying
streets, plazas, and even doorways. Martín flees to the Encina house, where
in a gesture freighted with meaning Leonor herself opens the front door,
which is usually guarded by a male doorkeeper. She admits Martín to the
enclosure of the home and hides him in her own bedroom, where the two
first openly assert their mutual love. Leonor thus has direct control over
the barriers between public and private space; in this moment of collapse of
public and private she is an autonomous subject who empowers others to
move from one space to another. She determines in this moment whether
Martín will live or die, an unprecedented ability to control male destiny and
another sign of the chaos that ensues when gender-normed distinctions
between private and public no longer prevail.

Yet Leonor's autonomy and control are fleeting. Soldiers enter the
Encina house forcefully, in a violent demonstration of the dangers of enabling the permeability of the barrier between public and private. These
soldiers stop Martín: "Las dos centinelas de la puerta se lanzaron sobre

él blandiendo sus tizonas. El joven, sin desconcertarse, apoyó la espalda a una de las paredes del zaguán y, desenvainando su espada, principió a parar los desatinados golpes que los policiales le descargaban" (The two sentinels at the door rushed at him brandishing their swords. The young man calmly set his back against one of the walls of the entry and, drawing his sword, began to parry the blows that the soldiers unleashed upon him; 324). Martín's own transgression of the public/private divide means that he can no longer easily cross boundaries between the two realms as he did at the beginning of the novel. Having violated the rules governing the passage from one space to another and the proper occupation of the two areas, he is no longer permitted to traverse these spaces without consequences. Just as Leonor strove to offer him the enclosure of the house to shelter him from public violence, Martín attempts to use the physical space of the house itself to protect himself when he braces himself against the wall. But the violence of the revolution is literally brought home. The soldiers remove Martín from the house, demonstrating that disruptive elements of public life that intrude on the private sphere must be isolated and expelled. It is perhaps even more dangerous to the orderly arrangement of public versus private that in this case men and women—Martín and Leonor—collaborate to enable the collapse of public and private spaces. The novel must then enact the return of order and the re-creation of firm boundaries between the two domains.

Martín fails to escape the consequences of his public actions within a private space. After the dramatic incursion of the public into the private initiated by Martín and facilitated by Leonor, Leonor herself ventures out once more to intervene in public affairs, arranging for Martín's escape from prison. She involves Edelmira Molina in her plans, creating a link, albeit temporary, based on female solidarity that trumps the class divisions that have kept the two women apart until now. Ultimately the insertion of the private into the public saves Martín. Yet even this unprecedented and successful involvement of the two women in the public sphere is heavily mediated. Leonor and Edelmira plan Martín's escape in the domestic space of the Encina home, and they do so for private, intimate purposes and using stereotypically female strategies, as Edelmira bargains for Martín's life by promising to marry another man. When Leonor and Martín are briefly reunited upon his escape, it is within the enclosed space of a carriage. While the carriage is a vehicle intended to occupy and traverse the street, it is also a private shelter, a domestic space in miniature and in motion. Its liminal nature allows Leonor to journey through the public spaces of Santiago at night. Every instance of female "crossing" from private to public and vice versa, then, is carefully constructed to show that such traversals do not permanently threaten the split between the public and private realms. The message is that intrusions of one sphere into the other are permissible only under carefully controlled circumstances and when they are meant to restore the appropriate separation of spheres. In a letter from Martín to his sister that serves as the novel's epilogue, he recounts how he and Leonor saw Edelmira and her new husband during a *paseo*. This brief scene is the last encounter among the four characters and the last scene of action in the novel, so it serves as the text's last word on gender and space. In it, Blest Gana underscores the proper occupation of public space by women: accompanied by men, in a space marked out for entertainment and feminine diversion, and, here, with each woman associated with a male partner of her own social class. The novel's resolution signals the reiteration of boundaries between the private and the public and makes it clear that such boundaries hold true across class lines.

A lesser-known novel published in Yucatán in 1861 serves as this chapter's final exemplar of the mid-nineteenth-century Spanish American fascination with private and public spaces and the ways in which gender roles are enforced and reenacted through those spaces. *La mestiza* was the first novel by the Mexican author, journalist, and government functionary Eligio Ancona (1836–93). A member of the Liberal Party, Ancona had previously published articles and stories, mostly satirical in nature, in journals in Mérida. He subsequently wrote several historical novels about the conquest of Mexico and the colonial period as well as the multivolume *Historia de Yucatán*.[24] He also held various political positions in Yucatán, was governor of the state twice, and ended his political career as a Supreme Court justice. His twinned literary and political careers demonstrate his deep interest in the racial and ethnic conflicts that racked Yucatán during the nineteenth century. In *La mestiza* those conflicts are projected onto and doubled by relationships between men and women; the novel is a cautionary tale about the abuse of lower-class mestiza women by upper-class white men. In it, the beautiful, orphaned mestiza Dolores is seduced by the white aristocrat Pablo, with the assistance of a middle-aged mestiza woman. He abandons her after the birth of their son and marries a white woman of his own class, but Dolores is rescued from destitution by her faithful suitor, Esteban, also a mestizo, who marries her and takes her to live in the country. In the novel's conclusion, the dying Pablo, whose own wife and child have already died, encounters the happy mestizo family and gives his biological son his blessing. In brief, the leitmotiv of the book has to do with the betrayal of virtuous mestizas who are the objects of white male upper-class sexual desire. Older women present themselves as protectors of these innocent girls, and yet they aid and abet the white men who seduce and abandon them. These go-between figures enable the penetration of what should be safe home spaces by men, resulting in what Ancona portrays as the inevitable victimization of lower-class indigenous women by elite white men. Ancona rails against these abuses but represents them as individual rather than systemic. In repeated but isolated cases, white men choose to take advantage of their privileged status to sexually persecute indigenous and mestiza women. By using this approach, Ancona both decries the abuses suffered by the lower-class women and avoids any calls for widespread social reforms that would empower indigenous groups to resist white dominance. In fact, I argue that Ancona's novel codifies hegemonic norms of racial and sexual control at the same time that it condemns the excesses resulting from those racial and social disparities.

Like *Aves sin nido*, *La mestiza* opens with a description of the neighborhood where much of the novel's action is set, in "una angosta callejuela del barrio de San Sebastián, formada por dos hileras de rústicas albarradas, cuya mala construcción desparecía en parte bajo un tapiz de silvestre enredadera" (a narrow alley of the San Sebastián neighborhood, composed of two lines of rustic walls, whose poor construction partially vanished under a tapestry of entwined greenery, 9). San Sebastián was a neighborhood of Mérida originally populated chiefly by displaced Mayan workers, and during the time of the action of *La mestiza*, it was still a suburb of the city inhabited by indigenous and mestizo people. In the novel, however, no Maya appear; indigeneity has been replaced by *mestizaje*. Ancona's description presents San Sebastián as an economically devalued area, run down and overgrown, not maintained by civil authorities. Nature intrudes inappropriately into dwelling spaces and public places.

A través de la verde espesura de sus hojas, y casi ocultas entre el follaje, descubríanse algunas de esas casitas de paja en que habita nuestro pueblo; pero a las cuales se entraba sin duda por otras calles, porque en la que estamos describiendo no se veía una sola puerta que hiciese sospechar en ella la existencia del hombre.

Through the thick greenery of its leaves, and almost hidden in the foliage, there were some of those little straw huts in which our people live but which one surely entered by other streets, because in the street we are describing it was impossible to see even one door that might betray the existence of a human being. (9)

The first person who appears in this quasi-pastoral scene, however, is not a humble peasant at one with nature, as Dolores, the mestiza of the title, will prove to be. Instead, the arrival of a handsome young white man causes all the singing birds to fly away. This man waits in the shade of an orange tree that, like the bushes and vines growing over the walls that are meant to define the limits of the street, intrudes out of private property into what should be the public space of the street.[25] The opening scene suggests that this hybrid, mestizo neighborhood is also a hybrid physical space, blending nature and culture, so that when the white man arrives, he represents the fully cultivated world of constructed spaces, and nature flees before him.

The "casita" or little house of Dolores and her family is guarded by a pair of enormous trees that create a transitional space from the street to the domestic enclosure. The household's interior is scantily furnished with one bed, a few chairs, and a hammock, another marker of indigenous identity. While nature reigns unchecked in the street outside the house, the cultivated land of the casita contains Dolores's garden, which is full of plants such as white lilies that metaphorically represent Dolores's virginal state, her aunt Marta's serviceable vegetable plot, and an orchard. These agricultural pursuits provide the family's sustenance and bring nature under man's (and woman's) control. Moreover, they provide a place where Dolores can engage with the natural world without entering the disruptive and threatening space of the street.

This pastoral scene is shattered when Dolores's father dies, leaving a letter that none of them can read. Along with the letter, Pablo, the young white man of the opening scene, enters the house in a way that underscores his superior place in the hierarchies of race, class, and gender: "Antes que le invitasen a sentarse, Pablo tomó asiento y se colocó entre Dolores y Marta" (Before they could invite him to sit, Pablo took a seat and placed himself between Dolores and Marta, 25). His casual assertion of his masculine, white, elite authority disrupts the family's efforts to maintain its privacy. Pablo affirms his dominance as a man, as a white, and as a reader, thrusting himself onto the scene and, by sitting between the two women, separating them. His ability to manipulate multiple codes of language, class, race, and gender depends on his privileged social position in Yucatán. It also underscores the decisive advantage he has in any power play or transaction. As we know, in the nineteenth century, reading aloud was often an activity that took place within the intimate space of the family, yet Pablo's irruption makes it something other than personal and private. He invades the domestic haven. He takes something from this space and from the family inhabiting it—the information in the letter written by Dolores's dying father that Marta and Esteban would have preferred to keep within the space of the family—just as later he will remove Dolores herself from the enclosing and protective space of the house.

In an extended parenthetical description of Dolores's adolescence, Ancona remarks on the solitary nature of her house. This seems contradictory given that at other moments in the novel it is clear that Esteban lives very close by and that when the women need help, numerous neighbors are quick to appear. Yet Ancona specifies that the house is so removed that Dolores grows up "casi fuera de la sociedad" (in almost complete isolation; 35) and that Marta begins sending Dolores to the market because she believes the street is safer than the lonely house. Nonetheless, Dolores meets Pablo in the street during her trips to and from the market, and when Marta once again goes to market and leaves Dolores at home, Pablo visits Dolores there. Her house is both isolated and a hub of activity. This contradiction reveals Ancona's conflicted position about appropriate domestic spaces for women, especially lower-class mixed-race women; they should emulate their elite counterparts and make their houses spaces of domestic bliss, but they should also be economically self-sustaining and separate from white society, which entails strengthening the mestizo community and differentiating it from white communities precisely so that mestizos can resist white incursions. Writing from a place where indigenous resistance to white control continued throughout much of the nineteenth century, Ancona struggled with how to represent mestizo autonomy in a way that would empower that group of Yucatecans without threatening the white elite of which he himself was a member. The result is that houses both protect and imprison their mestiza inhabitants in his novel.

Pablo's illicit nighttime entrance into Dolores's house is facilitated by the fact that part of the garden wall has crumbled; instead of barring his entry, the broken pieces form a sort of staircase that he climbs. Once inside the courtyard, "una alfombra de hierba y hojas secas apagó el ruido que debía producir aquella ligera caída" (a carpet of grass and dead leaves hushed the noise that his slip should have made; 65). The house that should protect Dolores betrays her and invites in her seducer, and the natural world in which she takes so much delight further enables his entry. Here, however, the interplay between the isolation of the house and its location in a neighborhood of concerned inhabitants comes to the foreground. The alarm raised by mestizo neighbors forces Pablo to flee and foils his attempt to break in. Yet the mestizo community is not robust enough to consistently present a unified front, and from the point of view of the lower-class indigenous and mixed-race women of the novel, it seems that neither private nor public spaces are safe from white male sexual desire.[26] Throughout *La mestiza*, spaces that should be inviolable are, instead, both violated and provide locations where violation of female bodies occurs.

At this point in the novel Marta narrates an interpolated history, a cautionary tale serving as an explicit parallel to Dolores and Pablo's relationship. In Marta's story, Juana, a mestiza like Dolores, lives with her father and goes to market every day, where a young white man meets and eventually seduces her. Marta refers to him as a Spaniard and glosses, "entonces todavía dábamos a todos los blancos el nombre de españoles" (in those days we still called all the whites Spaniards; 82). Her comment about all whites being Spaniards further emphasizes the divisions between whites and Mayas, the colonizers and the colonized, Spanish literacy and Mayan orality. The socioeconomic class divisions of the novel also are encoded in the tale of Juana and the "Spaniard"; economic necessity sends Juana to the market and leaves her vulnerable. In *María, Aves sin nido*, and *Martín Rivas*, the upper-class heroines have the choice of leaving the house or remaining within it; their struggles have to do with gaining social acceptance of their departures from the home and with their uses of private space. The lower-class indigenous women of *La mestiza* and *Aves sin nido* find themselves without options and must engage with the public spaces of the street and the market. In this vein Juana also visits her neighbor Cecilia twice a day to buy the bread that Cecilia sells. In Cecilia's house and with Cecilia's conniv-ance, Jaime, the white man, meets Juana repeatedly for conversations until one evening he rapes her:

> [S]intió Juana los pasos de una persona que se acercaba; alzó la ca-beza y vio entrar a Jaime quien cerró la puerta tras si, dándole una vuelta entera a la llave. Dio un grito al considerarse a solas con el jo-ven español; quiso levantarse de la silla que ocupaba, pero le faltaron las fuerzas. [...] ... Acababa de dejar su honor, para no recuperarlo jamás, en casa de su infame amiga."

> Juana sensed the steps of someone approaching her; she raised her head and saw Jaime come in and close the door behind him, turning the key to lock it. She shrieked, seeing herself alone with the young Spaniard; she wanted to get up from her chair, but her limbs failed her. [...] ... She had just left her honor, never to be won back, in the house of her infamous friend. (86)

In a lengthy—and literal—ellipsis, Juana is raped. Cecilia's actions permit the abuse of domestic space and of Juana's body. While Cecilia's role as a woman should be to guard the sanctified space of the home and to main-tain female chastity, economic considerations and her own inferior position in the hierarchy of race and class outweigh any solidarity based on gender she might have experienced.

Having been raped, Juana becomes Jaime's mistress, is impregnated, and no longer leaves the house so that her dishonor will not be known. Sexual shame is intensely private and confines her to interior spaces; public space signifies knowledge, revelation, openness, and social judgment, as will be the case for Dolores as well. Underscoring Juana's economic as well as sexual dependence, once the baby is born, Cecilia, too, abandons her, citing financial desperation, and Juana runs out of food. She faints from hunger and wakes to find that her house has been "invaded" ("gran número de sus vecinos había invadido su casa"; a large number of neighbors had invaded her house; 90). Juana's closely kept secret, guarded within the walls of her house, has been made dramatically public by the entry of the public into her home. The baby's existence and her inability to care for herself or for her child result in this dramatic rupture of domestic privacy and enclosure. Just as Juana's body was forced open and violated, her house is forced open and violated by the neighborly "invasion."

Juana eventually becomes a prostitute to pay her son's medical bills and has another baby; both children are taken from her due to her neglect, and Juana, "no teniendo ya hijos, no volvió a su choza" (no longer having children, didn't return to her hut; 95). Without her role as a mother, she no longer has access to the domestic, enclosed spaces that mothers occupy; she has no right to privacy, but lives in the public space of the brothel, where intimate acts of sex are public, economic transactions rather than private, familial interactions. When Juana becomes fatally ill, she returns to her home, but strangers—tellingly, a mother and children—live there and Juana's own children, now cared for by others, fail to recognize her and thus reject her. Her public life as a prostitute has led to her complete expulsion from the space of the house, from the family, and from the domestic realm.

Every time Juana ventures out into the street, even to seek a doctor for her sick child, she suffers a negative consequence, sexual in nature. The doctor takes payment in her body; news of Juana's beauty and availability spread throughout the city, and other men come off the street and into her house for sex, continuing the invasions and violations begun by Jaime. This is the cautionary tale Marta narrates to Dolores to underscore the dangers of continued association with Pablo, who, like Jaime, frequents the public space of the marketplace and inappropriately enters the homes of others, crossing thresholds and boundaries of all kinds.

Upon Marta's death, a woman claiming to be doña Elvira, Pablo's mother, removes Dolores from her house. Dolores has a deep sentimental attachment to her home: "El pensamiento de tener que abandonar [. . .] aquella casita en que había nacido y en que había vivido con su padre y con Marta, la hacía estremecerse" (The thought of having to abandon that little house in which she had been born and where she had lived with her father and Marta made her shudder; 110). Dolores displays emotions for the very spaces of the house itself; when she leaves, she bids farewell to the rooms, furniture, courtyard, and plants. In this scene Ancona represents Dolores as intimately bound to domestic space and life. Her sensitivity to domestic nuance is underscored when she observes that "Elvira's" house is modest and simple rather than the mansion she had imagined such a wealthy woman would occupy. When Dolores asks where she has been brought, the woman replies, "A mi casa" (to *my* house; 113). She then takes off her black dress and reveals herself in the typical white dress of a mestiza, just like Dolores herself. Like Cecilia in the interpolated history, this mestiza betrays female solidarity in favor of economic gain at the behest of a wealthy white man and inappropriately uses a domestic interior to facilitate the sexual exploitation of other women.

Pablo tells Dolores that "esta casa no es la de mi madre, sino un asilo risueño escogido por mí, con que te brinda mi amor" (this house is not my mother's, but an enchanting haven chosen by me, with which I bestow my love on you; 124). He strives to imbue the house with the same kind of emotional power that Dolores's own home held for her. When Dolores says she will go to the real Elvira's house, Pablo threatens that his mother's house will imprison Dolores, but she is already imprisoned. Lacking economic resources, Dolores is incapable of making a choice that would preserve her sense of self, her autonomy, and her virginity. The domestic space that should protect Dolores instead enables her exploitation. Like Juana, Dolores has a baby; after months of seclusion, she ventures out one day and sees Pablo, who has abandoned her. Tellingly, she sees him in a complex visual interplay rather than directly. While in the street she glances into the open window of a house, inside of which a huge mirror reflects someone standing in the doorway of a house across the street. Here other devices mediate Dolores's access to other people's private spaces: the window, which frames and restricts her access, and the mirror, which delivers only a reflection of the original, and an incomplete one at that, as Dolores cannot tell from the reflection what Pablo is viewing. "El original de aquel transunto que tan bien presentaba el espejo, se hallaba en el lado opuesto y Dolores no podía verle [. . .]. Los ojos de éste estaban clavados en algún objeto que no reproducía el espejo" (The original of the scene that the mirror presented so well was across the street and Dolores could not see it. His eyes were fixed on something that the mirror did not reflect; 148). When she crosses the street and attempts to enter the house where she has seen Pablo, he stops her on the very threshold. Dolores's one venture out of her house to engage in the public sphere after her seduction is disastrous. She is barred from her physical and emotional attempts to gain access to Pablo and to the elite lifestyle he and his house represent. She is not even allowed to enter the wealthy, ostentatious rooms of his mansion, but remains sequestered in a small, modestly furnished space while Pablo's legitimate wife occupies the grand parlor. The fact that Dolores's one effort to leave her own house ends in such complete failure signals Ancona's desire to communicate the message that women, even—or especially—lower-class women, should know their place and stay in it.[27]

In the conclusion to the novel, Esteban brings Dolores back to her original home. "Su jardincito, la huerta de Marta y los árboles frutales no solamente conservaban su verdura y primor, sino que habían recibido también innumerables y productivas mejoras que revelaban la mano inteligente del cultivador" (Her little garden, Marta's plot, and the fruit trees weren't just green and lush, but had been given numerous improvements that revealed the gardener's intelligent hand; 177). Esteban has faithfully tended the house and Dolores's beloved garden, and Dolores rewards his steadfastness through marriage. Dolores is at last returned to her appropriate physical and social space, dwelling in a "casita" and married to a fellow mestizo.

Like the other novels discussed in this chapter, La mestiza brings to the foreground topics of sexuality, race, and class and the ways in which those power dynamics (male/female; white/mestizo, Indian, or Afro-Hispanic; elite/lower class) map on to the physical spaces that people occupy. In many ways La mestiza recodifies traditional, colonial ideas about women's enclosure within the home, which may speak to the novel's status as the first published in the group discussed here and to Ancona's lifelong interest in regional history, as signaled by his devotion to writing a multivolume history of Yucatán and his several historical novels. Yet, as Ann Twinam points out, many of the strictures governing female comportment in the colonial era were true for elite but not lower-class women. The fact that Ancona projects those concerns about honor and purity onto poor women of color as represented by Juana and Dolores speaks to a more specifically nineteenth-century set of worries about the crossing of class and race lines. These concerns would also play out in Ancona's historical novels La cruz y la espada and Los mártires de Anáhuac, which dramatized his anxieties about racial mixing and set them during the conquests of Yucatán and Tenochti-tlán. In general Ancona was deeply preoccupied with the crossing of racial lines, which in *La mestiza* map onto class lines nearly exactly; whites are elite and wealthy, mestizos are poor and lower class. His white characters use their economic superiority in conjunction with race-based privilege to extract sexual concessions from lower-class women. Socioeconomic class is marked by the types of spaces that characters occupy and by their ability or lack thereof to violate spatial boundaries. Dolores is depicted in her home, in her extensive garden (which is the only place where she interacts with nature), and in the street for the sole purpose of going to the market. She never goes into a house in which she does not live. Esteban, too, goes to a similar list of places; he also enters both the houses where Dolores resides. His access to her homes is permissible within the novel's strict codes be-cause of his race and gender. When he goes into Dolores's dwelling space, it is to use his masculinity to protect her from the sexual depredations of whites. In these cases the solidarity of race and class is greater than the hierarchical inequality of gender. The physical spaces of the novel and the ways in which characters occupy, inhabit, and abandon them put into play attitudes about the proper occupation of space originating in Europe and North America. In *La mestiza* such ideas are displaced onto lower-class, ethnically marked women, making the projection of European ideals about bourgeois behavior an incongruent fit with the preindustrial reality of pro-vincial Mexico.

Pablo and Jaime wield too many advantages, and their power is overly determined because in all areas—race, gender, class—they enjoy privileges that their victims do not. Wealthy white men intrude into spaces where they do not belong, but lower-class mestizos either refrain from entering where they are prohibited or are barred from doing so, as Dolores is when she tries to enter Pablo's house. In *La mestiza* such limits on female physi-cal mobility are reinforced by the punishments enacted on the women who transgress them. Yet those women are also passive victims of white male mobility, as the spaces occupied by mestizos and especially by mestizas are too easily penetrated. While in other texts the porosity of the supposed barrier between private and public often facilitates women's entry into the public realm and allows them to take on functions within the public sphere, in *La mestiza* this permeability is always dangerous to women. Elite men and their mestiza accomplices fail to respect the separation of the private and public realms, which leads to the sexual victimization of women and to social decay. Ancona's novel frames the issue of female mobility, race relations, and the displacement of indigenous people from the countryside to a more urban environment in ways that forcefully disempower women, reinscribe the dominance of elite white men, and erase indigenous identity in favor of mestizos.

María, Aves sin nido, and *Martín Rivas* argue for the perpetuation of the separation of those spaces and of the gender roles assigned to each as a way to maintain and encourage the incipient bourgeoisie and its accompanying middle-class ideals. Moreover, the supposedly elite ideology of the separation of spheres also applied in literary texts to the lower classes. So, too, the lower-class women of *María, Aves sin nido, Martín Rivas*, and *La mestiza* are subjected to the separation of private and public. While the target audience of discourses emphasizing the sanctity of the home and the moral imperative that women stay in the home would most logically be the upper classes, who could afford nonworking women, many fictional works depict impoverished women who struggle to stay inside at all costs, even if their home is nothing more than a one-room shack. These texts contradicted the economic realities that dictated that many lower-class women left their homes to work, yet their message that a belief in the sanctity of the home transcended the boundaries of class, ethnicity, and race served to universalize, even naturalize, that ideal for readers, making it even more pervasive—and persuasive.

The separation of spheres functioned as a powerful trope in nineteenth-century Spanish American thought. Male writers projected ideals about the sanctity of the home to argue for women's ability to use their private influence on public actions. Paradoxically, authors positioned both types of discourse as obeying the demands of modernity: those who deployed more conventional notions about the separation of the public and private did so in an effort to gain the cultural capital of a certain modernity associated with Great Britain and Europe, while those who affirmed that the public/private split redounded to the benefit of women and thus of the nation laid claim to a progressive ideal of the nation that would include the participation of women. Finally, however, while the rhetoric of the separation of spheres could be malleable, it also proved restrictive, as it does in the novels analyzed here, which enforce and reiterate the idea that gendered activities, and the people associated with them, must be assigned to specific places. The insistent linkage of gender identity and space results in the enactment of restrictions on women's mobility, literal and metaphorical.

3

Constructions of Domesticity

It is by now a commonplace that in nineteenth-century Spanish American literature the family serves as a metaphor for the nation and that authors express their political agendas through allegories of courtship and marriage. In such readings, potential love matches symbolize the reconciliation of contesting political or ethnic groups and point to ways for the newly formed Spanish American nations to negotiate difference without falling into civil war. Most notably, Doris Sommer's *Foundational Fictions: The National Romances of Latin America* succinctly explains her project, subsequently taken up and adapted by a generation of critics, as one that wishes "to locate an erotics of politics, to show how a variety of novel national ideals are all ostensibly grounded in 'natural' heterosexual love and in the marriages that provided a figure for apparently nonviolent consolidation during internecine conflicts at midcentury" (6). At their core, Sommer's interpretations of what she identifies as the key novels in nineteenth- and twentieth-century Spanish America are concerned with courtship and the process of arriving, or failing to arrive, at successful matches. Her analysis concentrates on erotic love and the ways by which lovers overcome obstacles to marry and thus consummate the political unions signified by their personal relationships. Her work highlights the characters' struggles to lay claim to their love objects and on the resolution of those struggles in matrimony. *Foundational Fictions* offers a highly convincing analysis of Latin America's national novels and a rubric for further literary criticism that ties together representations of personal and political events.

Nonetheless, other critics have affirmed that Sommer's critical framework establishes a totalizing view of nineteenth-century Latin American literary production and also excludes multiple texts that, while influential or popular when they were published, did not achieve the status of canonical works. Historical novels, popular novels with stereotypically happy endings, and texts that present different views of interracial relations, for example, do not fit neatly into Sommer's persuasive schema.[1]

In Spanish America, men and women alike produced numerous texts revolving around the domestic theme. Many of these works, especially those written by women, failed to enter the literary canon that, in the early twentieth century, valorized what Sommer refers to as "national novels." The criteria established by later literary critics who prized features associated with realist and *modernista* literature rarely left room for writers whose works tended toward the romantic and the didactic. While Sommer emphasizes the search for successful (love) matches, nineteenth-century Spanish American narratives frequently display a persistent interest in describing what happens *after* the marriage. What I call a domestic discourse, a narrative thread or interpolated scenes representing established families, often runs parallel to the courtship narratives as young lovers make their way against a backdrop of domestic scenes; at other times, the home and the relationship between husband and wife or between mother and child form the centerpiece of the tale. Such constructions of domesticity appear both in Sommer's foundational fictions and in other nineteenth-century texts. Despite Sommer's assertion that domestic romances "end in satisfying marriage, the end of desire beyond which the narratives refuse to go" (6–7), many texts show the consequences of the productive unions that Sommer's foundational fictions advocate. Such domestic writings were an important part of literary discourses circulating throughout the nineteenth century. These stories and serialized novels, often published in journals and magazines with predominantly female readerships, were both popular and influential. Equally as important as the novels and stories depicting domesticity for male and female readers were the journal articles, conduct manuals, and visual imagery that produced representations of girls and women engaged in domesticity and that promoted and even critiqued the phenomenon widely known as the angel in the house, the self-sacrificing daughter, sister, or mother who worked to ensure household security and happiness. The exclusion of such works from the canon bespeaks neither a lack of popularity nor a lack of interest in domestic topics among the reading public at the time of publication. Like the national romance, domestic tales offered readers the means by which to imagine themselves involved in nation-building activities. At the same time, domestic ideology, with its rhetoric of self-abnegation for the good of the family, often came into conflict with the attributes of self-determination and single-mindedness necessary for the protagonists, male and female, of national romances. In either case, domestic discourses formed a vital element of the nineteenth-century Spanish American literary imagination.

Discourses of domesticity were embedded in a web of significance that connected them to modernizing ideals, resistance to social change, conflicts over gender and family roles, the desire to replicate European modernity, and the impulse to adhere to traditional Spanish and colonial values, and these meanings often existed simultaneously and even within the same text or cultural product. I argue that nineteenth-century men and women created specific images of domestic life in order to present persuasive arguments about the many issues to which they related domesticity and, often, to promote ideas about the potential or actual roles for women in society at large. The supposed ideals of domesticity, then, were subject to explicit and implicit manipulation and contradiction and the varied uses to which writers put those ideals reveal both the instability of such supposedly foundational rhetoric as well as its enduring power, which was the lure that attracted writers to it. The idealized images of domesticity deployed in numerous texts constituted a series of signifying shortcuts, and writers used them to establish commonalities with their readers at the same time that those same writers frequently critiqued, subverted, or contradicted the images and messages they invoked.[2]

The image of woman as the angel in the house became enormously popular in Europe, North America, and South America in the mid-nineteenth century. According to Bridget Aldaraca, domestic ideology in Spain was based in large part on the enduring concept of the perfect wife, "la perfecta casada," disseminated and systematized by Fray Luis de León's 1583 work of the same name (25). What differentiates nineteenth-century domesticity from earlier iterations is the concept that the private and public spheres are both crucially different and inextricably intertwined, as we saw earlier. The physical space of the house now has "a social content," as Aldaraca puts it (31). Within that space, the morally pure domestic angel creates a sanctuary from the public sphere and the pressures and potential vices of urban life. Nancy LaGreca states that the angel of the house is defined "in terms of the woman's relationship to those around her" (10); she is focused outwardly on the needs and wishes of others, not inwardly on herself. Through her beneficent influence her family maintains its spiritual and physical virtue and finds a respite from the contamination of public life. As Christine Stansell writes of North America, "Designating themselves moral guardians of their husbands and children, women became the standard-bearers of piety, decorum, and virtue" (xii). This perception was common in Latin America as well, where the 1859 publication of the Spaniard María del Pilar Sinués de Marco's *El ángel del hogar* and her subsequent prolific publishing career, during which she edited two journals, wrote over a hundred novels, and published widely in periodicals in Spain and Latin America, were instrumental in spreading the doctrine of the domestic angel throughout the continent. Arguing that women were best suited for the domestic role and that it was their social and spiritual duty to dedicate themselves to making the home a moral and physical haven, Sinués del Marco tapped into traditional Catholic beliefs idealizing motherhood and female purity as well as into newer discourses of modernity advocating the split between public and private and the ensuing relegation of women to the domestic sphere.

For many liberal thinkers, there was a potential ideological contradiction lurking here, in addition to the discursive contradiction just noted, in which domesticity's selflessness came into conflict with the exaltation of the self-realized individual required by the allegorical national novel. As noted in chapter 2, the division between the public and the private spheres that produced discourses about domesticity was associated with the onset of modernity. Yet women's roles as wives and mothers were traditional ones that they had held for centuries as caretakers and nurturers. Only with the apparent split between the public space of male commercial activity and the private space of female homemaking, which became visible as paid work shifted to spaces such as offices and factories that were outside the household, did the desire to convince both men and women that women belonged in the house take on urgency. Indeed, the perception that increasing numbers of women were leaving the space of the house to go to work in factories, schools, medical clinics, and offices helped create a counter-reaction that manifested in rhetoric that exhorted women to stay home and men to keep them there. Only the middle and upper classes had the privilege of acting upon this discourse, as lower-class families frequently depended on women's salaries. But the intellectuals who furthered the domestic ideal often worked to spread it to the popular classes as well.

Liberal intellectuals had to reframe the question of women's relationship to the home, even though the outcome was generally similar to that of the conservative view that maintained that women's place should continue to be in the home. Both conservative traditionalists and liberal modernizers connected national health and identity to women's place in the home. For the conservatives, women were to remain secluded, submissive to the male relatives, and to carry out their traditional duties. However, the liberals strove to resolve the potential ideological paradox by presenting the same situation as one in which women had the power of moral suasion and could rule over their domestic domain. By allotting women some capacity to act and speak within the space of the home, liberal thinkers could continue to attach the fate of women to national narratives of progress, rather than fostering an outdated idea of women as weak, inferior creatures who needed male protection within the enclosed space of the house.

The modern modality empowered women as spiritually superior beings who were responsible for domestic harmony, which then led to morally correct behavior in the public realm by their husbands and grown children. The home was construed as a space in which women exercised superior moral facilities and carried out the crucial role of raising the next generation of citizens. In this view, while men were the ultimate authorities, women had control over the emotional and spiritual areas that set the moral tone for their families. This allowed for the idealization of women as morally elevated and concerned with the physical and emotional well-being of others, a construction of which some writers would take advantage to posit more daring possibilities for women's roles. Envisioning women as both capable of and responsible for acting on behalf of others enabled liberal thinkers to take advantage of discourses of modernity based on the European and Anglo-American model, which included both an emphasis on the primacy of the domestic realm in women's lives and the belief that educated women who had some civil rights, albeit limited, were integral to projects of national progress.

This chapter reads novels and stories that invoke the domestic trope against this backdrop of nineteenth-century rhetoric about the private sphere, the home, and family. By claiming continuity between the home and the nation, authors of domestic narratives could make the case for the importance of women's role in constructing and maintaining the nation. On the one hand, then, domestic discourse and the theme of the angel in the home arose because of the division between private and public space. On the other hand, because that division was rhetorical in nature and did not mirror an objective external reality, many writers could envision a connectedness between the two realms that allowed for the possibility of women's seamless movement from the domestic to the public realm, rather than the disjuncture that other thinkers posited about modernity. The angel could enter the public hurly-burly, if not physically, at least psychically, and bring her moralizing, virtuous presence to the domain of business, politics, and commerce. By exercising her civilizing force within the home, her power also extended outward from the home.

In Mexico, a lively journalism industry sustained numerous newspapers, magazines, and serials throughout the nineteenth century. Laura Suárez de la Torre identifies *Diario de Méjico*, founded in 1805, as a key moment for Mexican journalism. Not only did the *Diario* give news and reports, but unlike its predecessors, it contained cultural reporting and serialized novels, which would be hallmarks of many periodicals throughout the century (11). After Independence, many more periodicals responding to the diverse political interests of their editors appeared, and beginning in the 1830s, literary magazines were especially popular. Suárez de la Torre argues that their very popularity led to an improvement in content and layout as the editors competed for readers and that these journals looked to newly literate groups such as women, children, and artisans to bolster readership (14–15).

Semana de las Señoritas Mexicanas (1850–52), edited by Juan B. Navarro, had both male and female readers. The subscription list shows the names of more men than women, which signals men's greater purchasing power; they were in all probability buying the magazine for their wives and daughters, who were less likely to have access to spending money. *Semana* was published in the capital and boasted nationwide circulation. An issue of *Semana* would usually contain essays on history, translations of French novels, poetry, recipes, household advice, sheet music, and illustrations, as well as opinion pieces. It typified the kind of printed matter to which women had access and which was likely to give voice to opinions about gender roles and the relationship of women to national identity and progress.

In the first issue the editor announced that the journal would fill the need for a women's magazine and show "a los claros talentos y perspicacia de nuestras bellas paisanas el movimiento intelectual del país" (the nation's intellectual movement to the clear talents and perspicacity of our lovely countrywomen; i), inform them of current events and important scientific discoveries, share Mexico's best literature, and disseminate ideas about piety and religion. The journal intended to educate its female readers, a declaration which makes it apparent that, at least in Navarro's view, women had not only lacked access to the kinds of information that *Semana de las Señoritas Mexicanas* offered but that they and their male relatives would benefit from such reading. His statement constructs a public push for female education and literacy as a desirable element of national progress. The journal consistently supported the doctrine of domesticity.[3] Instead of setting women up to compete directly with men, the writers strove to allay concerns about women becoming independent of men and threatening their dominance in the home or even outside of it. *Semana* did not aim to establish women's equality but to help them fulfill their natural role of bestowing charity upon all humanity. Writers often construed women's conventional role as extending outside the immediate space of the home to encompass the entire human race. In these ways the journal empowered women to take an active role outside the home as caregivers, but removed any possible threat of female independent agency by making that external role one that does not benefit women by improving their lot in life.

Twenty years later, *El Eco de Ambos Mundos: Periódico literario dedicado a las señoritas mexicanas* (1872–74) announced its goal of elevating women's status and explicitly connected that status to the fate of the nation, continuing the pattern of invoking the betterment of women's condition as a necessary component of the modern Mexican nation. The male editors claimed, "Dios al criar a la mujer, quiso darle al hombre un ángel protector. Ella, en medio de su debilidad, tiene algo de superior a nosotros" (God, upon creating woman, wished to give man a guardian angel. In the midst of her weakness, she has something superior to us; 3). Here again the rhetorical strategy that appears to empower women by elevating them removes them from a realm where they could directly influence male-dominated public affairs by making them distant angels, protective spirits who cast an amorphous positive glow over men, without actually enacting concrete change in the real world.

Woman's superiority lies in her loving, beneficent, protective nature, as she is "dispuesta a sacrificarse por su felicidad" (given to sacrifice herself for his happiness; 3), meaning the happiness of her male companion. But the editors distinguish between woman's voluntary self-sacrifice and her enforced subordination to men, as countries where women are "enslaved" show no signs of progress. Here, women's status is an indicator of modernity: "La condición de las mujeres es el termómetro que marca el grado de civilización y adelantamiento de un pueblo" (Woman's status is the thermometer measuring the degree of civilization and advancement of a society; 3). The editors even subtly nod to science by referring to the thermometer, a medical instrument, and likening women to it. Yet once again women do not participate actively in the modernizing project but represent modernity; this discursive formulation reiterates female passivity in the guise of making claims for women's active roles in the domestic sphere. Without having to call actively for an improvement in women's condition, simply reframing the terms in which that condition is described enables the male editors to participate in the movement toward modernity, exactly because women's status is so closely associated with a narrative of progress. For the editors of *El Eco de Ambos Mundos*, it is not necessary to implement, for example, laws guaranteeing women's rights or better education for girls; instead, they present women's traditional role within the home as one endowed with spiritual power. All that the editors need to do in order to stake their claim to modernity is to seize the opportunity offered by modernity's essentially rhetorical status and to say that they recognize women's moral superiority within the home.

The message is underscored by the fact that in the same issue, María del Pilar Sinués de Marco published an article titled "Libertad," in which she asserts, "La libertad no sirve de nada a la mujer, por el contrario, es para ella el mayor de los males" (Liberty is worthless for woman; on the contrary, for her it is the greatest of evils; 73). Sinués de Marco worries that if women win emancipation in the form of higher education, they will abandon the domestic duties for which they are naturally best suited. Woman's mission consists of giving her children a moral and religious education and training her daughters in particular to be good wives and mothers, so no further education or freedom is necessary or even desirable. While Sinués de Marco notes that women have the crucial task of running their households efficiently, she does not go into detail about the type of education a typical middle-class woman would need in order to keep a household budget on track, manage and oversee servants, administer basic first aid and medical care, and teach one's children to read and write. Instead, she emphasizes the decorative nature of women's roles. Women bring beauty and virtue to the home, which, as we saw in chapter 2, became an increasingly important and specifically feminine space in the nineteenth century. The inclusion of Sinués de Marco's essay, with its forceful rejection of emancipation for women and its embrace of what she herself calls the "yoke" of matrimony, sends a strong message to the female readers of *El Eco de Ambos Mundos* that their place truly is in the home.

La Mujer Mexicana enjoyed a four-year run, publishing eighteen issues between 1901 and 1905. It is notable for being published in Morelia, not Mexico City, which then as now was the country's capital in every area: political, social, economic, and artistic. The presence and success of *La Mujer Mexicana* in a secondary city demonstrates the way in which rhetoric about women's roles and the desirability of modernization and progress pervaded the national conversation.

Mariano de Jesús Torres (1838–1921), the editor, was a regionally known historian, journalist, and author of dramas and poetry.[4] He explicitly states in the introduction to the first issue that Mexican women emblematize the country's pride in its strides toward progress. Each issue usually included biographies of Mexican women from pre-conquest times to the present as well as those of other countries, poetry, household advice and recipes, essays, and news items. Both men and women published in its pages, but the image of women presented in the journal was essentially a passive one. Mexican women could be displayed as examples before the rest of the world, the journal's readers were educated by exposure to the edifying materials Torres published, and women adorned the home through their virtuous sacrifice of any personal desires.[5]

Rather than offer specific advice about what to do in order to achieve that status, Torres instructed his female readers in what sort of personality and emotional affect they should adopt. Women should not actively acquire knowledge but should focus on maintaining a state of emotional readiness that will impart tranquility and sweetness to their families.[6] Torres and his predecessors used a consistent set of strategies to enforce women's passive occupation of the domestic space, by assigning to the role of the angel in the house an elevated moral and spiritual dimension. When they endowed the domestic role with enhanced social cachet and described it as women's highest, purest mission, they constructed a vision of domestic femininity that was nearly impossible to avoid, because rejecting it would entail rejecting sacred rights, a noble mission, and the all-important cause of modernity, which even before Porfirio Díaz's thirty-year dictatorship and the associated explicit emphasis on positivism and science was a crucial element in the Mexican imaginary.

Such discourse is strikingly consistent across decades, even though the historical context was changing rapidly and dramatically. The department store La Gran Sedería published a free weekly advertising supplement with editorial content called *Femina* from 1910 through 1912, edited by Salvador Palencia y Llerena. During the span of its publication, Porfirio Díaz's rule ended and the cataclysm that would be the Mexican Revolution began. Yet *Femina*'s pages reflected none of this social upheaval; it echoed and produced normative discourse about women's roles. As the editor announced in January 1911, *Femina* was intended as a periodical for the home, particularly for mothers and for young women destined to become wives and mothers. While *Femina* did acknowledge that opportunities for women outside the home were increasing through articles such as "Nuevas carreras para la mujer" (New careers for women), which noted that women in other countries held jobs in such occupations as steamboat captains and diplomats (Oct. 9, 1910), the anonymous writers also asserted the primacy of women's roles in the home.[7] Women should be malleable, gentle, and submissive; the writers specifically rejected the notion that a woman could or should outshine her male counterpart. A woman's most important role is to create a domestic haven where her husband can find shelter and rest from the pressures of the outside world. They use the phrase "la verdadera mujer" (the true woman) to construct a forcefully normative discourse that categorizes all those who do not create this ideal domestic space as "false women" who cannot participate in the gender-stratified spaces of *fin de siglo* Mexican society. The placement of such arguments about women's subordination to male desires in what we would today call an advertorial gives valuable evidence about what kinds of rhetoric about domesticity remained popular into the twentieth century, as the marketers for La Gran Sedería clearly believed that voicing such sentiments would attract female buyers to their store.

Not only did ideas about domesticity and women's place in the home appear in a wide range of periodicals in Mexico, but writers also made use of the image of the angel in the house and all the associations that accreted to her in fictional works that served to advance associated arguments about national identity and the political direction they believed the country should take. One of the most striking examples is Ignacio Manuel Altamirano's novel *El Zarco*. A full-blooded Chontal Maya, Altamirano (1834–93) was a journalist and publisher, a professor, Supreme Court justice, congressional representative, diplomat, and prolific author of novels, essays, and works of history. He supported Liberal president Benito Juárez and strove to bolster the ideologies of an independent, liberal nation after the war with the Conservatives had riven Mexico.

In *El Zarco*, written in 1885 but not published until 1901, Altamirano turned his attention to the bloody and chaotic period of 1861–62, examining the effects of civil disorder on the small town of Yautepec and its inhabitants. Through the diametrically opposed characters of Manuela and Pilar, Altamirano also advanced his ideas about ideal femininity and the participation of women in public life and national discourse. In *El Zarco*, Manuela, a white, upper-class beauty, selfishly abandons her widowed mother and runs away with the bandit of the title, while the lower-class mestiza Pilar faithfully remains at home, takes care of Manuela's bereft mother, and eventually wins the heart of the novel's true hero, the Indian blacksmith Nicolás. When the young women are first seen, Pilar is making a crown of orange blossoms, signifying her purity and, as Manuela says scornfully, her desire to marry. Marriage is much on the minds of Manuela, Pilar, and Antonia, Manuela's mother; the last, because marriage affords protection by securing the domestic space and installing women safely within it. The defiant Manuela views marriage as a way to escape the confines of the home, while Pilar yearns for domestic stability. In Altamirano's novel, constructed so as to offer a viable image of Mexican national identity based on mestizaje and the hard work of the lower class, Pilar is figured as the feminine ideal and wins the love of the industrious Nicolás.

When Nicolás is imprisoned by an unjust military commander, Pilar adapts her domestic role to take care of him; she visits all possible authorities to plead his case, but the only action that has any meaningful effect on his prison conditions is that she prepares and sends food to him in jail. She uses her tears to win sympathy from the sergeant taking Nicolás to jail and to appeal to Nicolás's co-workers so that they will support him, manipulating her self-presentation as a vulnerable, emotional woman to make her sudden move into the public realm of male-dominated politics socially acceptable. Nicolás finds consolation in his knowledge of Pilar's love and care; "había un ángel que lo protegía" (an angel protected him; 45), he realizes in an explicit evocation of the angel of the house. Pilar also refuses to abandon Antonia, who, although deserted by her biological daughter, now finds herself comforted "sobre todo de aquel ángel, que más que su ahijada, parecía ser su verdadera hija, heredera de su virtud, de su sensatez y de su noble carácter" (above all by that angel, who more than her goddaughter, seemed to be her true daughter, heir to her virtue, her discretion, and her noble character; 48). Once again Pilar is figured as the domestic angel who puts the needs and desires of others above her own in stark contrast to the selfish Manuela. Such images consistently support the idea that the ideal woman devotes herself to caring for and nurturing others, from her parents to her male companion.

Furthermore, Altamirano uses these depictions of normative femininity to uphold the Liberal state and to advance his own ideas about nationalism and patriotism.[8] Manuela transgresses the social order by assuming agency, abandoning her angelic role, and eloping with El Zarco; such actions destabilize society by destroying multiple family units (mother-daughter and husband-wife, as Manuela and El Zarco never regularize their relationship) and, as Cruz notes, by crossing class lines (78–79). Pilar restores social order in conjunction with Nicolás as she both fulfills her feminine role as the nurturing angel and helps return Nicolás to his rightful place in society. Pilar works through existing social structures that have been disempowered and rechannels power through them, making the unsupervised army officials subject to civil control. It is perhaps this to which Sommer refers when she describes Pilar's identity as "gendercrossed," saying, "Her intrepid valor combines with an ideally sweet and submissive nature. It is she who organizes the popular resistance to the army that has imprisoned her man, mobilizing political and then paramilitary support" (227). On the other hand, Cruz describes Pilar's interventions as "súplicas y ruegos" more than concrete actions (pleas and petitions; 75). Whatever Pilar's degree of autonomy and agency early in the novel, at the end she is safely married to Nicolás and ready to formally take up the role of angelic wife and future mother that her crown of orange blossoms presaged. After all, women cannot be citizens in Altamirano's ideal Mexico, only mothers to future citizens. *El Zarco* consistently employs normative images of femininity to encode messages about national identity and the role of the family as a social unit comprising the nation, in a forceful argument that national stability depends profoundly on domestic stability and on women's acceptance of their domestic destiny.

Pilar manages to negotiate the outside world successfully because her ultimate goal is to return to and re-create the safe space of the home where she can live out her domestic idyll. The idea that the home constitutes the best and, indeed, only place for the domestic angel and that the physical and psychic worlds outside the home are fraught with peril for women features not just in Altamirano's novel but in other essays and stories throughout the continent. David Joaquín Guzmán's lengthy essay "Amor a las ocupaciones del hogar," published in *El Repertorio Salvadoreño*, touches many of these themes.

El Repertorio Salvadoreño, a publication issued by the Academia de Ciencias y Bellas Letras de San Salvador, appeared monthly from 1888 to 1894 and was a general interest periodical with sections on literature, the mathematical sciences, and natural science. A scientist with interests in botany, medicine, and zoology as well as the first director of the Museo Nacional of El Salvador, Guzmán (1843–1927) founded the Academia de Ciencias y Bellas Letras and gave the Academia's "Discurso Inaugural," also published in *El Repertorio Salvadoreño*, in which he praised mankind's inexorable march toward progress and called for El Salvador to develop its industry, infrastructure, and educational systems. A year later in "Amor a las ocupaciones del hogar," he reiterated the importance of national progress and executed several complicated and contradictory rhetorical maneuvers as he attempted to establish a sustainable model for Salvadoran women's role in the nation's advancement. He created a self-reinforcing cycle in which the home was the only safe and nurturing space for women, who needed to stay in the home in order to maintain its nurturing aspects. The home supported and protected women, and in turn women's occupation of the home made it a nurturing and caring space for their families. There was no need for women to leave the house, and, in fact, her job was to make the house such a benevolent, uplifting place that her family could find everything they needed and wanted within it:

> El sagrado vínculo del matrimonio exige [. . .] que la casa sea el centro de todos los atractivos, y por eso [la mujer] debe procurar embellecerla con ese arte que sólo las mujeres poseen, que sólo el orden conserva, que la verdadera felicidad doméstica fortifica, haciendo todo otro entretenimiento innecesario. Los festejos y reuniones de tono podrán proporcionarle los goces que la familia le brinda a cada instante. Esos entretenimientos, además, puede la familia procurárselos en el seno mismo del hogar, en esas reuniones de confianza que sirven para fortificar los lazos de la amistad y para pulir los modales y buenas costumbres.

> The sacred bond of matrimony demands that the house be the center of all attractions, and so [woman] should decorate it with the art that only women possess, that only order preserves, that true domestic happiness fortifies, making all other entertainment superfluous. Respectable parties and gatherings can offer the pleasures that the family enjoys. The family can hold such entertainments in the very bosom of the home, in intimate reunions that serve to fortify the bonds of friendship and polish manners and good behavior. (99)

Guzmán deftly weaves together several discursive strands here. He claims that women have a unique set of skills, an assertion that implicitly and explicitly imposes on them the responsibility of exercising those abilities to make the home a welcoming space for the family. He also associates women's domestic skills with words denoting attractiveness, beauty, and charm, typically feminine attributes ("atractivos," "embellecer," "arte"), and marks the home as a feminine space that is the extension of the female body ("el seno mismo del hogar"). This vocabulary reinforces the message that domesticity and femininity are intimately connected with each other and with the physical space of the house. The repetition of "fortificar" communicates the force and strength of women's activities while those activities themselves are couched in terms of the diversion and entertainment they offer ("festejos y reuniones," "reuniones de confianza," "pulir los modales y buenos costumbres"). Rather than being matters of great societal import or political heft, they have to do with emotional bonds and the construction and improvement of interpersonal relationships.

Guzmán locates women in the home, constructs that space as a nurturing, family-oriented place, and associates women's traditional roles as caretakers with these activities of consolidating bonds of family members and friends. By repeatedly emphasizing that women's vital tasks lie in the sentimental arena, Guzmán reinforces the idea that women are primarily emotional rather than intellectual, and he excludes them from the male-dominated, logical professions that exist in the public realm, underscoring further still the concept that women belong in the domestic space.

"Amor a las ocupaciones del hogar" then explicitly connects women's roles in the home, family, and nation with the national and continental project of progress and modernization. Guzmán writes prescriptively,

> El mejor modo de que la mujer trabaje con provecho y honra de la sociedad, es cumpliendo con todos los deberes de la familia, y que a la vez, coopere también en el movimiento general del progreso, que así lo hace al impartir a sus hijos, los futuros ciudadanos, una educación completa.

> The best way that a woman can work for the advantage and honor of her society is by discharging all family duties, and at the same time, cooperating with the general movement of progress, which she does by giving her children, future citizens, a complete education. (100)

With the conjunction "and" Guzmán links women's familial work with societal progress, specifying that mothers are the first and most important teachers of their children. Women themselves are barred from citizenship, an idea that always goes unacknowledged in Guzmán's essay and others like it, but that does not exempt them from the demands of the nation or from the responsibility of ensuring domestic harmony.

What makes such domestic harmony different for Guzmán than for other writers who adopt a more traditional view of society and gender roles is the series of explicit connections he draws toward the end of his essay among national progress, domesticity, the angel in the house, capitalism, and what we might call vocational training for women, home economics before the term was formally coined. In an apparent contradiction, Guzmán insists that women, suited by inclination and character to domestic roles, must nonetheless be trained in how to execute those roles. In order to maintain their families' positions in the burgeoning middle class, women need to learn how to run their households efficiently, to save and spend money wisely, and to respect work and workers. Here Guzmán's writing takes into account the shift that occurred in Latin America over the course of the nineteenth century as national economies began the long, slow transition from near-feudal agricultural economies in which the miniscule upper class lived off the labor of their tenant farmers to bourgeois capitalism in which a growing middle class saw greatly expanded opportunities for paid work in a range of occupations. His insistence that work is "un hábito honesto y agradable, útil a la existencia social" (an agreeable and honest habit, useful to social existence; 104) forms part of his argument, here and in other writings, that national progress depends on widespread participation in the capitalist economy via paid work, commerce, and consumerism. Women who teach their daughters to appreciate work and to be capable of working also teach them economic independence and participate in national modernization. Because Guzmán stresses that the goal is for women to remain in the home as watchful guardians of men's money, he also reinforces the standards of angelic domesticity, in which women actively enjoy doing household work.

> Dichosas las jóvenes que heredan o aprenden de sus madres el amor a los quehaceres domésticos, acostumbrándose, desde temprano, a no echar a menos las ocupaciones que contribuyen a la conservación del capital del padre, ocupaciones honestas y adaptables al sexo y a su dignidad.

Lucky are the girls who inherit or learn from their mothers a love of domestic chores, becoming accustomed from an early age to not ignoring those tasks which contribute to conserving their fathers' capital, honest tasks, appropriate to their sex and dignity. (105)

Mothers are responsible for transmitting to their daughters, through education, influence, and heredity, not just a sense of domestic responsibility but a love for those domestic chores. Guzmán specifies "ocupaciones honestas," thus underscoring the idea that paid work could be a respectable use of time for women and that they could leave the home to work without suffering a loss of reputation. Both domestic and extra-domestic work are activities that preserve and increase familial wealth. Guzmán in these ways uses conventional notions of domesticity and transforms them over the course of his essay to advance a very specific agenda about modernity and progress as tied to and dependent on market capitalism.

Another influential, prolific, and multitalented writer and intellectual was Soledad Acosta de Samper (1833–1913). The daughter of the Colombian general Joaquín Acosta and his Canadian wife, Caroline Kemble, Acosta de Samper was educated in Bogotá, in Halifax, Nova Scotia, and in Paris before returning to Colombia and meeting her husband, the writer and politician José María Samper, who supported her career. Trilingual in Spanish, French, and English, Acosta de Samper became a prolific writer in multiple genres. Fervently sure of the importance of understanding national and global history, she wrote numerous historical essays and biographies and fifteen historical novels. She also wrote short stories, plays, and essays on topics ranging from religion to education to women's rights. Acosta de Samper and her work, which explored the question of women's status, education, and rights, were vital participants in Colombia's robust intellectual community. Her writing appeared in the leading journals of Colombia and Spanish America, and she also founded and published several journals. During the first half of her writing career, she wrote many works of fiction focusing on women's lives, hopes, and goals, several of which will be treated here.

Acosta de Samper often questioned social norms and the widespread effort to instill in women habits and beliefs of conformity and submission. In her novels *Laura* and *Una holandesa en América*, first published in the

1870s, her protagonists struggle against society's expectations for female behavior and especially against the strictures of the doctrine of the angel in the house. While they do not rebel openly, narrative asides in both texts and the lives and eventual destinies of both women reveal a thorough critique of Colombian society's emphasis on limiting female participation and self-expression.

Laura was a six-part serial published under the pseudonym "Aldebarán" in *El Bien Público* in November and December 1870.[9] This journal, directed by José María Quijano, appeared twice a week from July 29, 1870, through August 6, 1872. Aimed at a general audience, it boasted the lengthy and descriptive subtitle "Periódico politico, literario, noticioso, y de ciencias, industria, comercio, estadística, costumbres y variedades" (Political, literary, news magazine, and science, industry, commerce, statistics, customs, and miscellaneous items; Alzate 12). The serial traces Laura's education into femininity and the course of her unhappy marriage, focusing on her emotional trajectory as she discovers that her adored husband is an adulterer. She nurses him through a near-fatal illness out of duty, causing him to fall truly in love with her, but by then Laura can no longer reciprocate his emotions. In the novel's conclusion Laura dies, granting her husband forgiveness with her last breath.

Laura does not begin life auspiciously as the stereotypical domestic angel; the early death of her own mother, the person who should naturally have shaped her personality and comportment, means that Laura has failed to become successfully integrated into feminine society. Acosta emphasizes that Laura's tendency to freely express her emotions, be they positive or negative, causes her to act rudely to those around her. In order to further her instruction in proper feminine behavior, Laura's father moves from their isolated hacienda to a nearby town where neighbors and company successfully domesticate her: "su carácter fue suavizando; los rasgos desagradables de él se notaban menos, y aprendió a encubrir hasta cierto punto la violencia de sus sentimientos. [. . .] fue creciendo y perfeccionándose" (her character was mellowing; her disagreeable traits were less obvious, and she learned to conceal the violence of her emotions. [. . .] she was growing up and perfecting herself; 33). Acosta draws attention to the fact that Laura must learn how to act like a woman, a strategy that shows that the domestic virtues are a social construct, not an innate set of characteristics naturally possessed by all women. Laura is interpolated into femininity; she must learn not how to become a woman but how to become the right kind of woman, to paraphrase Simone de Beauvoir. Acosta also critiques the particular ways in which such femininity is created by noting that others perceive Laura's emotions as excessive and "violent." If women are excluded from the realm of the rational and the intellectual because they are overly emotional, they are not permitted to experience the full range of their emotions (anger, sadness, passion), meaning that the domestic arena is also not a space in which all women naturally fit.

Laura's hasty marriage to Amadeo is attributed to her eagerness to accede to social norms and her learned willingness to ignore her own better instincts in favor of following social norms. Her new husband's neglect causes Laura to fail to create the domestic haven that would, if the proponents of conventional femininity were correct, entice him to remain with her. When she eventually discovers the extent of his infidelity, "su vida no tenía objeto ya" (her life lost all purpose; 52). Only at this point, when the domestic ideal has been thoroughly destroyed, does Laura begin to emulate the feminine models held up to her and to all women of her class. She finally dominates her emotions, just at the moment when societal expectations would have her give in to sentiment and to pardon her erring husband. Instead, Laura consciously decides not to love Amadeo and adopts a cool, uncaring demeanor, of which the omniscient narrator carefully comments:

> No queremos decir que nuestra heroína fuese un dechado de cualidades, no que así se debe manejar toda mujer; pues hay quien crea que la mayor virtud en la esposa es el olvido de los sentimientos personales: mostrarse en todo caso mansa, tierna y amable, no resentir agravio y permanecer siempre la sierva de su señor.

> I don't mean that our heroine was a paragon of virtue, or that all women should behave thus; for there are those who believe that the greatest virtue in a wife is to forget all personal sentiments: always to act as if she were meek, tender, and sympathetic, not to feel aggravation and to always be the servant of her lord and master. (58)

In refusing to adopt the pose of the "mujer abnegada" or long-suffering wife, Laura defies gender norms, and the narrator's remarks transmit implicit approval of Laura's attitude. The use of the phrase "hay quien crea" imposes distance between those who believe such things and the narrative voice itself, sending a delicate critique of the belief that wifely virtue consists in the erasure of selfhood.

Laura becomes the dominant person in her marriage, reversing the paradigm expressed by "those who believe" that the perfect wife is perfectly submissive. She controls her husband's access to money and grants him permission to live "donde prefiera, aquí en mi casa" (wherever you like, here in my house; 61) or elsewhere. By referring to their home as "mi casa" at a time when husbands controlled their wives' property, Laura asserts her own right to her space, ejects Amadeo from it, and definitively excludes the possibility of domestic paradise. Acosta de Samper emphasizes the transactional nature of marriage and exposes the discourse of angelic domesticity as a cover for mechanisms that ensure the transmission of capital from one man to another via the female body.

In what veers dangerously close to a parody of conventional discourse about marriage, Acosta de Samper uses the commonplace term "yugo de matrimonio" negatively as Laura tells her husband:

> El yugo del matrimonio no se puede sacudir sino con la muerte; procuremos hacerlo lo menos pesado posible, cumpliendo yo estrictamente con mis deberes, y usted procurando guardar a lo menos las apariencias de hombre casado: es lo único que debemos exigirnos mutuamente para que nuestra vida sea menos desagradable, ya que jamás será feliz.

> The yoke of matrimony can't be removed except by death; let's try to make it the least burdensome possible, I by complying strictly with my duties, and you trying to uphold at least the appearance of a married man; that is all we can expect from one another so that our life will be less disagreeable, given that it will never be happy. (61)

Marriage was frequently described as a yoke that could be borne lightly and that women were tasked with making a joyous and rewarding connection.

Here, however, Laura rejects her assigned role as the wife who suffers in silence at worst or who brings happiness to her domestic haven at best. By telling Amadeo that she will strictly comply with her duties, she underscores the ways in which marriage imposes unwelcome burdens on women. The use of the word "estrictamente" is double-edged: She will carry out her responsibilities exactly as she should, allowing no room for complaint from others. But she will not go above and beyond those duties to enhance her husband's domestic experiences. Social norms dictate that when a husband causes an unhappy marriage, the wife is responsible for creating a happy home. Here Laura firmly rejects such a possibility, affirming that their married life will never be happy. Acosta de Samper reveals the failures of domestic discourse through her heroine's noncompliance.

When Laura nurses Amadeo back to health, the narrator characterizes Laura as exercising the ultimate in self-control. Her long-postponed assumption of the role of the domestic angel is an almost crushing burden.

> Siempre cuidadosa, abnegada, admirable, nada olvidaba, ni desmayaba jamás; bien que, eso sí, ni una vez salía de sus labios la más leve palabra afectuosa, ni se la oía un suspiro ni un lamento: impasible, tranquila, severa como la estatua del deber, pero de un deber sublime, guiado sólo por la fría razón.

> Always careful, self-sacrificing, admirable, she forgot nothing, nor did she ever faint; but it is true that she never uttered even a word of affection, nor did she sigh or lament: she was impassive, calm, severe as the statue of duty, but a sublime duty, guided only by cold reason. (66)

Acosta de Samper insistently points to the stark division between action and motivation, exposing the hollowness at the heart of this particular domestic angel and at the root of domestic discourse in general. Laura epitomizes reason and logic, stereotypically male attributes, rather than love and emotion, feminine attributes. Only on her own deathbed does she manage to give the now-repentant Amadeo a loving glance, but tellingly, she never gives voice to her newfound sentiments; instead, she dies. The message is that love kills women. In the interstices between Laura's actions and her emotions, between lived reality and societal expectations,

Acosta de Samper inserts her critique of the restrictive gender norms that tell women not only what to do but how to feel and exposes the hypocrisy of these systems.

Six years later, Acosta de Samper serialized *Una holandesa en América* in *La Ley* under the same pseudonym of "Aldebarán." The novel was reprinted, with changes by Acosta, in Curacao in 1888 under her own name. Here is the story of Lucía, daughter of a Dutch mother and an Irish father, who is raised in Holland by her aunt. Lucía comes to Colombia as a young woman to join the father and younger siblings whom she barely knows. Her eccentric, laudanum-addicted father owns a ramshackle, isolated hacienda where her sisters have been allowed to roam unchecked in defiance of codes of behavior for upper-class woman and where her brothers and the servants treat one another as equals, threatening the social hierarchy. The novel focuses on Lucía's efforts to bring civilization and order to the filthy, chaotic hacienda by educating her six young brothers and sisters, to reform her father's laudanum habit, and to coax her errant older sister into some semblance of "correct" behavior. As her Colombian friend Mercedes advises her, "El deber cumplido es siempre dulce. [. . .] Si no hubiera que hacer sacrificios, ¿existirían acaso virtudes?" (A duty carried out is always sweet. [. . .] If one didn't have to make sacrifices, would there even be virtues? 131) In contrast to *Laura*, in *Una holandesa en América* the heroine manages to enact domesticity in both the letter and the spirit of the law.

Lucía's work acquires even greater significance, in contrast to Laura's frigid maintenance of the domestic façade, because it takes place in a time of political upheaval and national turmoil. When she visits Mercedes in Bogotá, civil war breaks out and the girls take refuge in a convent; Lucía's brothers join the Liberal army and are swept up in the fighting. Lucía's role is to nurture this next generation of Colombian citizens and, by bringing peace and order to her family's hacienda, to create a microcosm of what the nation as a whole should resemble. Throughout, Lucía remains conscious of her higher calling to bring order and tranquility to her disordered home. Indeed, in her letters to Mercedes, she frames her task in religious terms: "Tendré fuerzas, valor y perseverancia, si Dios me lo permite, para reformar con el tiempo esta familia" (I will have the strength, courage, and perseverance, if God allows, to reform this family in time; 142). At the same time she rejects the lure of the cloistered life of nuns, seeing them as inherently egotistical for not putting the needs of others above their own desires. Such comments shape a particular image of domestic virtue. The angel of the house sacrifices her own wishes to satisfy the needs of others, but even more, she raises others to a greater moral stature through her actions and examples.[10]

Finally, in the novel's epilogue, set seven years after her arrival in Colombia, Lucía has achieved the apotheosis of domesticity: "Nada podia verse más suave, noble y digno que la fisonomía de esta mujer, siempre activa, ocupada, diligente, aseada hasta la exageración, bondadosa hasta el extremo" (Nothing could be more noble or dignified than the face of this woman, always active, busy, diligent, clean to the point of exaggeration, generous in the extreme; 266). Indeed, her father explicitly addresses her as "ángel de mi casa" (angel of my house; 269). It is revealing that despite all that Lucía has done to convert the chaotic space of the hacienda into a tidy, well-run home, it remains her father's house, not hers. No matter what she does, she lives in her father's home as his dependent. Despite her lack of economic independence, she holds moral sway over the household, which, I will argue, provides more personal fulfillment than the destiny typically seen as best suited to elite women: marriage.

There are two counternarratives to Lucía's tale of domestic accomplishment in *Una holandesa en América*. In one, Lucía's sister Clarisa marries a carpenter against her father's wishes and constantly argues both with him and her husband. Her marriage is a doubly defiant act. Her father professes to be a true democrat, and one of the reasons for the chaos in his house is that he encourages his sons to mix with the servants as equals. Yet he is outraged when Clarisa marries far below their social class. By doing so, she not only selects her own husband rather than waiting for paternal approval but she also exposes her father's hypocrisy and double standards. Only at the end of the novel is Clarisa redeemed thanks to Lucía, who arranges for her to work as a seamstress in Bogotá. Thus she finally engages in meaningful work that is appropriate to her gender and her class. In a counterpoint to Lucía, the self-serving Clarisa puts her own wishes above the needs and happiness of others. Yet she herself is never happy, suggesting that Lucía's ability to subsume her own desires in her execution of her duties is a more valuable life skill than Clarisa's incessant egotism.

Mercedes, who marries the man of her dreams, provides the other alternative to Lucía's life of domestic spinsterhood. This should be the storybook happy ending, yet Mercedes writes to Lucía prior to her marriage that she believes her future husband would prefer her to be more submissive and less articulate about her own opinions.

> Los hombres me han dicho [. . .]: buscan en el ser amado absoluta sumisión; quieren ejercer un dominio completo sobre nuestra alma; figúraseme a veces que ellos querrían vernos moralmente a sus pies, a pesar de que se fingen nuestros vasallos y nos llaman ángeles y diosas.

> Men have told me . . . : they look for absolute submission in the woman they love; they want to exercise complete control over our soul; it seems to me sometimes that they would like to see us, morally speaking, at their feet, in spite of the fact that they pretend to be our vassals and call us angels and goddesses. (250)

Mercedes's assessment of male wishes contains a pointed critique of the dominant paradigm mandating that women cede to men in all aspects of their lives, even their thoughts. The domestic angel systematically erases her own subjectivity as she meets the needs of others. Mercedes's case, however, shows the limits of that erasure of self. If men construct their needs as requiring absolute control over their wives' very thoughts, then perfect domesticity means giving up any claim to intellectual independence.

Lucía herself is far from the submissive model that Mercedes grimly characterizes as the male ideal. If Lucía were to accede to her father's wishes as Mercedes describes, she would not be the moral paragon and reformer that the novel elevates as its female role model. It is because she repeatedly defies her father that she succeeds in her civilizing mission at his hacienda. She throws away his laudanum drops, thereby breaking his opium addiction and improving his temper. She also converts to Catholicism against his will and defies his atheism by bringing religion to the rest of the hacienda, saving the money she earns from domestic chores to sponsor a visiting priest. In a novel full of strong-minded women—even Clarisa has the force of character necessary to defy first her father and then her husband—Lucía is the strongest by far, controlling her own life and the lives of those around her. In the novel's conclusion her father laments the fact that in taking care of him and her siblings she has lost her chance for personal happiness, that is, fulfillment in marriage and motherhood. She responds that "lo único positive en este mundo es el íntimo sentimiento y la sincera convicción de haber cumplido estrictamente con nuestro deber" (the only positive thing in this world is the intimate sentiment and profound conviction of having complied with our duty; 270). Acosta de Samper's message is that moral duty is the most important force governing human beings and that Lucía is by this standard the most powerful person in the book. She controls and influences the lives of everyone on the hacienda. She exercises autonomy and power, and while not traditionally happy as her father might see it, she is certainly by far the happiest woman in the book, much more so than her married counterparts. In *Una holandesa en América* Acosta de Samper manipulates the conventional image of the submissive angel in the house to argue that it is possible to use the domestic role assigned to women by society to assert control over the lives and souls of others.

Twenty-five years later, Acosta de Samper remained occupied by questions of women's roles and the negotiation of gender norms. In 1902 she began publishing a monthly series of small volumes whose title, *Biblioteca del Hogar* (Bogotá: Imprenta del Vapor), indicates its purpose: to enable families to create their own library of works suitable for domestic consumption. Each volume contained a single narrative such as a fictional story, biography, history, or travelogue appropriate for all family members; it was material "que pued(a) introducirse en el hogar sin riesgo" (that could enter the home without risk; 65). One of these volumes featured her novella "Amor de madre: que todo lo demás es aire" (A mother's love: Everything else is simply air), which begins with a debate over duty and honor versus family affective bonds. While the male characters praise historical men who have sacrificed their children for a religious or political cause, the female characters and even some of the men condemn such men for their lack of compassion and caring. As one male debater explains this attitude, "las madres siempre han sido madres" (mothers have always been mothers; 5). This straightforward statement carries a host of implications: to be a mother is to incarnate and transmit all the qualities associated with motherhood, not just with parenting. Mothers always put their children first, and this focus on the individual means that they cannot see the greater social or national good; the speaker gives the example of the mayor's wife who, when her son is taken hostage by the enemy besieging the city, surrenders the entire town to save her child's life. Paradoxically, these conceptions of motherhood also mean that mothers conceive of virtue differently than men. Hence they may flout laws and regulations that interfere with the execution of their maternal responsibilities, and they act ethically if not legally. As the unnamed female narrator says, "Una madre [. . .] no ofrece voluntariamente la vida de sus hijos sino en casos muy extraordinarios. Una madre es capaz de cometer un crimen para evitar que sus hijos lo hagan" (A mother . . . does not voluntarily sacrifice her children's lives except in extraordinary circumstances. A mother is capable of committing a crime so that her children will not; 6–7). To illustrate this point, she then tells the story of Francisca, a widow during the War of Independence.

When Francisca discovers that her son plans to murder the man who ruined his father, she exclaims, "¡Daría mi vida por la suya!" (I would give my life for his; 18) and decides to take a course of action that will provide her son with "una lección que le mantendría en el camino de la virtud" (a lesson that will keep him on the path of virtue; 19). She then commits the murder herself and, although her life is spared at the last second, she goes insane and never recognizes her son again, in an ironic narrative stroke. Like Laura and Lucía, Francisca complies strictly with the ideology of the angel of the house, making the ultimate sacrifice for her child. Her example of angelic behavior is so extreme, however, that like Laura's sarcastically meticulous obedience to the domestic code, her actions serve as a decided critique of gender norms. After all, her adherence to the expectation that mothers provide examples of virtue for their sons leads her to commit murder, the ultimate crime. This cannot be what society expects, reads the subtext of the story, yet it is one of the many unwelcome results of a distorted system of beliefs about appropriate gendered behavior. Acosta de Samper's subversive narratives undermine and critique the prevailing codes of behavior for women.

Juana Manuela Gorriti, whose role as a journalist, magazine editor, and renowned hostess of literary salons was crucial in developing a robust community of intellectual women, similarly made use of domestic discursivity in ways that subverted dominant gender norms. Gorriti (Argentina, 1819–92) was a prolific author of short stories, autobiographies, biographies, histories, and even a cookbook.[11] She produced domestic narratives that frequently served as political parables in the well-known trope of the home as nation and that provided lessons—albeit often ironic ones—for women in providing domestic contentment. She wrote stories about families ripped apart by political dissent in which she employed the trope of the home as nation and invoked the concept of the angel in the house in order to create effective metaphors for political conduct and to impart persuasive messages to her readers about women's roles in the home and in the nation. The historical backdrop for many of these stories is the struggle in Argentina between the Federalists, who advocated a loose confederation of Argentine states, and the Unitarians, who sought to establish a strong central government in Buenos Aires, during the dictatorship of the Federalist leader Juan Manuel Rosas from 1831 to 1852.

Gorriti's stories dramatize the national struggle between the two parties by displacing that conflict onto the personal level. For example, in "El guante negro" (The black glove), which first appeared in *Revista de Paraná* in 1861 and was later republished in the collection *Sueños y realidades* (1865), Isabel, the daughter of a murdered Unitarian, is in love with the Federalist soldier Wenceslao. Her rival for Wenceslao's affections is Manuelita Rosas herself, who gives Wenceslao the fateful glove of the story's title. When Wenceslao decides to leave the Federalist army and join Isabel's Unitarians, his father, a Federalist colonel, vows to execute him. Wenceslao's mother kills her husband to rescue her son, who then renounces Isabel and returns to the Federalists.

The young women of the story are those who traditionally should fulfill the role of the angel of the house, and at first glance, both Manuelita and Isabel seem to carry out those duties. Each visits Wenceslao to provide comfort, Manuelita by expressing her gratitude and affection and Isabel by tending to his wounds. Isabel first enters as "una figura blanca, vaporosa y aérea como las Wilis de las baladas alemanas" and Wenceslao calls her "mi ángel hermoso" (a white figure, ethereal and airy like the Wilis of German ballads . . . my beautiful angel; 56–57). On the other hand, each woman subverts and undermines the role of domestic angel. Tellingly, both Manuelita and Isabel are dislocated, never seen within their own homes. All domestic scenes take place in the home of Wenceslao's family, affording the young women no physical space of their own in which to exercise domestic talents. By the same token, both are physically active when the bed-bound Wenceslao is recovering from a wound; they visit Wenceslao in his bedroom, affirming female agency and independence. This inverts the dominant paradigm in which women wait passively at home for men to take action. These visits to Wenceslao's sickbed bring bad omens and difficult decisions to Wenceslao, rather than providing the nurturing care that the domestic angel should administer. Manuelita leaves behind the titular black glove, which Wenceslao fatefully hides over his heart, foreshadowing both the emotional turmoil he will soon face and his own physical death, the stoppage of his heart. Likewise Isabel offers no domestic comfort. Despite her white garments, which should signal purity of body and soul, she is not an angel but a Wili, a female spirit who lures men to their deaths. Instead of curing Wenceslao's wound, Isabel discovers the glove and, racked by the jealousy that turns "al angel en demonio" (the angel to a demon; 59), demands that he abandon the Federalist cause for the Unitarian army. Isabel is ethereal and mysterious; she appears from a secret door in Wenceslao's bedroom and tells him about her ability to foresee the future. But her otherworldly gifts are decidedly not angelic.[12] The rage and jealousy that lead her to order Wenceslao into the Unitarian forces will also lead to the destruction of his entire family and her own heartbreak. Both Isabel and Manuelita take actions that destroy domestic peace rather than building it.

Instead, Wenceslao's mother, Margarita, incarnates the virtues of the angel of the house. She comforts him and affirms that being supplanted in her son's affections by Isabel does not matter to her. "¿Quién era esa mujer, que amaba tanto, pero cuya santa abnegación era superior a los celos?" asks the narrator, responding to the rhetorical question, "Era una madre" (Who was that woman, who loved so deeply, but whose saintly self-sacrifice overcame jealousy? . . . She was a mother; 60). By framing this statement as "she was a mother" rather than "she was the mother of Wenceslao," Gorriti accords to all mothers these qualities of selflessness and disinterested love.

While such maternal devotion mimics the kinds of discourses about the angel of the house that we have noted in so many other nineteenth-century texts, Gorriti, like Acosta de Samper, asserts that there are dire consequences of this utter dedication to the needs of one's children. Margarita and her husband, the Federalist colonel, debate the relationship between family responsibilities and personal honor. When her husband reminds her that early in their marriage she had commanded him to "muere, pero no te deshonres faltando a la palabra! Nada puede borrar las manchas del honor!" Margarita replies simply, "Era esposa, ahora soy madre!" (Die, but do not fail in honor by breaking your oath! Nothing can erase that stain from your honor! . . . I was a wife, now I am a mother! 64). Although her husband is willing to kill his own son in order to preserve family and military honor, Margarita believes that her son's physical well-being is more important than abstract notions of honor. Even more than that, her maternal role has completely taken over: "Era esposa, ahora soy madre"—the two roles are mutually exclusive when husband and son make competing claims. The term "mother" is applied as a totalizing category, affirming that all mothers would make the same choice to defend their children's lives above any other consideration. Indeed, Margarita makes the ultimate choice between husband and son: because she cannot win the verbal argument and her husband will kill Wenceslao rather than see him become a Unitarian, Margarita murders her husband to save her son's life, like Francisca in "Amor de madre." She has completely renounced her role as a wife and is subsumed into motherhood. Gorriti carries the implications of domestic ideology to the extreme in order to show their ultimate failure; if women are supposed to be endlessly self-sacrificing and utterly devoted to their children, they lose the sense of social responsibility that makes them adhere to laws conflicting with personal dedication to the ideal of motherhood.

"La hija del mashorquero," originally serialized in *Revista de Lima* in 1863, was subsequently also published in *Sueños y realidades* and, like "El guante negro," takes place during Rosas's dictatorship. The story focuses on a loving father-daughter relationship between one of Rosas's brutal enforcers and his daughter, whose very name, Clemencia, bespeaks her angelic nature. Even when she realizes that her father commits atrocities in Rosas's name, "era toda dulzura y misericordia" and her filial love does not wane; indeed, "deseó vivir para acompañar al desdichado como un ángel guardián" (she was all sweetness and mercy . . . she wanted to live to accompany the unlucky soul [her father] like a guardian angel; 121). Her self-appointed task is to care for the women and children left as widows and orphans after her father has assassinated their male relatives. The people she comforts see her as an angel: "¿Quién eres, criatura angelical?" asks one woman, later telling her children, "es un bello ángel" (Who are you, you angelic being? . . . she is a beautiful angel; 127). Finally, Clemencia enables the escape of a Unitarian's wife by taking the other woman's place in prison. The Unitarian woman elevates Clemencia from an angel to the Virgin Mary herself, saying, "La virgen del Socorro ha descendido a mi calabozo para librarme" (The Virgin of Socorro has descended to my prison to free me; 130). Yet when Clemencia's father mistakes her for the other woman and kills her, Clemencia becomes even more exalted and her blood cleanses her father of his sins as if she were Christ himself. "La sangre de la virgen [. . .] como un bautismo de redención, hizo descender sobre aquel hombre un rayo de luz divina que lo regeneró" (The blood of the virgin, like a baptism of redemption, brought down a ray of divine light that renewed him; 131).

Gorriti represents Clemencia as the absolute epitome of the self-sacrificing angel, who exemplifies the virtues of abnegation, purity, and innocence so well that she even dies for her father.[13] Clemencia relinquishes her own desires for a husband and children and her own domestic space in order to protect her father's victims, a discursive maneuver that asks the implicit question of how much sacrifice is to be demanded of the domestic angel. Gorriti interrogates the limits of domestic discourse by having Clemencia make increasingly more difficult decisions and sacrifices, all of which can be justified within the discursive range of angelic ideology. If the angel is never to consider her own wishes, Clemencia's hope for her own home must be discarded. If the angel is to serve as the supreme moral role model for her family, Clemencia must die to redeem her sinful father. At the same time, Gorriti shows that the supposed passivity of the domestic angel, who waits at home and reacts to the needs of others, is contradictory to the other demands placed on women to be spiritual exemplars and to serve others. Clemencia takes control of her own life and destiny in a variety of ways. She accesses multiple spaces, venturing into the homes of others to bring assistance and the typically masculine space of the prison. She also decides her own fate and that of others through her decisive actions. Once again, all these movements and decisions are made possible by the deployment of domestic ideology but also serve to question the imposition of that very same domesticity.

In these stories, political issues threaten domesticity in two ways: they break apart existing families and they prevent new ones from forming. But Gorriti cannot be arguing for the isolation of the domestic sphere from the public sphere, because of the active role she has her female characters take. In fact, it is their moral duty to undertake these political activities and to further them by using their domestic abilities. Women are the bearers of high moral standards, but they are not meant in Gorriti's scheme to use those standards to create protected spaces—the sacred space of the home—far from political activities. Gorriti instead demonstrates the interconnectedness of family and politics, of the so-called private and public spheres, in order to critique received gender norms that limit female autonomy. She shows both the impossibility of such limitations and the corrosive effects on female identity of received discourse about domesticity and women's roles.

A telling moment in Gorriti's *oeuvre* comes with the 1890 publication of a cookbook titled *Cocina ecléctica*. While *Cocina ecléctica* may at first glance seem to be an anomaly appearing toward the end of Gorriti's lengthy literary career, I read it instead as part of a long-term strategy in her work for encoding discourses of domesticity. Although Gorriti's name appears on the book's cover as the author, the recipes included were collected from women around Latin America, connections developed during a lifetime of nurturing female networks through her literary salons in Lima and her tireless work as a journalist and editor of periodicals. Nina Scott surmises that the idea for the cookbook came from the presence in Argentina of the teachers brought to the country from the United States as part of Domingo Faustino Sarmiento's efforts to modernize the educational system, as the community cookbook was unknown in Latin America in the nineteenth century (311). However Gorriti came by the idea, she took full advantage of the concept and its execution to position herself cleverly as a decidedly non-domestic woman who nonetheless was well aware of the vital nature of the domestic work carried out by women as a matter of routine.

The only part of the cookbook actually written by Gorriti is the brief prologue, which begins, "El hogar es el santuario doméstico; su ara es el fogón; su sacerdotisa y guardian natural, la mujer" (The home is the domestic sanctuary; its altar is the stove; its priestess and natural guardian, woman; 151). But Gorriti laments,

Ávida de otras regiones, arrojéme a los libros [...] sin pensar que esos ínclitos genios fueron tales, porque [...] tuvieron todos, a su lado, mujeres hacendosas y abnegadas que los mimaron, y fortificaron su mente con suculentos bocados, fruto de la ciencia más conveniente a la mujer. Mis amigas, a quienes, arrepentida, me confesaba, no admitierón mi *mea culpa*, sino a condición de hacerlo público en un libro. Y, tan buenas y misericordiosas, como bellas, hanme dado para ello preciosos materiales, enriqueciéndolos más todavía, con la gracia encantadora de su palabra.

Eager to learn of other places, I threw myself into books without thinking that those outstanding geniuses were so because they all had at their side hardworking, self-sacrificing women who spoiled them and fortified their mental labor with succulent mouthfuls, fruits of the science which is most becoming to woman. My friends, to whom, repentant, I confessed, did not accept my *mea culpa* except upon the condition that I make it public in a book. And, as good and merciful as they are beautiful, they have given me for it precious materials, enriching them even more with the enchanting grace of their words. (151)

Gorriti begins with a traditional rhetorical flourish evoking the image of the angel in the house. By specifying that the stove is the center of this domestic temple, she further exalts female cooks and elevates a task often seen as mundane. She then renounces any personal claim to the domestic sphere and reconstructs her life history as one of reading, not cooking. "Ávida de otras regiones" could mean that she wanted to explore other physical places, which she could do only through reading; it could also mean that she was eager to travel to regions other than the kitchen, that is, to spaces not gender-marked as female. Significantly, the writers Gorriti lists are all men, underlining her willing entrance into a masculine sphere of influence. She points out that these writers only achieved their genius status because of the domestic goddesses at their sides who spoiled them and fed them with "suculentos bocados, fruto de la ciencia más conveniente a la mujer." This may well be a self-deprecating statement about Gorriti's own inability to provide "suculentos bocados" and a veiled jab at a system in which only men are the recipients of such treats. But Gorriti is clearly also commenting on the fact that women's practical work has tended to remain unseen, at least—or not least—by men, even invisible.

While Gorriti says that she herself has been blind to the ways in which women's private work enables the public world of men to function smoothly, it is clear that other women have not been so heedless. Gorriti finds herself confronted by the need to confess her blindness to her female friends, who then punish her by forcing her into a public confession of her faults. In this reading, she admits to her sin of behaving, in short, like a man, never noticing the practical efforts that go into sustaining intellectual creativity.

Another reading of this passage would focus on the phrase "la ciencia más conveniente a la mujer." The "science" best suited, most appropriate, or even most convenient for a woman is cooking—the science or art that Gorriti herself has consciously rejected by throwing herself into books. Cooking is the proper occupation for a woman, but it is also the most convenient, suggesting that propinquity plays a larger part in the decision to devote oneself to the domestic arts than does biological sex. Gorriti slyly implies that women's supposed affinity for cooking and the domestic arts is a question of nurture rather than nature, as gender norms inculcate certain behaviors in both women and men. In Gorriti's formulation, literature and cooking become diametrically opposed and are associated with the two sexes: literature with the named men who produce books, cooking with the anonymous women who feed them. At the same time that she puts this opposition into play, however, Gorriti undermines it by refusing to fall into the gender-assigned category to which she should belong. She rejects the "appropriate" and "suitable" occupation of cookery.

Astute readers of the time would have recognized Gorriti as the prolific author of numerous short stories, biographies, and articles, not as a domestic goddess. Moreover, even as she issues her *mea culpa*, she pays it only lip service. Her way of making amends for ignoring women's labor is not to undertake those tasks herself but to create a cookbook containing the recipes of other cooks, almost all of whom are women.[14] Gorriti herself remains decidedly a writer and makes no moves to become a cook. Indeed, she does not contribute even one recipe to the cookbook; her role is to oversee the project and write a prologue that not-so-subtly distances her from the "mujeres hacendosas y abnegadas" and their "ciencia conveniente." Hence, at the moment when Gorriti seems to be drawing near to traditional domestic discourse, she erects barriers between herself and that discourse.

While Gorriti invokes and subtly critiques the trope of the home as domestic sanctuary in the opening lines to *Cocina ecléctica*, her other writings make it clear that this domestic sanctuary—if it even exists—is by no means apolitical. According to Doris Sommer, "For Gorriti, [...] the possible contest [between passion and politics] seems almost irrelevant, because both desire and power belong to the male world, as capable of producing horror as of winning glory" (107). Sommer argues that Gorriti's heroines do not fuse erotics and politics as the national novel requires. Nonetheless, I assert that it is the case that in her stories, moral and patriotic duties are intimately bound up with women's roles in the family, which Gorriti also uses to figure the nation. Rather than evading the passion/politics duality that Sommer describes, Gorriti encodes it differently, substituting familial love for the less reliable, more mercurial passions of romantic love.

Gorriti's work constructs a narrative space using domestic images that idealize and elevate the figure of the woman. By doing so, she is able to manipulate societal norms about women's behavior in order to impart certain messages about their moral and patriotic duties. Her heroines are deeply involved in the political life of their country, but Gorriti embeds the political message within the supposedly domestic plot. This double-edged message about domesticity is reflected in the prologue to *Cocina ecléctica* in which, as we have seen, Gorriti at once praises the "angel in the home" and carefully distances herself from that image of domestic perfection. The scene of the domestic in Gorriti's work allows, even demands, that women express and act upon political and moral beliefs. If the home is the domestic sanctuary posited, albeit ironically, in the prologue to *Cocina ecléctica* and woman is its priestess and natural guardian, the rest of Gorriti's work demonstrates that domestic rites are by definition political and moral as well and that the guardian of the home is also the guardian of the nation.

In conclusion, nineteenth-century texts about domesticity operated on multiple levels. They represented domesticity as moral lessons for their female and male readers and advanced the idea that domestic stability is the key to national stability. These ideas are interdependent: the authors argue that successful family life strengthens the nation, and they demonstrate how to achieve domestic happiness. Some texts, such as the women's magazines, are explicitly didactic in their descriptions of the features women needed to acquire to be good wives and mothers; others, such as Gorriti's stories, focus on the patriotic emotions that allow or force women to subordinate selfish personal desire to civic duty; and still others use descriptions of domestic scenes as the backdrop against which openly political events are enacted. In all cases, the domestic trope functions to impart lessons about private and public behaviors to the readers. These texts demonstrate that in the nineteenth century, the sequel to romance, the establishment of domestic tranquility, was a powerful means of communicating messages about familial and national roles.

In fact, the domestic image is often incompatible with the national romance. The rhetoric of domesticity focuses on the self-sacrifice of women and their willingness to put the needs and wishes of their husbands and children above their own. But the quest of women in national romances is not to create a domestic idyll but to win the love of, and marriage to, the hero. The national romance demands an almost obsessive selfishness. Since the national romance functions to bring couples together despite social and even familial pressures working to keep them apart, the heroines must seek to satisfy their own desires at the cost of all else in order for the desired end—the marriage—to take place. The domestic angel, faced with the choice between self-interested love and self-sacrifice, should always choose the latter, thus thwarting the required conclusion of the national romance. Domestic discourse was a powerful and important means in nineteenth-century Spanish America to advance ideas about women's roles in society, be those arguments conservative or liberal. Those who viewed women from a traditional perspective used domestic ideology to pay lip service to the notion of national progress related to women's advancement by asserting women's importance in society while also reinforcing the idea that the domestic sphere was the ideal place for women. Those who sought to create opportunities for women used domestic ideology to insert their potentially transgressive arguments about women's education and advancement into the space of the home and the family circle. Both demonstrate the primacy of domestic tropes in articulating arguments about the role of women in the home, in their society, and in the national community.

4

Women's Education

In 1888 the Mexican journalist Mateana Murguía de Aveleyra wrote, "Todos los modernos pensadores convienen en que la prosperidad social, y la felicidad individual y colectiva de la gran familia a que pertenecemos, dependen de la educación de la mujer. En efecto, siendo ella la legisladora de la familia, importa mucho educarla convenientemente para que, cuando reine en el hogar, su imperio sea dulce, pero sólido, seguro, irresistible" (All modern thinkers agree that social prosperity and the individual and collective happiness of the great family to which we belong depend on women's education. Indeed, since woman is the legislator of the family, it is crucial to educate her accordingly so that, when she reigns in the home, her rule will be sweet, but solid, sure, irresistible; 431). Her words encapsulate several of the central arguments used for advancing women's entrance into the public sphere in nineteenth-century Latin America—first, that modernity requires women's education; second, that women need education in order to be good mothers; and third, that the nation depends upon the families headed by those educated mothers. Most important, Murguía de Aveleyra paired the discourses of progress and motherhood to argue that these phenomena were compatible rather than contradictory.

Numerous writers, both male and female, used accepted rhetoric about gender roles in order to argue for women's entrance, albeit under rather rigidly controlled circumstances, into the public sphere and, more specifically, to connect progress to education for women, which is the focus of this chapter. Across the continent, the themes and the ways in which writers framed their arguments about women's education were remarkably consistent, despite the different sociopolitical contexts in which they were producing their essays, novels, and stories and despite the different goals they wished to achieve. Men and women debated whether women should have access to education and what kind of education was most appropriate for girls and women across different socioeconomic strata. The plasticity of discourses about modernity, just as it enabled competing views to coexist about gender roles and public vs. private space and about domesticity, also meant that those who favored women's full access to higher education and those who wanted more modest improvements that did not threaten the status quo deployed the same series of concepts about modernity, progress, and women's roles in the emerging nation-states. As authors advanced their own agendas for their countries and for the modernizing process, women's education became an increasingly vital element of the national conversation. I argue that this demonstrates that women's issues were essential to the ways in which modernity in the nineteenth century was conceived and communicated to a greater public.

This chapter examines some of the numerous texts that took up the question of education for girls and women throughout Latin America in their specific sociohistorical contexts and, in the case of journalism, in the context of the periodicals in which they were published. Just as arguments about women's education are inseparable from the greater context of arguments about nationhood, citizenship, and identity, so too are the essays in which those arguments appeared inseparable from the journalistic apparatus in which they were published, with their advertisements for leather gloves and French perfumes cheek-by-jowl with news about scientific breakthroughs, articles advocating breastfeeding, and Christian moralizing.

In 1863, the Ecuadorean author Miguel Riofrío (1819–81) published *La emancipada* as a serial in a journal in Quito (Rodríguez-Arenas xix).[1] Riofrío, the illegitimate son of two members of the landowning class, was a lawyer and journalist who held various positions in the Ecuadorean government. *La emancipada,* one of his few works of fiction, is a striking short novel about the difficulties faced by the heroine of the title as she struggles against her conservative father's efforts to control her self-expression and her access to the written word and to force her into marriage against her will. Rosaura's story symbolizes the conflicts that Riofrío perceived in Ecuador as a whole, related to the transition from a conservative, colonial, religious society to a liberal, postcolonial, secular world. When her father, the town priest, and local authorities work together to marry her to an equally conservative misogynist, Rosaura uses a legal loophole to declare herself emancipated and leaves her town, believing that Eduardo, the man she truly loves, will find and marry her. However, misled by her actions and believing she intended to betray him, Eduardo fails to meet her, causing Rosaura to become disillusioned with social norms and to live outside conventional strictures by consorting with the lower classes and people of color. Eduardo joins the priesthood, finds Rosaura's location, and writes her letters condemning her behavior. Eventually she commits suicide by drinking herself to death.

The daughter of a liberal mother and conservative father, Rosaura, whose story is told in part through her own memoirs and letters, suffers her mother's death and the limits placed on her intellectual expression almost simultaneously:

> Una semana después de haber sepultado a mi madre, [. . .] recogió mi padre todos mis libros, el papel, la pizarra, las plumas, la vihuela y los pinceles: [. . .] lo fue a depositar en el convento y volvió para decirme:—Rosaura, ya tienes doce años cumplidos; es necesario que desde hoy en adelante vivas con temor de Dios; es necesario enderezar tu educación, aunque ya el arbolito está torcido por la moda; tu madre era muy porfiada y con sus novelerías ha dañado todos los planes que yo tenía para hacerte una buena hija; yo quiero que tú eduques para señora y esta educación empezará desde hoy.
>
> Tú estarás siempre en la recámara y al oír que alguien llega pasarás inmediatamente al cuarto del traspatio; no más paseos ni visitas a nadie ni de nadie. [. . .] Lo que te diga tu padre lo oirás bajando los ojos y obedecerás sin responderle, sino cuando fueras preguntada.—¿Y no podré leer alguna cosa?,—le pregunté;—Sí, me dijo, podrás leer estos libros."

A week after my mother's funeral, my father gathered up all my books, paper, chalk, pens, guitar, and paintbrushes: he [. . .] put them in a closet and came back to tell me, "Rosaura, you are now twelve years old; from now on you must live in fear of God; your education has to be straightened out, although the sapling is already bent; your mother was very stubborn and with her new-fangled ideas she ruined all the plans I had to make you into a good daughter; I want you to learn to be a lady and this education will start as of today. You will always be in your bedroom and if you hear someone coming you will immediately go to the inner courtyard; you will no longer go out, visit anyone, or receive visits [...]. You will listen to your father with lowered eyes and you will obey without answering, except when you are asked a direct question." "And I can't read anything?" I asked him. "Yes," he said, "you may read these books" (indicating several books of sermons). (4–5)

At the significant age of twelve, when girls typically enter puberty, Rosaura is initiated into two types of adulthood: her father strives to inculcate principles of ladylike comportment in her as she goes through puberty and becomes a woman, subject to the pressures her society places on upper-class women. The literate, artistic education associated with the mother and the meticulously itemized tools (books, paper, chalk, pens, guitar, and paintbrushes) are denounced as new-fangled, that is, modern, trash, and replaced by a paternally dominated training as a traditional woman. Secular books and all writing are discarded. Rosaura will be enclosed and silenced.

La emancipada establishes a set of binarisms attached to the tradition/progress divide that associates tradition with a particularly oppressive strand of Catholicism, with rural village life, with a pro-Spain colonial bent, and with a conservative political ideology, while progress is connected to liberal Christianity and secular education, with the city, with a focus on the new nation of Ecuador, and with democracy and an open society. In this regard it is notable that before her death Rosaura's mother took a special interest in public affairs; as the father complains, "Ella en vez de hilar y cocinar, que es lo que deben saber las mujeres, le gustaba preguntar en dónde estaba Bolívar, quiénes se iban al Congreso, que decía la *Gaceta*" (Instead of sewing and cooking, which is what women should know how to do, she liked to ask where Bolívar was, who was going to Congress, what the *Gazette* was saying; 10). Superficially, Riofrío advocates that the limited scope of activities traditionally available to women be supplanted by an effort to participate in the greater political context and by improved access to the supposedly male-only knowledge sphere. However, in *La emancipada* men, be they liberal or conservative, dominate the conversation about education for women, an effect that undermines the novel's stated position. Rosaura is the only woman who takes action, who emblematizes Riofrío's stance in favor of education for women. She is even the only woman who speaks and literally has a voice with which to explain her own opinions. Assigning pro-woman positions to male characters makes the case that women's situation is a national and public concern and not just a domestic and private one. Yet by making Rosaura the only woman empowered to represent her beliefs, the novel also enacts the same conditions of oppression that it condemns and forces Rosaura into a position of singularity rather than solidarity.

Various male narrative voices in *La emancipada* condemn the father's repression of Rosaura's intellectual activities; one young man tells the town priest that "las hijas no son esclavas ni de sus padres ni de los curas" (daughters are not slaves of their fathers or of the priests; 8). He strongly asserts women's right to self-determination and adds:

> Si en verdad somos cristianos, debemos ser sustancialmente distintos de aquellos pueblos en que la mujer es entregada como mercancía a los caprichos de un dueño a quien sirve de utilidad o de entretenimiento, mas no de esposa. En contestación [el cura] me arremetió con distingos y subdistingos disparatados.

> If we are truly Christian, we should be different in substance from those peoples among whom women are handed over like merchandise to the whims of a master whom they serve as a useful object or as entertainment, but not as a spouse. In reply the priest attacked me with all sorts of illogical harangues. (8)

While the city-educated university student voices logical arguments about the proper treatment of women in Christian nations and connects that correct treatment to a highly moral and totalizing view of "real" Christianity, the priest cannot voice an articulate counterargument. Likewise, Rosaura's father informs her that "el señorío de esta jurisdicción es vizcaíno y asturiano puro, y desde el tiempo de nuestros antepasados ha sido costumbre tener las doncellas siempre en la recámara y arreglarse los matrimonios por [. . .] los padres" (the authority in this jurisdiction is pure Basque and Asturian, and since the time of our ancestors it has been our custom to keep the maidens in their bedrooms and to have [. . .] the fathers arrange their marriages; 10), creating a clear semantic chain connecting Spain ("viz-caíno y asturiano puro") with the past ("nuestros antepasados") and with the subjugation of women, a subjugation that includes their physical con-finement to the private space of the home and their domination by male relatives. Riofrío works to construct a progressive version of Christianity and of contemporary Ecuadorean society in which women's fair treatment is a Catholic virtue. But more than that, by presenting a condemnatory perspective of a society in which women are treated as chattel, he creates an implicit ideal world in which women have equal access to learning, to literacy, and to public affairs. While Rosaura, like her deceased mother, is exceptional because she has already gained privileged knowledge of and control over writing with the specific intent to communicate to another audience, Riofrío's explicit message is that all women, or at least all upper-class women, should be able to achieve the same.

Given that Riofrío constructs a fictional world that attaches progress for women to a progressive model of society, it may seem contradictory that the novel ends with Rosaura's precipitous descent down the social ladder and her death. Rosaura's so-called emancipation is not a successful negotia-tion of gender norms that permits her to choose her spouse and intellectual pursuits freely. Only by threatening violence on her wedding day is she able to free herself, brandishing a pistol and telling the priest, "Quiero descubrir lo que puede hacer el brazo de una hembra" (I want to find out what a woman's arm can do; 23). Rosaura's liberation comes from the combina-tion of her superior understanding of legal codes—she "reads" law better than her father and the priest—and her ability to wield a weapon. In this moment Rosaura is most "man-like" while simultaneously claiming femi-nine empowerment as she exercises power both in the traditional domain of violence and the modern domain of literacy. But what should be the apex of her success is instead the point at which she begins her entry into a dissipated lifestyle from which she turns away only when she receives reproachful letters from Eduardo.

Rosaura's ability to read and to reason now dooms her, and after recog-nizing the state of moral degradation to which she has fallen, she chooses to die, writing to her former lover, "He causado muchos daños que no habría conocido sin tus cartas" (I have caused great harm about which I would know nothing without your letters; 38). Crucially, if she were not educated, she would not understand the basis of Eduardo's criticisms. Although, as Flor María Rodríguez-Arenas argues, Eduardo's superior scholarship and training in rhetoric in comparison to Rosaura's more limited education give Eduardo a decided advantage in their debate (xlii), it remains the case that without education, Rosaura could not read the letters or follow Eduardo's reasoning in the first place. Her capacity to read and to grasp a sophisticated logical argument, which enabled her to free herself from an arranged marriage, now leads her to be persuaded that her "emancipated" life as a prostitute is irredeemably sinful. She writes to Eduardo, "Tú me has escrito en un lenguaje que me hace mucho daño" (You have written to me in a language that has hurt me very much; 35), emphasizing the power of the written word and her ambivalent relationship with it. She does not perceive her lifestyle as dangerous to herself or others until she reads it described in that way in Eduardo's letters. Literacy makes her rethink her life and comprehend her role in others' lives in a negative way.

Riofrío's novella condemns the restrictive patriarchy that attempts to force Rosaura and girls like her into passivity and subordination to their fathers and priests, who scorn the intellectual gifts of these women. Riofrío depicts Rosaura and her mother as victims of masculine control and power. On the other hand, Rosaura's efforts to live independently transgress the boundaries of acceptable behavior, even for Riofrío's liberal philosophy, and she is punished by being erased from the scene of the novel and of Ecuador. Her body, once the source of sexual pleasure, literally rots into pieces (Rodríguez-Arenas xxviii–xxxix). One way or another, then, women must be controlled by men, and the message of the text is not that women should be "emancipated" but that the source and type of control should permit women some small, circumscribed freedoms, such as access to reading and writing.

When women strive to be truly as equal as men, even proponents of modernizing women's living and educational conditions institute systems of control and repression. Women, Riofrío suggests, can be granted some educational progress, but they still must be subject to men's superior moral and intellectual domination. Rosaura's problem is not that her father controls her but that the wrong type of man—a conservative, regressive, colonially oriented man—exerts that control over her. By constructing a narrative in which the "emancipated" woman displays herself in public venues, becomes a prostitute, consorts with indigenous men, and engages in behaviors marked as lower-class and masculine such as horseback riding and attending cockfights, Riofrío critiques not just the conservative, backward-looking mind-set that seeks to confine women to the home but also the potential overreaching by women who take too much advantage of newfound freedoms. *La emancipada* demonstrates the precariousness of the balancing act in which advocates for women's education engaged and in many ways, especially in its ambivalence toward its female protagonist, exemplifies the struggle across Latin America to think through what women's education might mean for gender relations, family structures, and national progress and identity. In *La emancipada*, as in so many fictional and nonfictional texts, attitudes about gender support, transgress, and conflict with attitudes about modernity, progress, and national identity, bespeaking the contradictory and complicated processes by which Latin American intellectuals negotiated these issues.

While novelists used fictional story lines to dramatize the consequences of women having, or not having, educational opportunities, journalists explicitly laid out their arguments for and against women's education in essays, editorials, and news items. Nineteenth-century periodicals offered editors the opportunity to present their readers with a print experience that often seems now to be almost chaotic, as widely differing types of writing appeared within the same few pages of a magazine or newspaper. Magazines intended for a female readership usually contained fashion news, reports of recent cultural activities, and information about charitable societies and their doings, as well as didactic histories, brief biographies of illustrious men and women, household hints, and informative essays and opinion pieces. In terms of literature they often published poetry, literary translations, short stories, and serialized novels. The more successful periodicals also included advertisements ranging from dressmaking services, dry goods stores, and bookstores to shops selling luxury products such as kid gloves, hair treatments, imported clothing, health tonics, and patent medicines. Some readers read these elements separately, perhaps in different temporal moments; others read the magazine in its entirety. Still others heard selections from the magazine read aloud in the intimate setting of the home. All these modes of access to the journals allowed readers contact with a variety of texts, but those texts were often carefully curated by the journals' editors in order to transmit a particular set of messages. These cultural products enabled readers to access various types of knowledge and understanding, and many editors had the explicit intent of using their journals to educate their readers as well as entertain them.

In Argentina, journal publication skyrocketed after the dictatorship of Juan Manuel Rosas ended (1829–52). While during the 1840s there were fewer than a dozen new magazines, many of them short-lived, in 1852 as many as thirty new journals were founded.[2] Among these periodicals was the women's magazine *La Camelia*, which appeared three times a week for two months in 1852. In the journal, women writers took advantage of the rhetoric of national advancement in order to tie women's roles to activities in the public sphere. The editors of *La Camelia* maintained their anonymity throughout the journal's run but have been identified as Rosa Guerra and Juana Manso de Noronha (Greenberg 192).[3] They took as their slogan "libertad, no licencia" (liberty, not license), a maneuver that specifies from the outset the goals and limits to which they adhere, and complained that men had unjustly refused to share their liberty with women.[4] They argued that, like men, women had suffered under Rosas and that women were integral to the national project of reconstruction and consolidation. Indeed, Guerra and Manso appealed to the needs of "la Patria" and described the ways in which women could meet those needs. Thus they wrote, "La Patria precisa que se haga universal el conocimiento de las ciencias en ambos sexos, por que así puede esperar, la nueva generación de ciudadanos útiles, y capaces de sustituir, a los que hoy presiden los altos destinos de la República" (The Nation demands that knowledge of science be universal in both sexes, because that way we can expect the new generation of useful citizens, capable of taking the place of those who now preside over the highest destiny of the Republic; April 29, 1853, 33n9).

When women seek education, they are meeting the requirements imposed on them by their country, not seeking selfish personal fulfillment. Here *La Camelia*'s editors refer to a scientific education for both sexes. "Educación científica" was a common phrase among men and women who sought to wrest control of educational systems from the Church and to secularize instruction. When the editors use the term, they level the educational playing field and specify that equal access to progressive education means national progress. They also adroitly connect the topic of women's education to that of the post-Rosas national project; they continually evoke an image of Argentina consistent with what male liberal thinkers were proposing; and they insert phrases and words ("la Patria," "ciudadanos útiles," "la República") meant to prompt a favorable response in their readers. In the pages of *La Camelia* they create a consistent association between women's advancement and national identity in a way that prefigures later connections between women's education and national progress in particular. By attaching women to national identity, they insert women into the very heart of nationalist discourse.

The editors of *La Camelia* assert that women are as capable as men of participating in political discourse and in higher education, including the sciences. They show that education is necessary for women to carry out their domestic and patriotic duties alike: "Si nuestra educación fuese más esmerada [. . .] entonces seríamos más útiles a nuestros hijos, porque podríamos enseñarles y decirles: unos mismos alimentos os mantienen, y unas mismas leyes os gobiernan, amaos unos a otros, sed útiles y servid a la Patria, morid por ella si es necesario" (If our education were better [. . .] then we would be more useful to our children, because we could teach them and say to them: the same food nourishes you, the same laws govern you, love one another, be useful and serve your nation, die for her if necessary; April 29, 1853, 38n9). They compare the situation of Argentine women to that of their European counterparts, claiming that women in Europe have access to higher education and that "no somos las americanas de inferior clase que las europeas" (we American women are not of an inferior class to European women; 39). This comparison to a European ideal was a microcosm of other efforts to draw parallels between Latin America and Europe on a national scale, as Latin American intellectuals circulated the belief that Europe had already successfully achieved modernity. By asserting that Argentina should be similar to Europe in female education, *La Camelia*'s editors attach their rhetoric to the arguments advanced by their male counterparts. Moreover, should Argentine women be granted access to higher education, "veríamos [. . .] un nuevo progreso en las ciencias y las artes, que darían mucho más lustre a la heroica nación argentina" (we would see [. . .] a new progress in the sciences and arts that would give much more glory to the heroic Argentine nation; 39). Here too Guerra and Manso explicitly aver that women are integral in raising the status of their country, and they lay claim to patriotic discourse ("la heroica nación argentina"), demonstrating that women have a stake in the fate of their country.

The editors of La Camelia took advantage of the explosion in writing and publishing that occurred after the collapse of the Rosas dictatorship, which had imposed brutal censorship on intellectual activity. Furthermore, their frequent and explicit references to Argentine national identity and patriotism demonstrate their ability to tap into the post-Rosas national euphoria and related efforts to formulate a coherent, viable national identity. These writers ineluctably link together patriotism, domesticity, and women's education under the rubric of national progress. By articulating these democratic ideals, Guerra and Manso show that women, like men, understand and engage with sophisticated political ideas and concepts. Through their writing they display their own ability to interpret public political discourse. Guerra and Manso insert women into the new dialogues about national identity in order to stake out a place for women on the national stage and to reframe discourses of modernity.

Questions about how women could best participate in the national process and what type of education would best prepare them for that participation continued to appear in the Argentine press throughout the rest of the century. Twenty-five years after La Camelia ceased publication, such arguments focused not so much on Argentina's self-definition in and of itself, which had been a pressing issue in the political chaos that followed the end of Rosas's twenty-year dictatorship, as on Argentina's claim to be a modern nation. The presidency of Domingo Faustino Sarmiento (1868–74) was marked by notable changes in the areas of education, transportation, and communication; he established normal schools for training teachers, encouraged women to become primary school teachers, expanded the public library system and the railroads, and oversaw the development of the telegraph system (Shumway 253).[5] While Argentina was also coping with the repercussions of the war with Paraguay, which included a massive war debt, with outbreaks of cholera and yellow fever, and with a decreasing global demand for its products (Shumway 253), the rhetorical focus of many Argentine writers and intellectuals fell on making the shift from a discourse of patriotism to one of national progress, more loosely tied to patriotic nationalism but more closely linked to images of national success as dependent on Argentina's ability to make advances in standards of living, including women's education. Hence the ways in which writers took advantage of what were seen as the vital topics of the day in order to advance their own concepts about women's education remain remarkably consistent. For example, Josefina Pelliza de Sagasta claims in "Algo sobre la mujer":

> El ser más bello de la creación es la mujer; ella es el centro, en cuyo derredor giran las aspiraciones del hombre. Fundamento principal de la familia, es a un tiempo causa y efecto del móvil que agita la humanidad, de quien es madre. [...] Ella es un elemento radical del verdadero progreso.

> The most beautiful being in Creation is woman; she is the center, around whom revolve man's aspirations. Principal foundation of the family, she is simultaneously cause and effect of the motor that agitates humanity, of which she is the mother. [...] She is a radical element of true progress).[6]

These statements rewrite the traditional vision of women as marginal to male interests by placing feminine interests and influence at the center of private and public life alike. Moreover, Pelliza de Sagasta affirms that women are essential to the process of modernization. Her essay demonstrates similar tactics to those seen in other articles, as she refigures modernity as based upon female participation in modernizing activities. Women must be included in national activities in order for the society to be deemed modern, but their presence also creates and prompts the progress of modernity.

Across Latin America, both men and women were deeply invested in the question of women's education as it related to the image and reality of national progress. In Colombia, for instance, the periodical *El Museo Literario*, "dedicado al bello sexo" (dedicated to the fair sex), appeared for a total of forty-eight issues, edited by the conservative and very Catholic Manuel María Madiedo.[7] Beginning with its fifth issue on January 30, 1871, *El Museo Literario* published a series of articles about women's education. Such articles served to create and reinforce specific ideas about the pedagogical topics and strategies that were and were not appropriate for females. The first of these articles, by Fermín de Herrán y Tejada, begins with advice about appropriate clothing, hygiene, and physical activity.[8] Herrán y Tejada's article continued in the next issue, February 6, in which he discusses women's moral education, essentially outsourcing this to the Church, and in the February 20 issue, which he concludes with a discussion of women's academic education. After claiming that civilization is either at or close to reaching its apogee, he compares Colombia to more progressive countries:

> Las naciones más ilustradas han concedido a la mujer derechos en cuya adquisición esta ni siquiera ha soñado, todo hombre medianamente instruido, y amante del progreso y de la perfección, confiesa la necesidad de que la mujer sea educada, su inteligencia iluminada por la luz de los conocimientos.

> The most enlightened nations have given women rights of which our country has not even dreamed; all even semieducated men, lovers of progress and perfection, must acknowledge the need for women to be educated and to have the light of knowledge illuminate their intelligence. (58)

Herrán y Tejada invokes the standard set by those other, more advanced nations that have given women rights, and he further connects women's education to the narrative of progress by asserting that all men who love progress and perfection—the conjunction "y" equalizes the two phenomena—must acknowledge the necessity of women's education. By calling it a "necessity," he makes it an imperative; by referring to women's "inteligencia," he implies that women are innately intelligent and would benefit from education, rather than being intellectually inferior to men, in which case education could only be remedial at best. On the other hand, he defines sewing, embroidering, and ironing as arts, so they fall into the category of topics that women should study. He also thinks women should be able to read and to have some knowledge of geography, history, arithmetic, and grammar (58–59). If these are goals as yet to be achieved, education for women in 1871 Colombia is scant indeed.

In case his readers become alarmed at this expansion of educational opportunities, Herrán y Tejada quickly notes, "No pretendemos sin embargo que la mujer sea lo que se llama una *marisabidilla*" (We do not intend that a woman be what is known as a *bluestocking*; 59). The fear of educated men is that women will overreach themselves and strive to compete with men on an equal playing field, but by calling highly educated women "know-it-alls," Herrán y Tejada prevents advanced education for women from being seen as a viable possibility. Reading this line, a woman ought to realize that there is a possibility that she might become too educated (one cannot imagine a man being described as overeducated in the same way) and that too much education will make her socially repellent. A *marisabidilla* is a woman who makes a great show of her knowledge, so Herrán y Tejada's formulation also invokes the danger of women putting themselves forward and making themselves the center of attention, negative characteristics for the self-abnegating angel of the house. He goes on to say that being a female know-it-all is a flaw that harms the woman's family and her society, as it deprives everyone of the benefits that "en su esfera y condición podrían haberles prestado" (in her sphere and condition she could have bestowed upon them; 59). This statement also casts women's education as a function that serves others, not the woman herself. The *marisabidilla* is self-centered and self-aggrandizing, whereas the purpose of female education, identical to the purpose of female existence itself, is always to improve her family and, by extension, her society and nation.

Along very similar lines, Manuel Espinosa published "Importancia de la educación de la mujer" in the March 20, 1871, issue of *El Museo Literario*, arguing that "es preciso, es indispensable, ilustrarla [a la mujer] y moralizarla para que llene debidamente su santísima misión" (it is necessary, indispensable, to educate [woman] and moralize her so that she carries out her very sacred mission; 91). Woman is again the passive recipient of an education administered by men, an education whose purpose is to enable them to fulfill their "santísima misión." That mission, Espinosa glosses, is to be mothers in charge of educating their children and elevating the human race in a crucial, yet unspecified, manner. The use of the adjective "santísima" underscores the religious imperative of that project. Finally, Espinosa's essay consistently casts women as passive. They are the objects of education; men adore and worship them; and, as he concludes, they are destined for the domestic space, whether as daughters or wives and mothers. Their education is not meant to make them into active participants in society. Rather, their instruction and enlightenment show the modernity of their nation and help women better fulfill their traditional roles.

Only a week later, Severo Catalina's essay "La mujer: la educación" expressed similar ideas, emphasizing that education for women was essentially moral in nature. Catalina urges, "La *educación* es de más importancia que la *instrucción*. La primera se dirige principalmente al corazón; la segunda a la inteligencia. Eduquemos a las mujeres, e instruyámoslas después, si queda tiempo" (Education is more important than instruction. The former goes mainly to the heart; the latter to intelligence. Let us educate women and instruct them later, if there is time; 99). He does not list subjects or topics that women should master in order to be educated, but stresses that education consists of a certain moral elevation which remains unspecified in his formulation; this very lack of specificity allows him to present the idea of education for women as a social benefit without incurring the risk of proposing a detailed curriculum that could be criticized by more conservative readers.

Catalina continued his discussion of female education in November 1871, when he published "La mujer: el estudio." While he begins by asking, "¿Por qué las mujeres no habían de acudir a universidades y recibir grados y ejercer profesiones científicas e industriales?" (Why shouldn't women attend universities, receive degrees, and have scientific and industrial careers? 346)[9] and urging, "Ábranse universidades para las mujeres, confiéranseles grados; que ejerzan profesiones científicas e industriales" (Let the universities open to women, let them give women degrees; let women have scientific and industrial careers; 346), this is in fact intended to terrify his readers rather than to inspire them. Catalina makes the point that men do not want women to be intellectual peers and interlocutors and that since women cannot hope to dominate men in academic fields, they should naturally prefer to dominate in the sentimental realm instead. His formulation perpetuates the notion that women, no matter how well educated, are always intellectually inferior to men and that women who strive to compete intellectually with men are unnatural, not true women at all. As a counterpoint to the domestic ideal usually invoked, Catalina instructs his readers: "Figuraos un matrimonio en que el marido resuelve problemas de matemáticas, y la mujer estudia las *categorías* de Aristóteles;

o más bien, figuraos los hijos de ese matrimonio" (Imagine a marriage in which the husband solves math problems, and the wife studies Aristotle's categories; better still, imagine the children of that marriage; 346). Such a marriage would be dangerously unbalanced; the separation of spheres and duties must be maintained. Moreover, he argues that women are not biologically or physically suited to the study of the sciences or mathematics and that social conditions do not require women to be learned or to win attention for intellectual accomplishments. This last point harkens back to Herrán y Tejada's warning about the female know-it-all. A woman should be content with satisfying certain sentimental requirements: "Le basta con brillar por su humildad como hija, por su pudor como soltera, por su ter-. nura como esposa, por su abnegación como madre, por su delicadeza y religiosidad como mujer" (It is enough for her to shine due to her humility as a daughter, her chastity as a maiden, her tenderness as a wife, her self-lessness as a mother, her delicacy and religiosity as a woman; 346). While men should develop their intellectual faculties through rigorous study and practice, women should excel because of the innate virtues of their gender, not because of any particular effort or individual accomplishment; once more, they are passive instead of active. By consistently associating women with those virtues traditionally assigned to the domestic arena, such as humility, tenderness, self-sacrifice, and religiosity, Catalina communicates the message that a scholarly education is both inappropriate and unnecessary for them. Instead, like the other writers of *El Museo Literario*, he proposes an education limited in type and scope:

> Una regular instrucción, ni tan presuntuosa que raye en el orgullo de las letras, ni tan humilde que toque en la ignorancia de las últimas capas sociales, basta a la mujer para llenar sobre la tierra su noble misión de hija obediente, de esposa fiel y de madre tierna y próvida.

> A regularized education, not so presumptuous that it boasts of literary pride, nor so humble that it scrapes along the lowest social levels of ignorance, suffices for a women so that she can fulfill her noble mission as an obedient daughter, faithful wife, and tender, loving mother. (347)

Over and over again, he stresses women's roles within their families as daughters, wives, and mothers, with no part to play in the public sphere.

Throughout the articles published in *El Museo Literario* referencing education for women, the writers consistently extol the advantages of educating
women, link female education to national progress and ideals of modernity,
and carefully limit the education to be offered to women.

In these ways liberal authors took advantage of a narrative of national
progress that included increased educational opportunities for women
without threatening the status quo in which women remained restricted
to the domestic space and to their traditional roles as wives and mothers.
Their arguments favoring female education reproduced and reinforced existing norms that presented a conventional image of women as sentimental,
nurturing, and in need of male guidance and direction, and they described
the education that they thought women should receive in conveniently general terms. Their open-ended descriptions of what women should study
meant that their proposals could not be criticized for being too daring;
they rarely mentioned specific subjects and instead referred to "moral education" at the same time that they imposed strict limits on the amount and
type of education women should receive. Yet because they did advocate for
female education, they were still able to position themselves as advocates
of national progress. They took advantage of the rhetoric of modernity to
make discursive claims about women, progress, and national identity that
need have no basis in lived reality or material phenomena.

Such strategies were not limited to male writers, at least within the
pages of *El Museo Literario*. In 1871 Simona Jil de Martínez published a
two-part article titled "Reflexiones sobre la educación de la mujer," which
began with a forceful critique of the social injustices that had made women
"despreciable juguete del hombre" (a despised plaything of men; 194).[10] Jil
de Martínez goes on to assert that women would take all the strategies that
men had used to subordinate women and would use them against men
through their roles as wives and mothers so as to coerce men into paying
heed to female concerns. Jil de Martínez then explains that the problem
facing women has to do with the best ways to correct their society's "des-
bordado espíritu de individualismo, que amenaza pulverizar la masa social"
(unfettered spirit of individualism, which threatens to pulverize society;
195). Individualism could be seen as a social positive, as it was associated
with the North American work ethic that prized individual achievement
and success; that work ethic was in turn seen by many liberals as the factor

explaining North American political and economic dominance. By critiquing individualism, Jil de Martínez runs the risk of associating her argument with an anti-progressive stance that would condemn such unequivocal focus on individual improvement. Yet she brackets her criticism of individualism by restricting her negative comment to "unfettered" individualism, that is, individualism without any kind of social control, and she subtly invokes women's traditional roles as maintainers of social bonds and connectedness. Jil de Martínez calls for women to become educated not in specific topics such as literature, mathematics, or science but in "la verdad" and "la virtud"; as for her male counterparts, it is a question of educating the women's souls, not their brains. Such virtuous education will enable women to instill the values of brotherhood and patriotism in their children, thus ending civil strife and creating better civic leaders and national rulers.

In the second part of the essay, Jil de Martínez emphasizes that she values the separation of spheres and the development of different abilities. Complete equality would destroy the domestic sphere.[11] She frames women's education as intended to elevate their roles as wives and includes specific phrases such as "en el hogar" when writing of feminine responsibilities in order to underline her message that women's role is in precisely that place. Yet she also inserts language suggesting that from the domestic space, women can exercise enormous power over men. She concludes:

> Dejemos al hombre abstraerse para con el mundo, ensimismarse en cálculos científicos [...]. Para concluir no disputaremos al hombre sus propias funciones; pero seremos por nuestra elevación moral, árbitras de ellas, enderezándolas todas hacia el bien y hacia la virtud.

> Let us allow men to remove themselves from the world, bury themselves in scientific calculations [...]. To conclude we won't deny men their proper functions; but by virtue of our moral elevation, we will be their arbiters, steering them toward the good and the virtuous. (210)

Her dismissive phrasing when writing of male intellectual pursuits ("abstraerse," "ensimismarse") relegates men to the sidelines, where, as she says kindly, women will not "deny" men's rights to their own roles, terminology which places women in control. Women's superior morality makes them the supreme overseers of all activity, be it male or female, public or private. While Jil de Martínez often produces a justification for women's education that includes rather specific limits, as do her male counterparts, she also explains women's apparent confinement to the private sphere in terms of their moral power rather than their intellectual weakness, the strategy often employed by male writers. The outcome, nonetheless, is almost identical: these writers all argue that women's education enhances their activities within the domestic sphere but should not allow them to compete on an equal footing in the public sphere.

In Peru, too, as elsewhere, a national conversation about education generally occupied intellectuals. The liberal cleric Francisco Paula de González Vigil published *Importancia de la educación del bello sexo* in 1858, helping to stimulate national conversations about women's education, although concrete changes were slow to arrive. Concerns over the status of education in general were often expressed as concerns over women's education. For much of the century, girls' education consisted of domestic training, with classes about chores, cooking, drawing, poetry, manners, and a smattering of history and literature (Lergo Martín 2). Primary education for girls was not mandatory until 1872, but the success of the Partido Civil, led by Manuel Pardo, was crucial in the passing of laws to establish schools that trained both young men and women to become teachers beginning in 1873. The creation of these schools and the possibility of paid employment as teachers for female graduates stimulated public discourse about women's education.

Juana Manuela Gorriti, who arrived in Lima from Bolivia in 1847 and opened a private girls' school in 1850, was an integral member of Peruvian literary culture due to her activities as a writer, publisher of periodicals, and hostess of renowned *veladas literarias*, or literary salons, in the 1870s. Women's education was a common topic at the *veladas*.[12] At Gorriti's very first salon on July 19, 1876, the poet and journalist Abel de la E. Delgado read his work "La educación social de la mujer." Delgado, the editor of the journal *La bella limeña* during its brief but influential run in 1872, argues in his essay that women are equal but not identical to men and that they merit equal access to higher education for two reasons: progress is marked by women's active participation in matters of political and public import, but even more fundamentally, women enjoy the same liberties as men do, although, he is careful to note, this does not signify that women and men are the same.[13] Because he argues that women are essentially different, he can justify excluding women from areas such as politics, war, hunting, and flying hot air balloons.[14] Writing about projects of education and "un espíritu de ilustración" (a spirit of enlightenment), he points out that not only men are hard at work on this but that "la mujer, ese arcángel de dulzura que con su planta embellece la tierra que nuestras lágrimas riegan, la compañera del hombre [. . .], se presenta también para ayudarlo, eficazmente, en la jornada, y para prestarle auxilio" (woman, that archangel of sweetness who with her presence embellishes the earth that our tears water, the companion of man [. . .], appears also to help him in his day's labor and to support him; 39). Women do not initiate projects or act on their own, but fulfill their traditional role to assist male leaders. Delgado connects women's presence in literary circles such as the one in which he himself was participating to

> una verdadera revolución, cuya gloriosa bandera es la del progreso del siglo, puesto que esa revolución significa dos grandes preocupaciones vencidas; aquella de que la mujer no debe penetrar en el santuario de lo que se llama *alta enseñanza*, y la otra preocupación vergonzosa de que la mujer tiene su educación concluida, cuando sale aprovechada del colegio.

> a true revolution, whose glorious banner is that of the century's progress, since that revolution signals two great victories: over the idea that woman should not penetrate into the sanctuary of *higher education* and the other, shameful notion that woman's education is complete when she leaves high school. (39)

He links progress and modernity to national transformation, and national transformation to women's access to higher education and the discarding of the idea that a minimal education is all that women need. Delgado, probably taking into account his liberal, predominantly female audience at the salon, notes the inherent inequality in the fact that while educated men can exert influence in the public and private spheres, women are insufficiently prepared to help or advise their husbands. Hence, he argues, civilization as a whole will progress if women are well educated, because the benefits will redound via their male partners to the public sphere as well as to the private one. This is yet another variation on the idea that women exercise great influence on the public realm from their perch in the home, an idea that seems to empower women but that ultimately reinforces the belief that they are essentially domestic beings. Delgado does not believe that women should take on every job that men do, and he explicitly excludes women from working in finance and jurisprudence; but he does criticize those who, following the dictates of "good society," restrict women's access to education and to influence in the public realm.

Like Habermas, Delgado divides society into three facets, which he calls domestic, civil, and political. For the first, he recommends the kind of education of which other authors, such as those in *El Museo Literario*, also approve: an education of woman's character and sentiments. He defines civil society as the domain of business and law and affirms women's capacity to work in both; he also notes that women need to understand their legal status and rights in order to thrive. As for politics, Delgado prefers to keep women away from direct political activity, commenting that "dista mucho de serme simpático" (it's far from being appealing to me; 43). Indeed, Delgado employs emotional and personal terms to characterize his response to women in the public sphere. Earlier he announced, "Confieso que me halagaría muy poco ver a la mujer convertida en una notabilidad financiera" (I confess that it would hardly be attractive to me to see a woman as a queen of high finance; 41); likewise, he mocks the idea of women as military officers or politicians. His "I" appears throughout his essay; he is both delivering a series of justifications for women's access to higher education based on an appeal to logic and reason and connecting those justifications to his personal opinion and reaction. The use of emotionally charged words and phrases such as "mis más ardientes deseos" (my most ardent desires; 40), "la sociedad está horriblemente fraccionada!" (society is horribly fragmented! 41), "desgraciadamente" (disgracefully), "con entusiasmo" (enthusiastically), and personal reactions such as "me atrevo a decir" (I dare to say), "a mi modo de ver" (in my opinion), "yo reconozco en la mujer" (I recognize in woman), "no seguiré la opinión" (I will not follow the opinion), and "confieso sinceramente" (I sincerely confess), in addition to the deployment of exclamations and interjections ("¡Oh espectáculo magnífico de la civilización!"; Oh, magnificent spectacle of civilization!), transmit his sentiments and personalize the essay.

The thrust of Delgado's argument throughout is that in the ideal world, "la vida del sentimiento y la vida de la inteligencia, se penetran y se auxilian mútuamente" (the life of sentiment and the life of intellect intertwine and support each other mutually; 40), by which he means that women's emotional strengths complement men's rationality. His own rhetoric also mirrors this pairing, as he communicates his logical reasons for permitting women access to higher education with words and syntax expressing his powerful emotions. This in turn demonstrates the importance of reactions associated with the sentimental arena, which Delgado also attaches to the sphere of morality and ethics. Making use of the same emotive discursive range he attributes to women allows Delgado to privilege women's potential contributions to the public sphere, as his reader (or listener, at the literary salon) can follow the model that Delgado puts into play. Nonetheless, "separate but equal" remains the key concept in his work as he specifies the ways in which women will not compete with men; instead, furthering their education prepares them better to support their male counterparts from the safe space of the domestic realm.[15]

Six months later, at Gorriti's salon of August 9, 1876, Mercedes Eléspuru y Lazo complained that despite the progress Peru had made, in proof of which she adduced the arrival of gas heat and lighting in the capital, many citizens were not fully persuaded of the need for women's education. Eléspuru y Lazo laments that there are many men and women alike who preferred "la calesa verde a un wagon de ferrocarril" (the green wagon to a railroad carriage; 122). The "calesa verde" refers to the vehicle used by the Inquisition during colonial times to transport accused heretics for interrogation and torture; after Independence, allusions to the Inquisition were often used as a kind of shorthand to signify the backward traditionalism of men such as Rosaura's father and to associate those men with practices seen as barbaric, inhumane, and anti-Enlightenment.

Eléspuru y Lazo contrasts those horse-drawn buggies with the ur-symbol of modern capitalism, the railway. She criticizes those who automatically envision educated women as snobbish pedants who neglect domestic duties for the pleasures of books, and she equally criticizes the current state of education for women for producing girls who, while extremely religious, are frivolous and ignorant. She argues that educating a woman will make her both "un verdadero ángel del hogar" and "una estrella en el cielo de la Patria" (a true angel in the house; a star in the heavens of the Nation; 123), echoing the kind of language that many other authors used to advocate for women's education, and she concludes by calling for a library for women.

Eléspuru y Lazo does not suggest how such a library might be funded or what books it might stock, yet her call underlines the fact that elite women in Lima had trouble accessing educational materials beyond the basics. Her demand for a women's library invokes a multiplicity of meanings and implications. Libraries depend on a literate population concentrated within a relatively smaller geographic area, such as a city or town. Libraries operate within the public sphere as institutions in which multiple users participate. They make the private activity of reading public but also reinforce reading's intimacy; if the act of selecting texts is a public one, the widespread availability of texts that can be loaned to one user at a time means that reading can be private rather than shared. Eléspuru y Lazo's call for a public library for women invites them into the public sphere and grants women access to similar materials as men, but because it is a library for women, she also marks out a separate space for women's education, distanced from men's space. A feminine space gives women freedom to explore intellectual pursuits without male oversight, but might also suffer from an unequal distribution of resources and serve to perpetuate gender-based prejudices. Eléspuru y Lazo's efforts to negotiate the treacherous terrain of women's education reveal the larger-scale issues pertaining to gender, the public sphere, and the nation, as differing attitudes about the importance of the role of the individual versus that of the greater community and about the push to modernize and the pull toward traditionalism came into play, sharpened through the lens of gender and the even more specific topic of education.

On September 6, 1876, Benicio Álamos González, a Chilean journalist and politician visiting Lima, attended a *velada* and read his "Enseñanza superior de la mujer" (Superior education of woman). Like his counterparts, Álamos González argues that woman is vital to the progress of civilization because of her twin roles as wife and mother. But he goes further, questioning why women are limited to such roles. To those who fear that women's education will lead to a neglect of their familial responsibilities, he vehemently asserts, "El temor de que la madre descuide al hijo por la literatura y por la ciencia, es un absurdo" (The fear that a woman will neglect her child in favor of literature and science is absurd; 258) and that educated women will still attract romantic partners. He raises the ultimate terror, that education will make women unmotherly and ultimately unfeminine, because motherhood and femininity are read as synonyms, and then he rejects that idea utterly. In order to make an effective argument for women's education, he must dispel the worst possible scenario. Moreover, because their domestic duties do not tax their intelligence, women can execute their duties and also have time to study, observe, and produce great works (261). Álamos González takes for granted that woman are fully capable of working as doctors, nurses, shop clerks, and telegraph operators and in factories; they simply require an intellectual and moral education. Women need vocational training to prepare for those professions and to be excellent wives and mothers, but to contribute to the progress of the human race, which Álamos González sees as the greater goal, they need instruction in history, literature, mathematics, the natural sciences, geography, and astronomy. He explicitly connects women to world and national progress and to the modernizing agenda, but he does not radically rethink gender roles; in his scheme, women discharge their traditional duties and carry out new ones in addition to, not instead of, their domestic roles, in an early example of the now infamous "second shift" of women's working day. Finally, he charges his female listeners with the implementation of this program of education, a gesture which in itself speaks to his high opinion of women's capabilities; women should create a system of higher education rather than relying on men to do it for them. But it also puts the responsibility for rectifying a system of prejudice and bias on the victims, not the perpetrators, and allows oppressors to sidestep their own complicity in keeping women from accessing opportunities outside the home.

Álamos González's arguments seem to go far beyond those of other authors, and it could be argued that his apparently transgressive ideas found a voice because the venue in which he presented them, with listeners including some of the best-educated women in Peru and the elite's liberal thinkers, enabled him to advance these reforms. By the same token, however, his suggestions make alterations in a flawed system instead of creating a new system to replace the old one. Like the *Museo Literario* writers, Álamos González uses the rhetoric of modernity tactically, in order to promote particular ideas about the new nation and the public sphere.

Gorriti's literary salons and the debate about education for women they fostered took place within a larger intellectual context in Lima of lively foment about what the nation's future should hold and about the stakeholders who would participate in forming it. The general interest periodical *El Perú Ilustrado*, which Clorinda Matto de Turner edited between 1889 and 1891, was a crucial element in such conversations and addressed social questions including education. The journal used the idea that education was vital to national progress to advocate for education for women, both openly and subtly. For example, in an issue published several weeks after Castro's piece appeared, the editors inserted a congratulatory note to Felícitas Balbuena for having passed her first-year exam in dental surgery with excellence. "Parece," they continue, "que ciertas preocupaciones infundadas van desapareciendo, lo que redunda en pro del progreso general y el bienestar de las familias" (It seems that certain unfounded worries are disappearing, which speaks favorably of general progress and the well-being of families; December 15, 1889). They explicitly link progress to domestic welfare and both of those to the elimination of unspecified "concerns" about women's roles and capabilities. Comparing the enlightened present with the backward past, they comment that "hoy las cosas han variado de acuerdo con la razón y las ideas modernas" (today things have changed in accordance with reason and modern ideas). Their vocabulary links medical training for women in particular and higher education in general with logic, reason, and modernity, while those who oppose such opportunities for women are characterized as having ideas not based in reality. The description of Balbuena's achievement marginalizes anyone who does not approve of education for women. This news item appears in a section titled simply "Sueltos" (Loose ends), which consists of brief entries, usually only one to three sentences long, ranging from a thank-you note to a generous subscriber who has sent a box of art supplies to one of the journal's illustrators, to the announcement of the death of a child, to greetings to a visiting intellectual. By embedding Balbuena's accomplishment in this section, the editors both make it routine and note its exceptionalism.

As well as editing *El Perú Ilustrado*, Matto de Turner, a guest at Gorriti's literary evenings when she visited from Cuzco, also edited *El Búcaro Americano* from 1896 to 1908. In 1898 she described it in these terms:

> Una revista nacida al calor de generosos ideales a favor del mejoramiento intelectual de la mujer americana, fundada con la vocación del arte del artista llamando en fraternal invocación a todos los hermanos que en América cultivan la gaya ciencia y la prosa vivificante.

> A journal born in the heat of generous ideals favoring the intellectual improvement of the American woman, fused with the artistic vocation of the artist calling in fraternal invocation to all siblings who in America cultivate science and enlivening prose. (274)

The journal itself had the edifying and pedagogical intention of producing educated Latin American women. Here Matto de Turner calls to male and female intellectuals alike to incorporate women into the project of female education, and *El Búcaro Americano* enacts that call by featuring writers of both sexes. Matto de Turner also links women's education specifically to the ideals of progress and to the discourse of positivism, as when in 1896 she wrote that the journal's fundamental ideal was "la educación de la mujer en el rol que le depara el movimiento del progreso universal para que pueda cumplir satisfactoriamente los deberes que esa misma corriente evolutiva le señala" (woman's education in the role assigned to her by the movement of universal progress so that she may carry out satisfactorily the duties that this same evolutionary movement indicates to her; 275). By ascribing women's roles in their nations and on the continent to "the movement of universal progress," Matto de Turner creates the image of a process in which progress motivates, demands, and depends on women's educational advances, rather than arguing that female education is an appendage, however welcome, to an insistent and inexorable forward progress that would have happened regardless of female involvement. At the same time, her language casts women in a passive role. Her women do not strike out to seek new opportunities; they accept the responsibilities thrust upon them and discharge their assigned duties. Similarly she states in 1901, "La mujer productiva es el nuevo elemento de progreso de que se gloriará el siglo XX" (The productive woman is the new element of progress in which the twentieth century will glory; 275). Here women exist to demonstrate a facet of modern life and progress, in another iteration of woman as decorative object. Matto de Turner's very phrasing speaks to the inherent limits of rhetoric that strove to wed traditional gender roles and images of women as essentially domestic with the modernizing discourses about social progress and national advancement.

Yet another one of Gorriti's guests was Mercedes Cabello de Carbonera (1849–1909), a prolific writer of novels and journalistic writing, covering topics such as literary criticism, culture, history, and politics. She too was an advocate of education for women, arguing in her essay "Influencia de la mujer en la civilización" that all social ills could be cured by instructing women.[16] She connects the education of women with modernization and progress, but also with religious duty, saying that educated women are best able to combat agnosticism and telling her male readers: "Acercad a la mujer al santuario de la ciencia, para que ella a su vez pueda acercar al hombre al altar de Dios" (Bring woman to the sanctuary of science, so that she in turn may bring man to the altar of God; 115). She concludes:

La inteligencia de la mujer no es hoy más que la crisálida que guarda la brillante mariposa, que libera el néctar delicioso de las magníficas flores de la virtud, fecundadas por la ciencia y producidas a la sombra de la paz y la felicidad de la familia.

Woman's intellect is today no more than the chrysalis that protects the shining butterfly, which is freed by the delicious nectar of virtue's magnificent flowers, fertilized by science, and grown in the shadow of peace and family happiness. (115)

For women to reach their full potential, they must be accorded the access to "ciencia" that men have historically enjoyed. Cabello de Carbonera unites praise of science with the near-ritual invocation of the domestic realm and counters possible arguments about women's failure to achieve to date by presenting women, like Peru itself, as full of potential to be realized. With this gesture toward the future she, like her peers, connects women to education and education to progress in an irresistible logical chain. Yet again, however, women remain tied to their traditional roles; while Cabello de

Carbonera's ideal woman may learn about science, she returns the favor by helping men become more spiritual, and even their cerebral capacities are passive objects of beauty.

Lima and Buenos Aires boasted active and influential literary circles that included and sometimes even welcomed women as participants. While in other countries there may not have been as many women intellectuals, women were present as both objects and subjects of public discourse. Thus, for example, in Mexico City, the weekly magazine *Violetas del Anáhuac* appeared from December 1887 to June 1889, directed first by Laureana Wright de Kleinhans and later by Mateana Murguía de Aveleyra. Typical of women's magazines in Mexico and elsewhere, *Violetas del Anáhuac* contained society news, fashion, stories, poetry, biographical sketches of notable women, instructional material about science, history, and art, and household hints.[17] In addition, numerous editorials by the publishers express ideas typical of Porfirian and positivist discourse, as they argue against what they frame as the barbarous practices of bullfights, the death penalty, and duels. These activities, say various authors, are unacceptable for a nation en route to true modernity and progress. Such articles clearly situate the journal's position as an advocate of modernity and place into the intellectual context of the Porfirian dictatorship the frequent articles advocating education for women that also appear in the magazine's pages. Wright de Kleinhans, Murguía de Aveleyra, and their associates aligned themselves with the rule of Porfirio Díaz and with the philosophy of positivism that he and his governmental bureaucrats espoused, as well as its slogan of "Order and Progress," enthusiastically adopted by Díaz's "científicos" from Auguste Comte himself. The Mexican affinity for positivism led to the renovation of the system of higher education and placed educational reform in public view, allowing proponents of female education such as the editors of *Violetas del Anáhuac* to attach their own agendas for women's access to education to the greater scheme for modernization and progress. The focus on logical, scientific education propounded by positivists could be easily incorporated into arguments for women's practical education.

Arturo Ardao has argued that in Latin America in general, "positivism anticipated and precipitated scientific culture, instead of resulting from scientific thought as in Europe" (12). Positivism arrived in Latin America as a rhetorical phenomenon instead of growing organically from material conditions, in similar fashion to the inverted chronology of modernity and modernization. This too allowed for proposals about women's educational advancement to be affixed to the more global arguments in favor of rational, scientific education that were associated with Latin American positivism. Leopoldo Zea discusses the specific case of positivism in Mexico, asserting that positivist ideology facilitated the transition of power to the liberal bourgeoisie after 1867 and that secular education was a crucial element in strengthening the incipient middle class (85, 107–9). In the process by which the Mexican state was ever more defined as an abstract force rather than as an individual, wider access to education was vital in creating a ruling class. The Escuela Nacional Preparatoria, the flagship institution of the positivists, instructed students in the sciences and social sciences. Positivist education united the country by imposing order on individuals and, by extension, on a previously disordered society (164). Some intellectuals argued that women were an integral part of this project of creating order and impelling national progress, both in their traditional roles as mothers of Mexican citizens and in their newer avocations as active contributors to an economy that would be based on the movement of industrial capital. Such concepts appeared frequently in *Violetas del Anáhuac* and other writings by the magazine's editors and contributors.

One such article, "La señorita María Yáñez," used the case of María Yáñez and her successful defense of her nomination as a school principal to expound the argument for higher education for women. The article includes the new principal's own narrative of her desire to enter school administration, in which she presents herself as motivated by "el deseo de hacer uso de un derecho por tanto tiempo conculcado a la mujer: el derecho de penetrar en el templo de la ciencia y procurarse por sí misma su subsistencia" (the desire to make use of a right forbidden for so long to women: the right to enter the temple of science and to earn her own living for herself; Domenella and Pasternac, 447). Neatly bundled into this single sentence are three crucial ideas: the concept that women's education is a right, albeit one historically and unjustly denied to women; the importance of scientific education in particular; and the emphasis on women's economic self-sufficiency. By invoking "la ciencia," Yáñez appeals to the positivist passion for science and technology and makes an implicit contrast with what had typically been seen as acceptable education for women—they were taught, at best, to read and write and were given religious instruction. The use of the word "penetrar," too, signals an appropriation of male power—in fact, of the most elemental male power—and even refigures science as feminine, the object of penetration. Finally, by carefully noting Yáñez's desire to win her own "subsistencia," she underscores the limits of her ambition: simply to provide for herself. She thus takes a step back from what might have been a daring intrusion (penetration) into a province of male power.

At the same time, the author tactfully notes the "sacrifices" made by Yáñez: "No puede ser más loable ni más santa la idea que la ha decidido a consagrarse al trabajo, en la flor de su juventud y belleza" (There can be nothing more praiseworthy or saintlier than the idea that she has decided to dedicate herself to work, in the flower of her youth and beauty; 448). What could have been construed as a selfish desire for independence is thus reconstructed as a near-divine calling. The rhetoric of feminine sacrifice would have been familiar to the readers of *Violetas del Anáhuac*, although women were typically portrayed as sacrificing themselves on the altar of domestic service. By transposing the concept of the self-sacrificing woman to the public sphere, the author of the piece uses an idea from the private sphere of the home to justify Yáñez's double move into the public area as she becomes both the head of a school and the subject of an article published in a circulating magazine.

Such discursive combinations show the authors not only repeating the rhetoric of modernity but also manipulating that rhetoric in order to appeal to a widespread audience. Women's advancement is tied to national progress and to domestic ideals. Writers counteract potential arguments about the unsuitability of women for the workforce in two ways: they link women's education to the hegemonic discourse of positivism and argue that women's roles in the public sphere are a natural extension of their roles in the private sphere. This balancing act helps ensure the acceptance of the ideas couched in the pages of *Violetas del Anáhuac*. Marysa Navarro and Virginia Sánchez Korrol have pointed out that, while in nineteenth-century Latin America a small group of progressive women argued that total gender equality constituted the ideal relationship between the sexes,

> significant numbers of women [. . .] opposed such views, fearing that equality spelled the initial breakdown of home and family. Many

women supported traditional gender roles that oriented the female toward the home, while men [...] were understandably reluctant to compromise their legally sanctioned power. The majority of women who sought advancement and increased rights for [their] sex sought to mediate between two extremes: they advocated neither for "sameness" with men nor for a status quo that perpetuated female legal, professional, and economic inferiority. (82)

Those writers seeking to advocate for women's increased access to education could not, then, assume that all their female readers were in agreement with their agenda, should it be posed as a radical challenge to prevailing social norms. They carefully navigated around the potential dangers of appearing to overtly defy their society's standards for acceptable feminine behavior and of simply sustaining an oppressive model that barred women from educational opportunities.

Again, the most common strategy for avoiding these perils involved linking female education to women's vital roles in the family. In an article titled "Educación doméstica," Mateana Murguía de Aveleyra defends women's learning by asserting that educated women are crucial for raising appropriately domesticated daughters, capable of running the complex affairs of the home. She lists the main elements of women's domestic duties:

Si todas las madres tuvieran presente que sus hijas también desempeñarán algún día el mismo sublime papel, les enseñarían a fondo todas las importantes obligaciones que tienen que llenar como madres, como amas de casa, como educadoras de sus hijas.

If all mothers kept in mind that their daughters would also one day carry out the same sublime role, they would teach them all the important obligations that they have to fulfill as mothers, as housekeepers, as teachers of their own daughters. (431)

Women's education is important not because women selfishly desire their own advancement but because by being better educated they are more capable of discharging their domestic duties, which include raising the next generation of domestic angels. Murguía de Aveleyra stresses that mothers are the teachers of their daughters, not of their sons and daughters, as other nineteenth-century women argued; hers is a strictly feminine gene-alogy. In brief, the ideal advanced by the editors of *Violetas del Anáhuac* depicts a space in which women devote themselves to the well-being of others rather than privileging their own wants and desires, thus invoking once more the image of the angel of the house. At times this is the domestic space of the home; at other times it expands to include public space as well, a natural outgrowth of women's household roles. Moreover, the authors argue that the family is the linchpin of society and that women's familial roles are by necessity public roles as well. These apparently contradictory viewpoints are, as we have seen, reconcilable within the rhetoric of moder-nity as adapted to the Latin American context. Even more, their mutual reconciliation under the rubric of modernity demonstrates the importance of gender to the rhetoric of modernity and enables us to see modernity in late nineteenth-century Latin America as a fluid concept that had to be associated with the traditional in order to become intelligible to its Latin American consumers.

Wright de Kleinhans, however, would come to advance a more radical notion of female emancipation and potential. In 1891, several years after she had left *Violetas del Anáhuac*, she published "La emancipación de la mujer por medio del estudio" (Woman's emancipation through education), a scathing critique of male privilege and sexism. Her sophisticated and subtle argument anticipates the feminist movements of the mid-twenti-eth century; she deconstructs the ways in which biblical and mythologi-cal discourses have been used to justify women's oppression, critiques the idea that women are morally superior as a way to perpetuate masculine domination in other spheres, accuses men of using women for their own aggrandizement, and offers a historical overview of accomplished women. At the same time she affirms the overwhelming importance of motherhood and calls it "el empleo más arduo y más grandioso sobre la tierra" (the most arduous and grandest task in the world, 43). Wright de Kleinhans attacks men for depriving women of their right to participate in all aspects of hu-man creation and intellectual capacities and for enslaving women rather than treating them as the equal partners they deserve to be. Writing, "En la familia, lo mismo que en la nación y que en la sociedad, el hombre que ostensiblemente ha cumplido con sus deberes, interiormente ha sometido a la mujer a la misma supuesta inferioridad, privándola hasta de los derechos íntimos que le concede el privilegio de la maternidad" (In the family, just as in the nation and in society, the man who ostensibly has carried out his duties has subjected woman to the same supposed inferiority, depriving her even of the intimate rights that the privilege of motherhood grants her; 47–48), she deconstructs the most common argument for the relegation of women to the private sphere, which is that women were meant to rule in the domestic arena, leaving men to the public world. Yet Wright de Kleinhans asserts that men have replicated the same systems of oppression in the family as in greater society: not only do they deprive women of their rights as intellectual equals but they even take away the rights they have earned as mothers. Thus the supposed justification for keeping women in the home and allowing them only domestic work collapses.

Wright de Kleinhans brings together several discursive threads in her essay, first daring to argue that women are unquestionably the intellectual and moral equals to men and that they should have equal access to all areas of activity and work, then claiming that women's most important function is as mothers and guardians of their families. Rather than crafting an argument based on a moral imperative—that men must do what is right—she relies on an empirically based argument to show that women are demonstrably equal to men. In this way, her rhetorical strategy aligns with positivist discourse. Like authors across the continent, she holds up the United States as a positive model, in this case because in the United States women can work in all the careers and professions that men do. Ultimately, in this first section of the essay, Wright de Kleinhans avers that "en lo concerniente al amor, a la ternura del hogar y a los lazos íntimos de la familia, la mujer nunca dejará de ser mujer" (as for love, the tenderness of the home and intimate family bonds, woman will never stop being woman; 53). While women are equal to men, they retain their essential, innate femininity. Contradictorily, Wright de Kleinhans insists on the inherent difference between men and women in the same essay in which she affirms their fundamental equality. This slippage occurs because Wright de Kleinhans herself is caught in a contradictory position: she wants to argue for true female emancipation while using a set of rhetorical tropes about motherhood and femininity that serve to reinscribe women's de facto subordination.

That is, her essay posits both equality and difference, as is evident in this passage:

> Es necesario que [la mujer] trabaje por su regeneración intelectual ilustrando su mente con la luz de nuevas ideas, fortaleciendo su alma con la fe de nuevos principios y nuevas aspiraciones. Es necesario que deje de considerar la instrucción como herencia particular del hombre y que en las horas que sus quehaceres domésticos le dejen libres, si tiene familia que atender, o en su tiempo todo si carece de ella, trabaje por su mejoramiento renovando la viciada atmósfera que respira, regenerando su ánimo. Es necesario que deje de considerar la instrucción, el adelanto y la ciencia como bienes hereditarios del hombre, y que en vez de entregarse por completo a la molicie de fútiles entrenamientos, como adulta, penetre en todas las cátedras del estudio; como madre, lleve a sus hijos sin distinción de sexos y según sus facultades a los planteles de educación científica, literaria, o artística que los pongan al corriente de todos los conocimientos teóricos y prácticos de que hoy sólo disfruta el hombre, colocándose ella en situación de cumplir gloriosamente con su verdadera misión de alma y guía de la humanidad, que tiene que desempeñar en el mundo.

> Woman must work toward her intellectual regeneration, illuminating her mind with the light of new ideas, fortifying her soul with the faith of new principles and new aspirations. She must cease thinking of education as the special heritage of man and in the time she has free from domestic chores, if she has a family to take care of, or in all her time if she doesn't, she must work to better herself by renovating the vice-ridden atmosphere she breathes, regenerating her soul. She must cease thinking of education, progress, and science as hereditary rights of man, and instead of giving herself up to the tumult of useless diversions, as an adult, she must enter all areas of studies; as a mother, she must take all her children, regardless of sex, and according to their abilities, to be educated in science, literature, or art, which will put them in the forefront of the theoretical and practical knowledge that today only man enjoys, and which will enable her to carry out most gloriously her true mission as the soul and guide of humanity, which she must discharge in the world. (58)

Wright de Kleinhans invokes positivist rhetoric with a semantic chain that connects renovation, enlightenment, intelligence, and progress with words such as "regeneración," "ilustrando," "la luz de nuevas ideas," and "renovando la viciada atmósfera." This vocabulary evokes the positivist mission of "curing" Latin America's social ills and of moving forward into a new, scientifically based era of governance. At the same time that she works to connect Mexican women with the dominant rhetorical mode of the epoch, she also firmly reasserts their primary function as members of families, as mothers above all, charged with educating their own children. This is signaled through another semantic chain, one with words and phrases such as "quehaceres domésticos," "como madre," and "alma y guía de la humanidad." Men are not the "soul" of humanity, and they do not have this lofty destiny—a framing of women's role which Wright de Kleinhans implicitly condemns earlier in this same essay when she critiques as restrictive the idea that women are morally superior to men. Here, in her concluding paragraphs, she reenacts the same restrictions. Women should have unlimited access to all kinds of educational opportunities, but again, it is so that they can fulfill their destiny as literal and metaphorical mothers in and of their nations. This profound ambivalence indicates the difficulties that even the most progressive thinkers had in conceiving of truly substantive female equality in nineteenth-century Latin America.

The question of education for women might have seemed to be straightforward: women's education was a factor in modernizing the nation and the continent. However, when Latin American thinkers began grappling with the topic and possibility of providing women with more education than they had previously enjoyed, their engagement with the topic resulted in approaches of widely varying sophistication and ideological bent. This is precisely because men and women, conservatives and liberals, associated education with national progress and, often, with the advancement of the human race. Their rhetorical arguments with respect to the latter phenomenon often tap into the discourse of futurity that Carlos Alonso has described, in which America is seen, first, as the future to Europe's present and, second, as a space of ever-postponed potential, which Alonso calls "a concrete sense of the future as the realm of the possible-but-not-yet-realized" (9). As he also indicates, "The discourse of futurity [. . .] became the essential framework for the construction of novel ideological narratives during the postcolonial phase of nation-building" (17). In this conception, Latin America was a new dawn, the future of the entire human race. Women were strongly associated with this because of their roles as mothers, who literally brought new people into the world. This may explain the fact that discourses about women's education were frequently framed in terms of future contributions that these potential mothers would make. While in some cases writers praised educated women for their specific work as teachers or doctors, for the most part men and women alike created images of an ideal future in which educated women gave birth to and raised morally outstanding, patriotic, hardworking citizens. Women's role in creating the "possible-but-not-yet-realized" future was both physical, as they would bear the children of the new society, and intellectual, as they would inculcate these future citizens with appropriate ideologies.

This formulation meant that women remained strongly connected to the domestic sphere, a connection that, as we have seen, involves numerous contradictions. In the particular case of education, such education would normally allow women to leave the private sphere. But in order for women's education to be socially acceptable, it had to be framed in such a way that it enhanced and reinforced women's roles within the home and family. Some writers strove to maintain the traditional role of women within the home; others responded to social pressures that increasingly saw middle-class women leaving the home to work and tried to cement in place certain strictures for female (and, by implication, male) behavior that would keep women within the family. Still other writers saw in the manipulation of rhetoric about domesticity the possibility for female empowerment. Rather than using arguments about women's ideal roles as wives and mothers to argue for a limited education in morality and virtue, such authors pushed the limits and advanced more radical notions of what might constitute an adequate, reasonable education for women, while justifying this on the basis of women's domestic roles. Strikingly, in all these cases and with all their varying desired outcomes, writers consistently linked women to social and political matters such as national consolidation and modernization and asserted not only that women should benefit from the opportunities afforded by national advancement but also that the nation itself would profit from women's inclusion. Indeed, the argument is a double-pronged one: the nation must prove its modern condition by educating women, and educating women is necessary for the modernization of the nation. Finally, through their writings these women enacted what they hoped to bring about. By addressing the questions of national progress, modernity, and women's roles in those processes, the writers helped shape debates about modernization and gender roles. They recast the rhetoric of modernity in such a way as to make female education, whatever outcome they envisioned for that education, a necessary element of modernization.

5

New Technologies, New Work

Two of the most dramatic changes in late nineteenth-century Spanish America were the acceleration of technological innovation and the associated pervasiveness of new technologies in everyday life and the entry of middle-class women to the labor market. These phenomena were intimately connected. Across the continent and over the course of the second half of the century, ever-larger numbers of women found paid employment, often in public domains as teachers, telephone operators, or sales clerks, allowing them an expanded set of options other than the traditional ones of marriage or the convent. Not only did women gain access to a preexisting job market, but new types of work appeared as the physical processes of modernization and new technologies increasingly penetrated South American countries. The mechanization of production and the appearance of factories, both small- and large-scale, as well as the growing popularity of inventions such as the telegraph and the telephone, demanded additional workers for what were often repetitive tasks. As cities became more urbanized, the growth of the bourgeoisie accompanied a marked surge in commerce, the production and importation of luxury goods, and the availability of such goods to a larger public, which in turn meant a rise in stores where items such as clothing, shoes, books, and home décor were sold. Women often worked in these stores as salespeople, a newly respectable occupation. In general, women eager to gain economic independence or to improve their families' financial condition took advantage of these new options to vie for employment outside the home.

Public opinion about women's newfound economic independence ranged from frequent condemnation to much rarer praise. Despite the proliferation of articles in periodicals and other public discourse about women

Figure 3. Illustration for "Teléfonos y telefonistas" in *Zig-Zag* 1, no. 1 (February 19, 1905)

entering the workforce, discussions of women as workers and representations of women's work exhibit two striking characteristics: despite the increasing prevalence of women's participation in the workforce, women's work, paid or unpaid, was rarely represented in works of literary fiction, and fictional and nonfictional texts alike tended to ignore or obscure the ways in which women participated in work within and outside the home. For example, the focus on middle-class employment by some journalists elided the fact that lower-class women had always worked for pay as domestic servants, food vendors, and textile workers, among other occupations. It also concealed the unpaid work that lower- and middle-class women alike had always carried out in the home. The concentration on domesticity and women's supposedly natural affinity for domestic tasks served to categorize domestic labor as the fulfillment of a near-sacred mission rather than as chores or even drudgery, further disguising women's work from view. Those authors who did represent women's work typically took pains to do so in ways that showed women's work as an extension of their traditional roles in the family or as a continuation of their conventional labor as seamstresses or childcare providers. Upper-class women who worked for pay in these texts did so only out of dire economic necessity. All these elements send the message that women's work is not valuable or important, that women should avoid work, especially paid work, as much as possible, and that men should help them stay out of the labor force and the capitalist job market. In this regard, such statements can be read as contesting certain discourses of modernity from the metropolis that privileged women's entry into the public sphere via paid employment as a vital component of the modernizing project, but they also took advantage of modernity's newfound emphasis on domesticity, as we saw in chapter 3. Such writers selectively used particular elements of the rhetoric of modernity related to gender, demonstrating once more that modernity was a malleable concept in nineteenth-century Latin America.

These forcefully expressed opinions about women at work are especially noteworthy, given that women were indeed working outside the home throughout the nineteenth century and the entry of middle-class women into the workforce was a fact rather than a possibility. In the transition to urbanization and industrialization, traditional forms of work did not disappear. The demographic changes that saw the increasing concentration of people in urban centers and that facilitated the growth of industries and job opportunities related to new technologies expanded work possibilities for men and women alike but did not eliminate the home-based labor that now was often taken up by women. At the same time, Latin America's gradual shift to an urban, industrial economy permitted the entry of greater numbers of middle-class and lower-middle-class women into the workforce and allowed lower-class women to move from agricultural or artisanal work to factory labor.

According to Carmen Ramos Escandón, the focus on mechanizing and standardizing modes of production that had been related directly to female-assigned tasks frequently facilitated women's movement into the industrialized workspace. The modes of production that most readily employed women included large-scale food preparation and sales, domestic services, childcare, and textile work (273). Women's systematic movement into the labor force was more feasible when they were shown to be engaged in extensions of work that had typically been coded as female. Similarly, Marysa Navarro and Virginia Sánchez Korrol note that near the end of the nineteenth century across Latin America, "increasing numbers of women were employed as seamstresses, artisans, and food processors. [...] Teaching, nursing, and clerical employment offered the first opportunities for middle-class women to work outside the home, while factories and cottage industries incorporated women of the lower classes as a cheap source of labor" (80), and Nancy LaGreca indicates, "Early modernization required female labor, and women took underpaid jobs in textile and tobacco factories and, if more educated, as office workers, telegraph operators, schoolteachers, porcelain painters, or workers in photography" (34). In sum, in the nineteenth century women continued to work, paid and unpaid, as they had for centuries. Those arguing against women's paid work, in other words, were not trying to keep women in the home; they were trying to put them back there and to reverse a widespread social shift that was already well under way. Arguments that working mothers were more prone to neglect their children and that women's primary duty should be to tend to their children rather than to earn money were prevalent, as were worries that women who left the home for paid employment were or would become sexually active.[1] The paradox, then, remains that while women's work was a concrete phenomenon throughout Latin America and attracted significant attention from writers and thinkers from across the ideological spectrum, the labor of women remains for the most part unrepresented in much of nineteenth-century literature. Yet women's incursion into the labor market toward the close of the nineteenth century revealed the schisms and fissures in discourses that worked to classify female work as something other than work itself.

As urban areas grew in size and importance and as new technologies penetrated Latin American economies, women's roles and public perceptions about those roles and duties changed as well. At the same time, the discourses about women's employment changed in response to the pressures of modernization and to rhetoric about progress and national modernity. Such discursive changes are as uneven and contradictory as the very economic processes that brought industrialization. This enables us to understand modernity as continually rhetorical in nature, despite the growth of the physical, concrete phenomena of modernization. Modernity—and the ideas about gender that became associated with modernity—remained essentially unfixed and malleable. Reactions to the idea that women, especially middle-class women, were entering the paid labor force ranged widely as some writers strove to maintain conventional gender norms that dictated that women should remain home-bound while other writers advanced notions of female progress, often tying such gendered ideologies to concepts of the imagined nation and its role on the global stage.

Both men and women participated in shaping viable discourses about the notion and impact of progress, technological advances and changes in the work environment, and the relationships of these phenomena with gender, revealing anxieties and hopes and striving for impact on national conversations about these many innovations. To trace the effect of technological innovations on these writers, I highlight several technologies related to transportation, notably trains and trams, and communication, the telegraph and telephone. More generally, this chapter also analyzes representations of new modalities of everyday life and work that were brought about by the spread of new technologies in order to demonstrate that concepts of gender influenced those representations just as writers' ideas about social changes influenced the ways in which they presented gender and gender roles to their audiences.

In terms of transportation, the railroad was seen both to bring and to incarnate progress; it made the distribution of increasing quantities of industrially produced goods across greater and greater distances possible and was itself an industrial product. Steam power could overcome nature (Schivelbusch 10), an aspect that acquired value on a continent whose inhabitants perceived themselves as struggling to overcome an untamed and wild land. Domingo Faustino Sarmiento famously complained of Argentina's lack of a transportation network and attributed his country's supposed barbarism to this, among other factors. Yet by 1880, Argentina's railway system was perhaps the most extensive in Latin America, covering almost three thousand kilometers. Railroads carried export goods to market and brought imported goods to the interior, allowing for the greater dissemination of such products to cities that did not enjoy the advantages of coastal ports. In Chile, the copper mines of the north flourished with the development of railway transportation (Bushnell and Macauley 231–35). Elsewhere, the construction of railroads facilitated large-scale, monoculture agricultural industry; in Guatemala, coffee exports almost tripled in a decade in large part due to the new railroads (Bushnell and Macauley 284–85). The concentration of industry and agriculture also meant that workers could continue to cluster in one area, furthering the concurrent population growth of towns and cities as opposed to people's widespread distribution over a large rural area. Towns and cities afforded many more opportunities for commercial and cultural enterprises, from department stores and specialty shops to bookstores and opera houses. Trains facilitated all these developments by helping goods and people gather together in ever more centralized locations.

In 1888, Rosa Navarrio published a poem titled "A la locomotora" (To the locomotive) in the Mexican magazine *Violetas del Anáhuac*. The poem

begins, "Te saludo, del Progreso / Mensajera bendecida, / Y te doy la bi-
envenida, / Nuncio de prosperidad" [I salute you, blessed Messenger of
Progress, and I welcome you, envoy of prosperity; 356]. Navarrio continues
in this vein for twenty more stanzas, saluting the locomotive as a beneficent
harbinger of modernization to her city, Guadalajara. She associates the
train with an elite project of progress when she notes that not all understand the significance of the railroad: "Mas nada importa que el vulgo / Ig-
norante como necio / Tenga al Vapor menosprecio / si inmensos bienes le
da!" [But it doesn't matter that the masses, / ignorant and foolish, / disdain
the Steam Engine, / if it gives them wonderful benefits! 356]. Her poetic
"I" positions itself as the arbiter of social value, judging the railroad's effects
on all sectors. Navarrio also inserts an emotional response to the train's
arrival. She presents the fact that her narrator weeps with joy at the sight
of the locomotive as a reaction to be expected, normalizing the emotional
connection between regional and national pride, technology, and progress
that Porfirio Díaz's government sought to encourage.

Trains were an important symbol of Porfirio Díaz's oft-stated project
to bring Mexico out of its backward state and turn it into a modern nation
that would vie with Europe and North America. Between 1880 and 1884
Mexico's railway system grew from a few hundred miles of track to more
than fifty-seven hundred kilometers and ran from Mexico City to El Paso,
Texas. This allowed for the further development of the mining industry
and the export of mined metals to the United States (Bushnell and Macauley 207), which in turn increased commercial development both in Mexico
City and in the northern states. In Mexico City, for example, the central
Zócalo housed dozens of stores, large and small, including the city's largest
dry goods store (Johns 10). At the turn of the century shoppers could visit
over a dozen modern department stores on the way from the Zócalo to
the Alameda, selling goods imported from Europe and the United States.
Importers also shipped products all over the country (Johns 15–16). Navarrio's poem makes the connection between trains and progress explicit. "A
la locomotora" foregrounds the preoccupation of Latin American writers
with the process of modernization, almost always associated with the notion that Latin American countries could and should become more like
Europe and with the concrete phenomenon of increased industrialization,
which often played itself out in nineteenth-century texts as an interest in

the use of technology. Finally, her poem demonstrates that women were deeply concerned with these issues, as were their male counterparts. Navarrio was writing for the predominantly female audience who read *Violetas del Anáhuac*.

The interest in technology and travel appears in novels of the time as well across the continent. Clorinda Matto de Turner's 1889 novel *Aves sin nido*, discussed in chapter 2, contains a long description of a journey by train as Lucía and Fernando Marín, accompanied by their indigenous foster daughters Margarita and Rosalía, travel by horseback through the Andes to the train station.

> [D]e improviso se distinguen dos sierpes de acero reverderantes extendidas sobre la amarillenta grama, y sobre éllas el humo del vapor que, como la potente respiración de un gigante, da vida y movimiento a grandes vagones. De súbito se oye el resoplido de la locomotora, que con su silbato anuncia el progreso llevado por los rieles a los umbrales donde se detuvo Manco Capac.

> Suddenly two steel serpents appear, extended over the yellow fields, and over them the steam vapor which, like a giant's breath, gives life and movement to huge cars. Then one hears the whistle of the locomotive, which announces the progress brought by the rails to the threshold where Manco Capac paused. (197–98)

The train's presence is intimated before it becomes a reality, heightening the drama of its appearance. By invoking Manco Capac, the last Inca emperor, Matto de Turner signals the arrival of modernity to the benighted villages of the Andes, one of the central themes of *Aves sin nido*. She denotes the lost indigenous past and nods to the impoverished indigenous present while promising the appearance of progress that the train represents. The train connects the past to the future, and the steel rails provide a visual echo of this permanent connection.

Matto de Turner then describes the train journey itself, complete with details of the women changing into appropriate train-riding attire. They must physically transform in order to experience the transition to modernization, just as the physical presence of the train and the railroad permanently transforms the Peruvian landscape. Another revealing detail is the

Maríns' choice of reading material: Lucía opts for Carlos Augusto Sala-verry's *Poesías*, while Fernando decides upon Ricardo Palma's *Tradiciones*.[2] Palma was one of Matto de Turner's literary mentors, and this was her way of paying homage. But it is also noteworthy that Lucía and Fernando are reading works by contemporary Peruvian authors as they journey on the ur-symbol of progress to Lima, a place held up throughout the novel as the center of civilization. At the same time, these characters, who symbolize the future of the nation, read Peruvian literature that has a strong flavor of the past. Palma based many of his stories on his historical research, and Salaverry's poetry was strongly associated with the fast-fading Romantic movement. Like the train itself, then, reading connects past and future in a seamless unit, and it is telling that these acts of reading take place in a mobile vehicle, an enclosed space that is associated with no fixed location. The characters are between spaces and regions physically and mentally, not tied to a hegemonic concept of past, present, tradition, or modernity. Moreover, these scenes of reading counterpoint Matto de Turner's own project of creating national literature. As she proclaimed in the prologue to *Aves sin nido*, she intended to signal "puntos de no escasa importancia para los progresos nacionales y [hacer] a la vez literatura peruana" [points of no little importance for national progress and at the same time create Peruvian literature; 52]. By inserting other authors into her text, Matto de Turner places herself in the same literary tradition and differentiates her novel from theirs. Her characters acknowledge the past but are not bound by it, reading as they do on the train. Indeed, one might even say that they are traveling, like Peru itself, to the future.

The lengthy nature of the train episode is particularly striking when one takes into account the fact that the Maríns spend five days traveling by horseback from Killac to the train station and that Matto de Turner dispenses with this lengthy journey in a few brief paragraphs. The train episode continues when the locomotive collides with a herd of cattle on a bridge and is threatened with derailment into a river. However, Mister Smith, the train's engineer, manages to avoid any loss of life by steering the train into the riverbank, not the river itself, and shooting out the boiler that is about to explode. Smith is a stereotypical gringo, mangling Spanish, barking orders, and fixing the engine with panache. The narrator points out that Smith's asseveration that "el culpa no es mi, ¿entiende? Culpa los vacas, e fácilmente se remedio" (No fault of me, got it? Blame the cows, an' it get fix easy; 209) soothes the passengers precisely because his poorly spoken Spanish reminds them that he is an American.

The derailment of the train is the episode that has caused readers the most consternation, as it seems to serve little or no narrative purpose.[3] The chapters describing the train journey are interspersed with ones explaining events in Killac, the town the Maríns have left; perhaps, then, the train episode is meant to heighten suspense. But the episode is instead—or also—linked to Matto de Turner's other preoccupation, clearly evident in the novel: the desire to advance a particular modernizing project, one that incorporates women into the national agenda. Efraín Kristal notes that in *El Perú Ilustrado*, the journal she edited from 1889 to 1891, Matto de Turner argued that an active industrial sector would result in greater social justice (153) and claimed that foreign investment in industry and growth of capital would be the salvation of Peru. If we read the seemingly anomalous train episode of *Aves sin nido* in light of Matto de Turner's other statements about industrialization and the future of Peru, and if we see the novel as a coherent whole rather than as a collection of apparently disparate episodes, then it becomes clear that the train incident expands upon rather than distracts from the rest of the novel's arguments about what modernization entails. Hence "Mister Smith" is present not merely for comic relief but also because he represents the American ideal of progress, modernity, and technology. He directs a reassuring comment to one of the female passengers, tying women once more to the national conversation about progress. The train collides with a symbol of the past, a herd of cows, on an old-fashioned bridge of wood and iron, in contrast to the steel rails of the train lines (204). This is the literal clash of the rural and the urban, of the past and the future, the primitive and the modern. The cow dies but the train is restored to "life" within a couple of hours and resumes its journey to Lima, leaving behind the backward world of the countryside.[4] The episode of the train serves as a concrete reminder of the importance of technology to nineteenth-century Latin American writers. Read against the backdrop of the lively conversations taking place in the nineteenth century about industrialization and modernization, it becomes apparent that Matto de Turner, like others, worked to shape the very premises of that discussion.

While the previous examples highlight the increasing importance of railways in the Latin American literal and figurative landscape, the development of new modes of urban transit also figured in the transformation of the geographies of cities and in the way people perceived the urban environment. Manuel Gutiérrez Nájera, Mexico City's noted chronicler and poet, traced a complex relationship with the city and with the technologies that made urban life what it was in the 1880s and 1890s. In his essay "La novela del tranvía," which appeared in *Cuentos frágiles* (1883), Gutiérrez Nájera marked out an early approach to issues of transportation. Questions of travel and transportation within cities were crucial to the processes of urbanization. Mass transit meant that large numbers of workers could live at a distance from their places of employment. Transportation systems in turn depended upon streets that could be traversed by vehicles larger than the carriages that typically carried the upper class from place to place. Porfirio Díaz's modernizing project for Mexico City included paving the streets. Thanks to those improved streets and access to mass transit, Gutiérrez Nájera's essayistic "I" traverses the city and reports on what he sees, a Mexican version of Baudelaire's *flaneur*. This reporter is, by his own confession, "desocupado," not busy, signaling that he enjoys some of the newfound leisure time that modernization helped to bring (6). His very lack of busy-ness prompts him to get on the nearest tram, from which he can observe "el delicioso cuadro que la ciudad presenta en ese instante. El vagón, además, me lleva a muchos mundos desconocidos y a regiones vírgenes" [the delightful picture that the city offers in that instant. The wagon, besides, takes me to many unknown worlds and virgin regions; 6]. The tram facilitates the subject's access to hitherto unknown areas of the city, expanding possibilities and knowledge; it enhances the writerly project rather than detracting from it. The journey through the city also makes the urban landscape a passive, implicitly female object to be consumed by the narrator's active, questing "I." He views the "delicious" picture presented to him and discovers "virgin" regions. Moreover, the process of travel both dislocates and relocates passengers, removing them from their accustomed locales and transferring them to new ones. As the textual "I" rides the tram, he examines not just the city but its inhabitants, focusing on his fellow passengers—both men and women—and inventing a narrative and history for each of them. In this way the hybrid experience of the tram journey makes possible the private, creative moment that in turn results in a public product, the *crónica* that Gutiérrez Nájera would publish.

La Ilustración Guatemalteca, a biweekly journal dedicated to literature, commerce, and industry, highlighted another new form of transportation, the bicycle, in its regular column on cycling. *La Ilustración Guatemalteca* ran for roughly a year in 1896 and 1897 and was clearly on the forefront of contemporary discourse about social change. Moreover, it took advantage of new technologies in printing to reproduce visual images on its glossy pages that included both illustrations and photos. Bicycles became wildly popular in Great Britain and North America after the invention of the safety bicycle, which allowed for a comfortable ride and greater ease of use, as well as being cheaper to manufacture and thus more accessible. *La Ilustración Guatemalteca* reported on Guatemalan bicycling with great satisfaction, pointing out in "Notas ciclistas" that while other scientific advances had met with resistance in Guatemala, the bicycle had proven enormously popular. The author queried why more women were not seen riding their bicycles, as cycle importers reported having sold more than fifty bicycles to women, and assured his female readers that, were they to ride out, they would be "el objeto de la admiración y de las más galantes atenciones de todos los caballeros ciclistas" [the object of admiration and the most gallant attentions of all gentleman cyclists; 13]. Such statements make the potential women cyclists into the focus of male sexual evaluation and present female bicycle riding as an acceptable activity that brings women under male surveillance. If a possible objection to women cyclists was that access to this individualized mode of transport gave them increased independence and autonomy, the writer's inscription of female cyclists into the male sexual economy casts women in a subordinate position to masculine desire. As cycling is depicted as a leisure activity for those with sufficient money to purchase one of the expensive machines, rather than as a means to travel to work, women's only purpose for venturing out on their bicycles is to give men visual pleasure. On the other hand, *La Ilustración Guatemalteca* actively encourages women to take advantage of this new technology and to participate alongside men in the sport, albeit as decorative objects serving male pleasure.

In addition to its regular column on cycling, *La Ilustración Guatemalteca* also published articles on notable male and female Guatemalans, poetry, general news, and summaries and comments on the activity of the stock market. It featured other articles highlighting Guatemalan industry, as in "La Unión Industrial," which described a shoe factory employing over 120 workers.[5] Among those workers were 28 women who stitched shoes, a task that was a natural extension of their traditional domestic chore of sewing. The writer comments on the women's work uniform, "un traje sencillo [. . .], casi todas portaban al cuello una cinta negra con una pequeña cruz" (a simple dress . . . , almost all the women wore a black ribbon with a small cross around their necks; 71). By emphasizing their physical appearance, the writer distracts the reader from the fact that these women are laboring for wages in a factory; he also draws attention to their religiosity. The fear that factory work would make women licentious and sexually free is thus counteracted by the reference to their modest dress and Catholic virtue, as well as by the careful note that the women work in a separate area from the men. The article further praises the shoe factory as a model of industrial progress and proffers the employment of women at the factory as an essential element of that progress. Women's work is potentially dangerous to conventional social mores at the same time that it constitutes a vital element of national progress, so it must be couched in terms that enable readers to perceive such work as a normal extension of women's traditional roles within their households. The journal promulgates a vision of female employment in the new factory as inevitable, appropriate, and even desirable, connecting women, industrialization, and modernization.

La Ilustración Guatemalteca's fascination with the industrialization process and with the new consumer goods and technologies that resulted from industrialization and made it possible was common in fin-de-siècle Spanish America. In 1905, the Chilean magazine *Zig-Zag* began publishing. Founded by Agustín Edwards, it was co-directed by Joaquín Díaz Garcés and Carlos Silva Vildósola. *Zig-Zag* and its sister magazine, *Familia*, which was initiated in 1910, highlight the intersections among technology, modernization, and female employment. Perhaps even more important, these journals showcase anxiety about changes in women's roles in the home and at work while at the same time appearing to advocate for such changes.

Zig-Zag, a general-interest journal, published essays on culture and current events, satirical pieces, short stories, and fashion news and advice, signaling clearly its intended audience of middle- and upper-class men and women. Edwards, a banker turned newspaper owner, had traveled to the United States and Europe to study printing technologies and purchased the newest printing presses and machinery for reproducing color and black-and-white images.[6] In the first issue, the editors immediately announced that the journal would participate in a modern and modernizing project of developing its readers' good taste by providing the illustrations that its up-to-date reading public demanded. They pointed out that *Zig-Zag* enjoyed superior technology, thanks to a special arrangement with the most notable photography agencies in Europe and the United States, which had been arranged through communication via cablegrams (2). Not only did *Zig-Zag* possess the latest technologies as represented through its invocation of the trailblazing North American inventions, but it also used new technologies (the cable) to obtain them. The journal is thus painted as the product of modernizing advances in multiple ways. Such advances permit *Zig-Zag* to supply its illustrated pages to as many people as want to consume them, bringing all potential readers into the modernizing project.

Modernization was in full swing in Santiago by the end of the nineteenth century. Historian Bernardo Subercaseaux explains that the urban space had undergone significant changes by 1900. The street system, now traversed by both horse-drawn and electric trams, had been regularized and paved, and parks and plazas had been built. Other public spaces also allowed the different social classes to partake of high or popular culture, from the opera house for the elites to the streets and cantinas around the Estación Central where the lower classes would gather and listen to songs and broadsheets being sung or read aloud (78). Quite likely in response to the rapid growth of the middle class, *Zig-Zag*'s editors demonstrate a deep concern with the project of nurturing its readers' good taste, which is, like the creation of new technologies, a recent development. Employment statistics show the increasing numbers of the middle class, a phenomenon both partly due to and traceable through the tremendous expansion of the national government, which grew tremendously in size toward the end of the century. While the Chilean population in general rose 25 percent between 1865 and 1895, the number of merchants more than tripled and the number of office employees, both public and private, almost quadrupled. Reflecting the expansion of print opportunities in particular, the number of typographers went from 364 to 1,223 over the thirty-year period (Subercaseaux 80).

Zig-Zag establishes a normative discourse about "taste," meaning artistic and cultural judgment and selectivity. Although it does not specify what that good taste comprises, the journal closely links taste to modernity. Good taste is exclusive and special. Those who demand that their periodicals be illustrated are following the examples of their elite, advanced counterparts in Europe and North America. This viewing/reading public is also capable of choosing the best magazines and appreciating the many superlatives with which *Zig-Zag's* editors congratulate themselves. "La publicación de ZIG-ZAG forma parte de este movimiento universal en que las más ingeniosas invenciones mecánicas, las más felices y audaces adaptaciones del dibujo, los últimos adelantos de la fotografía, del foto-grabado y del grabado en general, se ponen al servicio de la reproducción artística y de las informaciones gráficas" (*Zig-Zag's* publication forms part of this universal movement in which the most ingenious mechanical inventions, the happiest and most daring adaptations of drawings, the latest advances in photography, in photogravure, and in engravings in general, are at the service of artistic reproduction and graphical information; 3). Here Díaz Garcés and Silva Vildósola proclaim the magazine's participation in a universal trend toward the newest and best technologies available. They connect this appreciation for what is novel and progressive with the cultivation of their readers' aesthetic senses and with a larger cultural and national trend toward modernization, all in unequivocally glowing terms. From its opening salvo, then, *Zig-Zag* affirms its stance in favor of all things modern and creates a normative discourse that incorporates its readers into that cosmovision.

This editorial pose is borne out by an article in the first issue titled "Teléfonos y telefonistas" (Telephones and telephone operators). If the train "annihilated" time and space by radically compressing distance (Schivelbusch 33), telecommunications played a similar role in enabling long-distance conversations and accelerating the pace of both business and daily life. The first telephones appeared in Chile in 1880, thanks to a North American businessman living in Valparaíso, but it was not until a decade later that telephone companies were able to expand significantly. At the turn of the century the federal government began granting and regulating telephone concessions. Once this happened in 1904, the Chili [sic] Telephone Company, a North American–controlled business that held the right to build and maintain telephone lines throughout the country, started to expand.[7] In *Zig-Zag*'s article, a writer visits Chili Telephone's Oficina Central, managed by "señor Jhonston [sic]." The Anglo-Saxon name signals the ongoing North American investment stake in the Chilean telephone system. *Zig-Zag*'s writer equates telephones with modernity by noting that much of contemporary business, commerce, and government is conducted via telephonic communication, which makes possible the rush of modern life, contemporary governance, and a strong economy. Were the telephone suddenly to disappear, "[l]os días, que tienen ahora cuarenta o cincuenta horas, volverían a ser esos infames días de antaño que apenas contaban doce horas hábiles" (the days, which now have forty or fifty hours, would go back to being those infamous days of yesteryear which barely had twelve useful hours; 6). The accelerated pace of communications enables more and more work to be done. The past is slow, conservative, and even contemptible, whereas the telephone office is the epicenter of all things new, progressive, and praiseworthy.

In this modern space, which emulates those of its North American models, women take a central role. The technological innovation of the telephone in itself provides a way for women to enter the workforce. Instead of taking jobs traditionally held by men and competing with their male counterparts for employment, women find paid positions in brand-new fields. At the telephone office, women are the only staff; the operators are even overseen by another woman, rather than Johnston himself.[8] This all-female space both privileges and protects women. They have access to paid employment, depicted as mostly congenial here, but they do not share that access with men.

Women working side by side with men was a common source of worry for turn-of-the-century observers, who feared the loss of female virtue in such situations. Yet *Zig-Zag*'s writer adduces other reasons for approving of the female-staffed telephones. According to him, all the callers needing to be connected are male. Never once does he admit the possibility that a woman other than one of the operators might use the telephone. This allows him to cast the scene in the telephone exchange as one in which women serve men, a strategy that makes their employment more permissible. Rather than using their employment to gain social and economic autonomy, the operators continue to enact traditional scenes of female submission by waiting upon men and by facilitating men's conversations with other men. In this way their office work is an extension of the labor performed in the home. The *Zig-Zag* writer further strategizes to make female employment acceptable by stating that male callers complain less when female voices greet them and that women respond more pacifically than male operators would to the shouts and complaints of irritated telephone users. Women here are not simply *allowed* to work—they are depicted as the best suited for this new kind of work.

Finally, the statement that the male callers flirt with the operators also diminishes the significance and threat potentially posed by the female workers. The operators never respond in kind to men's questions about their appearance or requests for dates. Still, like the Guatemalan women cyclists, they are the sexual object of male desire, as when the caller says, "Si usted tiene [. . .] tan hermosos ojos como linda voz, no vacilaría en dedicarme a usted por entero" (If you have eyes as beautiful as your voice, I wouldn't hesitate to spend all my time on you; 7), or he suggests, "Conversemos sobre el amor" (Let's talk about love; 8). While the operators are strictly forbidden to answer such comments, the very fact that it is acceptable, even normal, for men to treat female workers as sexualized objects makes their presence in the workplace less threatening to male privilege. Objectifying women subordinates them to male dominance in multiple ways. They serve men by obeying their orders and by functioning as potential sources of carnal pleasure. The ultimate centrality of men is illustrated by the cartoon that closes the piece (fig. 3): here, the operators smile and read *Zig-Zag* while the bust of a man, who occupies the center of the cartoon and who is larger than any of the women, shouts "Aló!" repeatedly into his phone. Ironically, the cartoon also undermines male supremacy as the operators ignore the man's shouts in favor of enjoying their leisure time reading. The article encodes social anxieties about the modernizing process and about women's role in the changing labor market. Technological progress is indispensable if Chile is to achieve the same success as the United States and Europe, and the writer boasts, "Ni en Buenos Aires, ni en París, ni en Nueva York el servicio telefónico es mejor que en Santiago" (Not in Buenos Aires, nor Paris, nor New York is the telephone service better than in Santiago; 8). Yet women's involvement in such progress must be controlled and mediated, and Zig-Zag's representational tactics emphasize the restrictions under which women enter the labor force and participate in modernization.

Five years later, the publishers of Zig-Zag founded another journal. *Familia: revista mensual ilustrada dedicada solamente al hogar* ran in parallel with Zig-Zag itself. The inaugural issue announced that the periodical had replaced the book as the readable item of choice in modern society and pointed out that, with the glaring exception of the family, all other subgroups enjoyed periodicals dedicated to their interests. The rise of journal reading was connected to modernity: "Dentro de las atenciones de la vida moderna y de sus exigencies multiples, es difícil encontrar medio mejor que no sea una revista para verlas tratadas en forma amable" (Among the duties and many demands of modern life, it's difficult to find any means better than a periodical to discuss those duties in an amiable form; 1). While Zig-Zag was a general interest periodical with appeal to a broad section of the middle class, *Familia* directed its message to the increasing number of women readers. As the editors explain, women in North America have long enjoyed numerous books about domestic happiness and how to maximize it, but Chilean families have lacked those advantages until *Familia*'s appearance. The editors position *Familia* as responding to the necessities of modern life and progress and as helping women, responsible for domestic stability, adapt their homes to changing external circumstances. *Familia* was one of the first magazines in Chile dedicated to women, and together with *Revista Azul* it would become known for its support of women's emancipation. Targeted to middle- and upper-class women, *Familia* attracted male and female writers, and a typical issue contained commentary on literature, music, and scientific advances; serialized stories; essays on love, marriage, religion, and the home; household hints and recipes; articles on fashion and social life; and a section of "Letters from Paris."[9]

Familia's first issue, like Zig-Zag's, clearly expounds its simultaneous commitment to and ambivalence about modernization and the associated phenomena of technological innovations and women's connection to the modernizing project. That first issue began with a futuristic comedic play set in far-off 1930, "El vértigo de la vida" (Life's dizziness) by J. Jacquín, which dramatizes the conflicts between the novelty of the modern era and traditional values. In the play the female characters display marked autonomy and agency and deftly use technology. The heroine and her mother both travel unchaperoned, and, indeed, the mother is absent through the play, having journeyed via airship from Paris to Yokohama for a conference. The very relationship between the heroine's parents is modern and inverts gender norms, since the mother's absence means that the father arranges the daughter's marriage and plans the wedding. These domestic undertakings are embedded in his business dealings, and modern technologies of communication facilitate an ironic return to the preindustrial model in which work and family life occupied the same physical space. Thanks to telephone and gramophone recordings, the businessman can transact commercial business from his home rather than his office. Similarly, the traditional and the hyper-novel meet in the mother's chosen profession of "chemical cuisine," which, while never described in the play, seems to unite the conventionally male discipline of science with the conventionally female chore of cooking.

Despite the presence of two suitors who represent modernity as defined by the space of the play, the heroine opts for her childhood friend, a poet. The sole character to renounce the luxuries of modern life, he prefers to write his poetry by hand instead of making a phonograph recording. Nor does he travel by air-car as do the other characters. Yet this character is represented as the most authentic and deserving of the heroine because he is the only one who uses his phonograph message to her to make a physical, permanent record of his devotion and love for her. While Jacquín's vision of the future is one in which women are employed, autonomous, and even scientifically minded, the play's conventional resolution strongly implies that women find happiness only in true love and successful marriages.

This last idea is underscored by the following article in this issue of *Familia*, "Consejos a una novia" (Advice to a bride), which follows the well-worn device of a letter from "doña Pabla" to her goddaughter Frida about marital happiness. In addition to giving Frida specific tips on household management, Pabla tells her: "Cuide de su casa. ¡Deje que las neofeministas chillen! . . . El hogar será siempre la gran pasión de la mujer" (Take care of your house. Let the neofeminists scream! . . . The home will always be woman's great passion; 7). The idea that women are best suited for domestic life and that their duty should keep them there, tending to their family's needs, runs through all of Pabla's advice, which echoes conventional tropes: the new wife should always give the appearance of happiness, she should create an orderly, clean house, she should manage her servants wisely, and she should save money by not spending a lot on clothes or following fashion trends slavishly. At the same time, a ruthless pragmatism surfaces at key moments. Pabla tells Frida that marriage is a sacrifice and a yoke, invoking traditional imagery of women's abnegation in matrimony, but adds that Frida should enter marriage without any sentimental illusions and even recommends that she make practical use of the tactic of dissimulation and lies of omission (6). While "El vértigo de la vida" suggests that women of the future, notwithstanding their new employment possibilities and comfort with technology, will still find their most supreme fulfillment in love and marriage, the practical, even cynical, nature of "Consejos a una novia" recommends resignation to the inevitable fate of marriage, as it is the only possible outcome for elite women. This attitude does not rely on religious traditionalism, however, as earlier invocations of female self-sacrifice often did; instead, the new bride's acceptance of marriage as a necessity rather than a joy is represented as an acknowledgment of fact. In some ways "Consejos" is more transgressive than "Vértigo." The latter assumes that romantic love is still a requirement for marriage, while "Consejos" knows that it is not and advises female readers to make the best of the inevitable. Here a reminder that *Familia* was the first magazine specifically for women in Chile is salutary. The first time that Chilean elite women have access to writing designed particularly for them, they confront first an ultimately sentimental depiction of marriage in an unrealistic future and then a cynical representation of the need to accommodate a potential husband's whims, desires, and quirks.

While *Familia* unlinked the concepts bound up in words such as technology, progress, and the modern from the idea that women could or should work for pay, more and more throughout Spanish America those concepts were being connected, explicitly or implicitly, even earlier. Indeed, *Familia's* editorial stance may have been in some ways a reaction against the movement of middle-class women into the workplace. Although *Familia* does not portray women working for money, many other texts, both fictional and nonfictional, created such representations. Yet even when journalists and novelists depicted women in positions of paid employment made possible by innovative technologies, their stance was equivocal. Just as authors increasingly viewed modernization itself dubiously, so too ambivalence about women's potential roles in the new economic structure reveals itself in fissures and contradictions in texts about the seemingly inevitable march toward modernity.

In 1888, Juana Manuela Gorriti, by then living in Buenos Aires after decades in Bolivia and Peru, published the short novel *Oasis en la vida*. This text, produced under the sponsorship of the insurance company La Buenos Aires, lauds the modern advances of the city and lays bare the ramifications of the transition to market capitalism for men and women alike. Gorriti uses the novel to advocate for women's full participation in economic activities and forcefully critiques the structures and social norms impeding their access to meaningful, paid employment. Yet she also casts a skeptical eye on the ways in which market forces affect human interactions and emotional states and alter people's relations to their physical and social environments. Given this, the introduction to the novel, written by Santiago Vaca Guzmán, reads as a much more straightforward take on modernity and progress, perhaps precisely because Vaca Guzmán does not address issues of gender. Instead, he counters Proudhon's argument that poverty is irreversible and inescapable and avers, "La industria, con sus innúmeras palancas de impulsión; las ciencias, con sus multiplicados alfileres de exámen; el cálculo, con su previsión y su aritmética; todos estos agentes de la vitalidad social, han venido a operar el milagro de la multiplicación del pan" [Industry, with its innumerable levers; the sciences, with their many examining needles; calculus, with its precision and arithmetic: all these agents of social vitality have come to produce the miracle of the multiplying of the loaves; 159]. Social change, associated here with industry, science, and math, the new areas of study and proficiency of the time, signifies not increased poverty but increased wealth. Scientific and commercial advances substitute for religion and supply human needs in ways that once would have been considered miraculous, thus invoking the pragmatism of positivism against the irrationality of faith-based beliefs. Vaca Guzmán's assertions bespeak a positive attitude about the benefits of modernization that predisposes the reader to understand Gorriti's novel as echoing the belief that new technologies and employment opportunities will necessarily lead to widespread social prosperity. Yet *Oasis en la vida* itself problematizes this idea through its representations of industry's multiple and varying effects on individuals, be they male or female. In the novel men and women alike negotiate the repercussions of the increasing development of a capitalist and mercantilist economy.

Oasis en la vida is the story of a journalist, Mauricio Ridel, who was sent to Paris from Buenos Aires as a child at the behest of his avaricious stepmother. When his father dies, leaving enormous debt, Mauricio uses an inheritance from his mother to satisfy his father's creditors and return to Buenos Aires, where he finds employment at a newspaper and begins writing novels. He finds lodging in a boardinghouse for women only and a love interest in one of the other lodgers, Julia, who teaches piano. They are eventually able to marry thanks to a windfall, a previously unclaimed insurance policy taken out by Mauricio's father, and the novel ends with their wedding.

Oasis en la vida opens as Mauricio hands in the last page of his latest serialized novel and another character comments that Mauricio works fourteen hours each day. Writing is immediately a public commodity. Mauricio's words are for sale, and indeed he must sell them for economic survival. The novel displays a deep interest in finances and women's role in local and national economies, as both mother and stepmother are key movers in controlling Mauricio's life and choices through their oversight of his finances. His youth in Paris, a city that for Latin Americans symbolized high culture and true progress and modernity, exiled him from home and family but gave him a cultural education and access to the intellectual life and modern attitudes that Paris represents. Mauricio returns to Buenos Aires because, as his financial advisor informs him, "en Buenos Aires que se agita a impulsos de un inmenso progreso, podrá Ud. con el trabajo rehacer la fortuna" (in Buenos Aires, which vibrates with the pulse of an immense progress, you can re-earn your fortune by working; 168). Paris is a city of intellectual learning and elite leisure; Buenos Aires, an evolving center of industry and financial activity where people improve their material status and socioeconomic standing. As Mauricio discovers, the city has also enjoyed the benefits of improved urban administration: "tan grande y bella, la gloriosa metrópoli habíase tornado. Las calles niveladas, llenas de luz, surcadas por vías férreas, con anchas veredas y rico pavimiento" (the glorious metropolis had grown so large and beautiful. The even streets, full of light, lined with tramlines, with wide sidewalks and rich pavement; 172). This description draws attention to the increased ease of transit through the city as greater numbers of inhabitants move through the urban sphere in mass transit vehicles, on paved streets illuminated by artificial lighting. In this praiseworthy urban space, the sign for the insurance company La Buenos Aires stands out, denoting a company that includes powerful capitalists both Argentine and foreign (172). Mauricio enters a city dominated and physically marked by the acquisition and growth of capital, a city that also facilitates such acquisition.

Mauricio is not the only worker in the novel. The women in the boardinghouse are also employed and self-sustaining. All these workers are controlled by a schedule, signified and made tangible in the text by clocks, bells, and timetables. Both the daily routine in the boardinghouse and Mauricio's newspaper job fall under the tyranny of the clock. Mauricio must absent himself from the boardinghouse during waking hours and he writes to strict deadlines. In another instance of the requirement to adhere to an externally imposed schedule, a woman exclaims at the swift passage of time when she hears the boardinghouse lunch bell. The bell and the woman's comment draw attention to the inflexible schedule that organizes the characters' lives. Similarly, Mauricio is roused from his thoughts by the clock striking a full two hours after his work has been completed, and he is "avergonzado de aquella inexactitud" (ashamed of such inexactness; 182). He has lost time, an act that causes shame in a society that places a monetary value on its workers' time. Gorriti highlights the development of accurate timepieces, their ubiquity in the city, and their consequences, the regimentation of time, schedules, and human lives.

The characters in *Oasis en la vida* consume luxury goods in a way only possible in this urban environment. The young women eat sweets from La Confitería del Lampo (177), commenting not just on the deliciousness of the candy but on the elegance of the sweetshop and its plan to create a space solely for women. Their purchase of the desserts and the potential female-only restaurant space speak to women's increasing economic power in the city, as they have the financial wherewithal to patronize stores in large enough numbers that a shop would consider building an area for their particular enjoyment. They also purchase candies and, later, bring Mauricio iced horchata from another sweetshop (186). These women enjoy the luxury of not having to prepare their own sweets or any food at all or to clean up. Their meals are cooked and served at the boardinghouse. Instead of spending their valuable time on uncompensated domestic chores, they work for pay. Even once Julia and Mauricio are engaged, she suggests that she continue working as a piano instructor after their marriage, while he swears that he will not allow her to "desafiar las humillaciones, a que el trabajo expone a la mujer en el áspero contacto con la vida" (confront the humiliations to which work exposes a woman in that rough contact with life; 190). His avowal, however, ignores the fact that Julia has been successfully working and "confronting humiliations" and that she is more than capable of dealing with the job market.[10]

A narrative twist made possible by the insurance company that patronized both the publication of the novel itself and the characters within it (we will remember that the sign for La Buenos Aires hangs over the city) puts Julia and Mauricio's debate over the appropriateness of women's work on hold. A chance encounter with an insurance company executive at the post office allows Mauricio to learn of his father's insurance policy, issued, of course, by La Buenos Aires. The post office, too, is a space born out of the new need for efficiency and of the concentration of people in the urban sphere. The postal system itself is not novel, but the method by which urban dwellers interact with it has changed. Large numbers of unrelated, unacquainted people regularly congregate at the post office, facilitating Mauricio's happy encounter there, and the novel concludes by paying homage to the power of insurance to assure familial security. Still pending is the question of Julia's right to work for pay. The *deus ex machina* of the insurance payout ends that debate without resolving it and leaves the last word to the priest celebrating their wedding and his praise of familial stability and happiness. Modernization thus both enables female participation in the workforce and ends it. Yet Mauricio and Julia are exceptions. The other women in the boardinghouse remain single and self-sufficient, and all the workers in the city are still subject to the routinization and mechanization that the rigid schedule of the clock signifies. Although Mauricio returned to Buenos Aires because hard work is rewarded there, he regains financial stability through a fluke, not through his own efforts. His hard work is not, in fact, rewarded. *Oasis en la vida* advances an optimistic vision for Buenos Aires as a model of progress whose inhabitants earn money that they can spend on creature comforts (sweets, cigarettes, the cashmere robe Julia dons), but there is no meaningful path to exit the ongoing routine of work. Modernization simultaneously improves people's lives and traps them.

Twenty years later, Argentine journalist and novelist Emma de la Barra found commercial and critical success when she published her novels *Stella* (1905) and *Mecha Iturbe* (1906) in Buenos Aires.[11] Writing under the name César Duáyen, she addressed Argentina's continued industrialization, the effects of European immigration, the changing political landscape, and women's capacities to contribute to national progress. Both novels feature female protagonists with Argentine mothers and European fathers who have been brought up in Europe and who return to Argentina, determined to make meaningful contributions to their new nation. These quasi-immigrant women are presented as feminine ideals, combining an angelic capacity for self-sacrifice with an understanding of women's work as an activity that takes place outside the home, in the professional sphere. In *Stella*, Alex sets up a school for her young cousins, helps her uncle in his business, and finally partners with her love interest, a doctor. In *Mecha Iturbe*, Hellen Buklerc is a skilled surgeon, having chosen her profession not only due to her aptitude but also her family circumstances, which require her and her sisters to earn their own living. Alex and Hellen are contrasted with the indolent, self-centered Argentine women who surround them. This is particularly true of *Mecha Iturbe*, much of which takes place in the fictional industrial suburb of Itahú, where several male protagonists have established a factory. This allows Duáyen to comment as well on the massification of labor, the potentially dehumanizing aspects of industrialization, and the benefits of technological progress. In both novels Duáyen consistently advances a notion of ideal femininity grounded in a vision of socially meaningful work and contributions to the community. More, this vision should form the ideal for all members of society, men and women alike. Her image of society is egalitarian inasmuch as her most positive characters expect and deliver the same dedication to social improvement regardless of gender.

Mecha Iturbe is organized around the work and love lives of several men and woman. Pablo Herrera is a young inventor who establishes a factory and surrounds it with a model town for workers in partnership with the doctor, Marco Silas. Hellen Buklerc works with Marco and marries Pablo; her counterpart is the title character, a beautiful but uneducated woman. While Pablo, Marco, and Hellen all strive to improve their society and work for social justice, Mecha is self-centered and disdains the lower classes. The novel ends with Mecha's death and the birth of Marco's daughter with another high-minded Argentine woman, Esperanza. Throughout the book, Argentina is marked by and adapting to technological and social change. Characters communicate via the telegram and telephone. In the opening pages of *Mecha Iturbe* a telegram summons one character back to his province. People shuttle between Buenos Aires and the workers' suburb of Itahú via the daily trains, which follow a fixed schedule thanks to the precision of clocks and timepieces. "A las diez en punto el largo tren expreso detúvose en la estación" (At ten on the dot the long express train stopped at the station; 109). In fact, railroad schedules demanded that time become fixed from one town or province to the next, so that times of departure and arrival would be valid in all the stops on the railway line (Schivelbusch 43). Trains make the characters' bi-located existence possible, allowing them to travel swiftly and dependably between Buenos Aires and Itahú. The railway system both connects the characters to multiple spaces and disconnects them, as they are continually in transit from one place to the other and frequently are absent when others want or need them. In this way the train collapses space by bringing Buenos Aires and Itahú temporally closer yet also bifurcates it. This tension is never resolved, only managed. At the end of the novel, Hellen and Pablo live among the social and political elites of Buenos Aires, where Pablo pursues a career in politics and Hellen holds social events to further her husband's ambitions. Once a week, however, they take the train to Itahú and work in the hospital and factory, returning to the city in the late afternoon where "nadie hubiera pensado, al verlos en la noche en su palco, que venían de llenar tan útil y rudamente su día" (no one would have thought, seeing them in their box at the theater in the evening, that they had come from spending their day so usefully and laboriously; 213). In Buenos Aires they work for social and political improvement generally. In Itahú they apply these grand principles practically, healing the sick and giving meaningful employment to lower-class workers. On the one hand Itahú serves as a laboratory for Pablo's and Marco's theories about progress; on the other, what happens there does not, perhaps cannot, happen in Buenos Aires, so Itahú does not offer a translatable model for urban transformation.

Stagnation and the difficulty of implementing change are also focused through Mecha herself, who represents a traditional model of femininity. Strikingly beautiful, her path to upward mobility lies in marriage to a much older Spanish aristocrat. Even her poverty-stricken childhood is the result of a conventional fall from economic security. After her father's death, her mother cannot support herself and her child because her only skills are sewing and laundry. The mother cannot perform these individualized service activities rapidly enough or in great enough quantities to pay the rent. Mecha grows up both decorative and wholly without purpose in life, unable to understand the charitable impulses and desire to further national progress that drive those around her. Even the clock in her house is personal rather than industrial. Elsewhere in the novel clocks set the beginning and end of the work day and control the schedules and lives of hundreds of workers with unfailing regularity, but Mecha's clock produces a tick-tock sound like a beating heart rather than marking time, telling the hour, or determining Mecha's activities in any way (41). The clock, like Mecha herself, is a decorative object rather than an aid to work or a tool for industry. Likewise, the men attracted to Mecha are members of the elite who live off their inheritances without producing goods or services, and their admiration for Mecha's physical beauty reflects their own—and her—superficiality.

Mecha stands in stark contrast to the selfless, industrious Hellen, whose many accomplishments include performing the operation that restores sight to Pablo's mother, Emilia. Moreover, the men with whom Hellen associates engage in socially meaningful work. Marco is a scientist and doctor who perfects surgical techniques to cure blindness, and Pablo is a mechanical genius who not only opens a factory but creates a planned community of homes and services for his employees and later parlays his industrial success into a political career. Duáyen fosters an image of ideal society as one in which progressive men and women partner, albeit not as complete equals. Of the factory town she writes, "En Itahú todos trabajaban" (in Itahú everyone worked; 99), emphasizing that the ability and desire to work spans all classes and both genders. Male and female workers participate in the creation not just of mechanical devices but of an engaged, socially aware community.

Mecha Iturbe consistently advances ideals of scientific progress and attempts to show what a country that makes significant technological innovations looks like through the utopian microcosm of Itahú. In addition to well-regulated factories staffed by contented workers, Itahú boasts a bridge that is a miracle of engineering. Yet this technological achievement leads only to the neighboring factory of the Lamparosa family, who have not made material improvements in working conditions or invested in industrial innovations that would better their mechanical processes: "El soberbio Puente, con sus cien metros de largo, unía el pasado y el future representado en las dos fábricas vecinas" (The proud bridge, one hundred meters long, united the past and the future represented in the two neighboring factories; 100). Connecting past and future, the bridge does not meaningfully help the inferior past transform into the more perfect future. The Lamparosa factory and workers are a fossilized, static remnant of past bad labor practices and failure to innovate that exist to provide a more striking contrast with Itahú's novelty and futurism.

Pablo designed the bridge, and his well-trained workers constructed it, so his decision to destroy it when the Itahú workers threaten to join the Lamparosa workers in a labor protest is a deeply emotional moment. More, this scene points to Duáyen's efforts to bring emotional content to the supposedly abstract topic of industrialization and to portray the owner/worker relationship as paternalistic and caretaking rather than cold and abstract. The problem with the Lamparosa family's managerial methods is not that they control completely their workers' lives and conditions of employment but that they do so capriciously and uncaringly. Pablo's employees enjoy their work because Pablo has decided to offer education, health care, and well-maintained homes, but such benefits are not guaranteed by contracts. Instead, they depend on Pablo's good will and continued control. Similarly, women's status remains linked to that of men and of male patronage. Hellen's abilities are recognized and praised by the men around her. Without Marco's mentoring she would not become a successful surgeon, and without Pablo's encouragement she would not continue to work in the medical clinic after marriage. Other women in the novel, including one of Hellen's sisters, suffer the stifling of their abilities precisely because men control and oppress them. Duáyen represents social change as dependent on individuals in order to stress the importance of individual action in societal transformations, but one of the effects is to reinforce a system of elite male patronage that ultimately disempowers both women and the working class.

Almost simultaneously with Duáyen's best-selling progressive novels in Argentina, the Mexican novelist and diplomat Federico Gamboa published his bleak naturalist novel *Santa* in 1903 and met with almost immediate success.[12] *Santa* tells the story of a young woman from the countryside who, upon being expelled by her family for losing her virginity, becomes a prostitute in Mexico City. Santa tries to leave the brothel on two occasions by forming stable liaisons with men but is forced to return when those relationships fail. Finally only the blind, ugly piano player remains to love her, staying by her side even while she dies of venereal disease in the novel's conclusion. *Santa* details the squalid urban settings where her decline into vice takes place. In Gamboa's deeply skeptical vision, modernity and modernization are represented as negative, and there is a deep anxiety about the consequences of an unthinking rush toward all things modern, including the increasing secularization of society, the growth of the urban sphere, the failure to delimit the boundaries of the public and private spheres, and the penetration of capitalism, which allows for humans as well as goods to be bought and sold in the market economy. While Gamboa was a supporter of Porfirio Díaz, he parted ways ideologically with the "científicos" and their program of social Darwinism, returning to his fervent and traditional Catholic beliefs (Ordiz 14).[13] Gamboa's reservations about modernization and progress play out in and on the body of Santa herself, as her beautiful, pure body gradually decays into a prostituted object handled and contaminated by men and finally into a cancer-ridden corpse. The plot and purpose of *Santa* echoes that of other naturalist novels. As J. P. Spicer-Escalante explains, Hispanic naturalist writers examined their individual societies with a focus on "the trials and tribulations of those societies as they sorted out their transition through modernity and post-coloniality." They saw their mission as one of observation but also of passing judgment on what they saw (19). Gamboa's novel participates in this project of critique and assessment, notably through his dissection of the urban sphere, its inhabitants, and Santa's interactions with that space and the people who occupy it.

When Santa arrives in Mexico City, she is plunged into a neighborhood of small businesses, including numerous butcher shops and a tombstone maker. These businesses in particular foreshadow Santa's destiny as a bodily object and her death (24–25). The street also boasts a tramline and electric lighting (25). At noon, the workers in these factories rush onto the street (27), causing Santa to fear that she will be seen going into the brothel. This opening scene presents the brothel as one of many businesses and foregrounds the capitalist impulses driving the city and its objectified dwellers.[14] It also presents daily urban life as mechanized and routinized; the workers obey the clock en masse and are controlled not by their own desires but by the arbitrary schedule imposed by the needs of the factory (Castillo 183). The workers are dehumanized and objectified by the massive processes of industrialization, just as Santa is dehumanized and objectified by prostitution.

Santa is subjected to other manifestations of modernization. To become a prostitute, she must register with the public health service, obtain an identification card, and undergo a gynecological exam.[15] Further, the medical officers take a lithograph of her (34). She is thus involved in the public health system in multiple ways: her body is directly subjected to the routine physical exam, her presence is installed within the medical/government system, and a faithful representation of her physical appearance is created for permanent enshrinement in public records. In short, Santa's body is made public and made known to the authorities. Later, she suffers the enforcement mechanisms of the public health systems even more directly: having failed to present herself for her weekly health inspection, she is imprisoned in a hospital. The small, dirty inspection office there features implements for the oversight and regulation of sexual behavior: "un mapa de las demarcaciones en que la ciudad se encontraba seccionada por la policía" (a map of the regions into which the police had divided the city; 169), which signals the symbolic and actual domination and regimentation of the urban space by public authorities and the apportioning of systems of control across different urban zones. Areas in which prostitution regularly occurs and where prostitutes are made known to governmental authorities are plotted onto the city map, showing the erasure of privacy in sexual behavior and the extent of public intervention in personal lives. The office also features a lithograph of Miguel Hidalgo, Mexico's great hero of Independence, and "una especie de armario suspendido, con el registro telefónico en su interior, cuyas brillanteces metálicas, diminutas ruedas dentadas,

alambres y rótulos microscópicos: 'Inspección General,' 'Bomberos,' y 'Gobierno del Distrito,' dan al aparato apariencias de reloj en compostura" (a
sort of hanging closet, containing the telephone apparatus, whose metallic
brilliance, tiny toothed wheels, wires, and microscopic labels, "General Inspection," "Firefighters," and "District Government," give the telephone the
appearance of a clock under repair; 169). These new technologies facilitate
the enforcement of codes related to sexual behavior and make the private
public. The telephone's almost menacing appearance, with its little fanged
dials and mysterious wires, bespeaks its importance in the officials' ability
to carry out their operation of surveillance and control. Machinery allows
the authorities to intervene more directly and forcefully in women's lives
and bodies. All is overseen by the mechanical reproduction of Hidalgo.
The reproducibility of the lithograph means that authority is widespread
and pervasive. All these technologies work to enforce systems of control,
regularizing and regulating what should be individual, private expressions
of sexuality.

Santa's life oscillates between enclosure in the brothel and her lovers'
homes and exposure in and to public spaces depicted as places of deca-
dence and dissipation. During the celebrations for September 16 that com-
memorate Mexico's independence from Spain, Santa travels to the Zócalo,
Mexico City's central plaza. The city's urban development is highlighted
here, literally, as electricity illuminates the city: "los enormes focos met-
ropolitanos [. . .] mezclados a las innúmeras luces incandescentes que
cubrían caprichosamente las fachadas del comercio rico [. . .] prestaban a la
metrópoli mágico aspecto de apoteosis teatral" (the enormous metropoli-
tan lights, mixed with the innumerable incandescent bulbs which covered
capriciously the facades of wealthy stores, loaned the city a magical aspect
of theatrical apotheosis; 102). Such a scene would have been impossible
without the Porfirian dictatorship's project to physically modernize the
city. But this image of modernity is presented as false and impermanent. It
is on loan, magical and deeply theatrical, a performance and imitation of
modernity rather than a lasting reality. Gamboa's city is a chaotic, crowded
place. The streets are so jammed with people on foot that only the trams
can pass, forcing Santa and her companions to abandon their plans to join
the celebration. The scene is one of disorder rather than the order that

Díaz's government had pledged to bring. Gamboa thus critiques both modernity's failure to carry out its promises and the lies that modernity tells in order to perpetuate itself.

Restaurants, too, are represented negatively. The Café de París is a vulgar place in large part because of its electric lights, which shed too much light on its dissipated clientele, while the Tivoli Central is "nocturno y pecador" (nocturnal and sinful; 111), made possible only by modernization. It is illuminated by electric lights and populated by a clientele that can come there before or after their day (or night) of work in the urban setting. As the Tivoli awakens for night, an action facilitated by the establishment's artificial lighting (112), so too does the city:

> Por ahí la calle abalanza sus ruidos: mucho rodar de tranvías y coches, mucho pataleo de caballos, mucho charlar y mucho reír, mucho griterío y mucho voceo de diarios:—!El *Tiempo* de mañana! El *Mundo* de hoy!

> There the street is a rush of noise: much coming and going of trams and carriages, many hoof beats, much talking and much laughing, much shouting and much crying of newspapers: "The *Time* of tomorrow! The *World* of today!" (113)

This is a space created through the technological innovations of electricity, improved streets, and newer, faster printing presses, yet it is not an inviting, welcoming space. Instead chaos reigns and time is sped up artificially by the technologies of transit and printing. Gamboa highlights the pace of change through the titles of the newspapers being sold. Now it is possible to own the world and to get tomorrow's time today, breaks with the chronological continuity that assured people of the stability of their lives.

Modernization affects both men and women negatively in *Santa*. The primary male characters, Santa's lover the Spanish bullfighter and the blind pianist of the brothel, lead lives that would be impossible outside the urban sphere. Yet their work contributes nothing to social productivity. While the bullfighter enjoys the wealth and social cachet of his profession, like Santa he serves as a luxury item, an entertainment rather than a necessity. The newfound access of the lower and middle classes to leisure time and disposable cash to purchase entertainment options such as visits to prostitutes or bullfights allows the toreador to profit from Mexico City's entry into modernity, but he himself refuses to participate in the social economy.[16] He remains devoted to his country of origin and lives in a boardinghouse peopled completely by Iberians who are likewise clinging to traditions seen by others as outmoded, marking him and other Spaniards in self-imposed exile as retrograde representatives of a way of life that has long since passed. Once again, Europe, especially Spain, is the land of the past, while America represents the future. Yet the bullfighter and his companions refuse to live in that future and thus contribute nothing to it. Similarly, Hipólito takes advantage of the black market of prostitution and plays the piano for the whores and their clients. Without the extensive network of brothels, an exclusively urban phenomenon, Hipólito's employment options would be nonexistent. Despite this he is unproductive. He never manages to establish a physical relationship with Santa and is last seen in the cemetery, a literal dead end for both the characters and the book. Men, like women, fail to adapt to modernization, yet as Gamboa argues, modernization is itself an illusion at best, a source of regimentation and hegemonic control over individual private behaviors at worst.

Despite the novel's emphasis on the increasingly urbanized space as infiltrated and shaped by market capitalism, it is telling that the text presents no alternative for Santa other than prostitution. Santa has no access to the jobs that other women had at the turn of the last century in Mexico City. Carmen Ramos Escandón writes that during the Porfirian period women often found work in industries that had mechanized work traditionally assigned to women, such as food preparation and sales, domestic services, childcare, and textiles, the last of which turned the individual activity of sewing into a production line (237). Yet such jobs are not even represented in the book, as if they did not exist. It is not enough that Santa cannot access them. Gamboa must eliminate any possibility of their appearance in the book, seemingly to dispel any question about why Santa does not seek out work in a factory or store. She herself says, "No sé trabajar" (I don't know how to work; 31). This statement in and of itself presents prostitution as something other than work, and indeed, Santa earns no salary separate from her room and board and whatever gifts the men who patronize her see fit to bestow upon her.

Santa has no access to modernity, which functions only to oppress and regulate her and other women. She is reduced to her sexuality, which falls under male control, and has no way to express herself other than through her body, over which she has only the illusion of agency. The urban space gives more men more open access to her body rather than providing her with autonomy or choices. Santa never considers employment in any of the new ventures that were increasingly open to women in the late nineteenth century, nor do new technologies benefit her. Her sickness cannot be cured, for example. Modernization is negative in that the urban space allows for the double commodification of Santa, the transformation of her body not just into an object (traditional) but into an object to be trafficked (modern). She is put on display in the public spaces of the city (restaurants, brothels) and sold for cash. Yet this construction destabilizes Gamboa's arguments decrying the pace and type of modernization in Mexico City.

If prostitution is not a job in the way that work in a factory or a butcher's shop is a job, then Santa's depersonalization and objectification do not function as a metaphor for the dehumanization that industrial capital imposes. Instead, prostitution becomes a moral choice. Santa is consistently presented as having a great deal of personal agency, although her ability to make choices about her life is determined by her inferior status as a woman. Gamboa's female characters are inherently limited and psychologically weak, always inferior to superior male intelligence (Ordiz 10). Gamboa's attitudes about women, and his consistent polarization of women between chaste and unchaste, mothers and whores, threatens to undo his attack on the modernizing project in Mexico, as his critique is based on reading Santa as emblematic of the Mexican populace subjected to that modernizing project. Anxieties about gender and gender norms thus displace worry about modernization to a large extent, although not completely. *Santa* demonstrates a deep-seated male anxiety about female power and sexuality that marks and even contaminates the novel's concerns about the processes, pace, and very nature of modernity and modernization.

By the close of the nineteenth century, at least some of the physical processes of modernization were in place in Latin America. Innovations in technology and industry created new opportunities for work, and cities expanded geographically as people moved away from rural areas to take advantage of these new possibilities for employment. Services were created or expanded to meet the needs and wishes of the newly urbanized population, ranging from mass transit to popular entertainment. Intellectuals, writers, and others involved in cultural production observed and participated in these changes and responded in ways that frequently had to do with their attitudes about gender, class, tradition, and progress. Not all writers at the end of the nineteenth century inserted themselves and their concerns into the ongoing debate about technology and the nature of progress in Latin America, but those who did often took a more radical view of women's roles in the process of modernization. Such writers argued that women, like men, would benefit from industrialization and that society should actively encourage women's participation in modernization by giving them access to scientific knowledge. The logical extension of this argument was, of course, that women should no longer be confined to the home but should make use of their newly won knowledge in the public realm. The fact that writers were affirming that women had a role in the public sphere and that they were connected, like men, to the industrializing project demonstrates that national debates about technology and its relationship to modernization in nineteenth-century Latin America afforded people a space from which they could assert the value of the shared participation of men and women in those debates and in their nations' future.

Throughout the second half of the nineteenth century in Latin America, writers and intellectuals thought deeply about questions of national identity, progress, modernity, and gender. As we have seen, these issues were intertwined on many levels. They appeared in discourses about the appearance, use, and occupation of public and private spaces. The theme of domesticity provided a means for writers both to critique and to advance their own concepts of modernity. On the battleground of women's education, thinkers fought over what constituted appropriate instruction for women in societies where men's and women's roles were both changing rapidly and not changing quickly enough for some. And as the century drew to a close and the twentieth century dawned, material changes in the conditions under which people lived and worked amplified, exacerbated, and contradicted preconceived notions of progress and social advancement and caused men and women to rethink the functions they and others should carry out. This book has sought to elucidate some of those arguments, ideas, and preoccupations in order to show that gender was a crucial factor in numerous discussions about national identity in the present and the future. These discourses did not disappear in the twentieth century; rather, men and women continued to ponder and argue over gender identity and roles as the feminist movement developed, as women won the right to vote, as sexual liberation disassociated women from reproduction, and as the gay rights movement made inroads in *machista* culture. The ways in which arguments about gender and modernity were made in the nineteenth century still influence conversations about public policy, family structures, and the definitions of masculinity and femininity that take place today.

Notes

Chapter 1. Introduction

1. See Gerber for a detailed discussion of Bachelet's communication strategies.

2. Bulmer-Thomas 23–31 passim.

3. In this vein, Néstor García Canclini criticizes both "the tendency to view our modernity as a belated and deficient echo of the countries of the center" (44) and "the crude determinism according to which certain socioeconomic conditions 'produced' the masterpieces of art and literature" (45).

4. See, e.g., Hale 384–86.

5. *Modernismo* was one of the most pronounced manifestations of the reaction to modernity but not by any means the only one.

6. See, e.g., Davies et al. 18–20.

7. Although the journal was published over a three-year period, only twelve issues appeared; publication was suspended several times for lack of funds, and when the twelfth number appeared, the editors announced that, having fulfilled their promise to those who had subscribed for a full year, *Lectura y Arte*'s run had come to a close.

Chapter 2. Public Space/Private Discourse

1. Ileana Rodríguez, Catherine Davies, Naomi Lindstrom, and Marzena Grzegorczyk are some of the critics who have addressed this topic in the Latin American context.

2. Manfred Engelbert also compares two of these novels, arguing that *María* and *Martín Rivas* should be read as responses to and participants in the modernizing process. For Engelbert, *María* depicts the failure of that process, while *Martín Rivas* demonstrates the success of capitalism. Lisa Reyes analyzes the representation of women and female agency in *María*, *Martín Rivas*, and *Aves sin nido*, as well as in Ignacio Altamirano's *Clemencia*.

3. *La mestiza* has suffered from critical abandon to the extent that several authors write that the book was first published in 1891, the date of its second edition, or even that it appeared in 1929 (see Loewe, who also places the action in the eighteenth century rather than the nineteenth).

4. Among the many critics who have written about *María* are Donald Mc-Grady, who provides a syncretic overview of the novel, its historical context, and Isaacs's life, as does Susana Zanetti; Doris Sommer, who includes a chapter on *María* in *Foundational Fictions*; and Gustavo Faverón Patriau and Eva-Lynn Alicia Jagoe, who analyze the role of Judaism in the book. Gustavo Mejía takes a Marxist approach in his prologue to the Ayacucho edition of *María*; Viviana Díaz Balsera (1998) analyzes the fissures in the novel's efforts to portray an idyllic existence; John Rosenberg (1994) discusses the excessive control exercised by the father over other characters in the novel; and Ivonne Cuadra compares *marianismo* in the novel with several other texts. Both Alfonso Múnera and David Musselwhite write of the interpellated episode of Nay and Sinar and its relationship to the rest of the novel, while Antonio García-Lozada, Lucía Ortiz, and María Mercedes Ortiz focus on national identity in the book. Jonathan Tittler discusses nature in the novel, while Gustavo Llarull gives a more explicitly ecocritical reading.

5. Rodolfo Borello, María-Inés Lagos-Pope, and Sylvia Molloy have all written about the exercise of patriarchal power in *María*.

6. I have written elsewhere of the ways in which the exterior landscape in *María* reinscribes hierarchies of gender and class (Skinner 2014).

7. Maribel Florián Buitrago connects the strategic deployment of gendered norms in *María* to the Colombian nation-building project: "La construcción de una identidad nacional, soportada en un sistema de diferenciación a partir del género, en el que cada uno de los sexos cumple un rol determinado dentro del grupo familiar, podría garantizar la adquisición, transmisión y duración de los valores o rasgos culturales que, en esa época, se pensaba podían llevarnos a cumplir con nuestros deseos de contemporaneidad histórica" (The construction of a national identity, sustained by a system of differentiation based on gender, in which each of the sexes complies with a determined role in the family structure, could guarantee the acquisition, transmission, and durability of the values or cultural features which, at that time, were thought to be capable of enabling us to fulfill our desires for historic contemporaneity; 2).

8. Doris Sommer has written extensively of María's outdoor adventures and what they may symbolize.

9. I have written elsewhere of some of the other implications of that scene (Skinner 2008).

10. Many critics have discussed the father's role in the family's eventual economic collapse. Manfred Engelbert argues that the father represents the first generation

of postindependence leaders, who began by advocating for liberalism and ended by promoting authoritarianism. Similarly, María Fernanda Lander asserts that in the novel's struggle between tradition and modernization, the father represents the latter, Efraín the former, and that "el obstaculizar los amores de María y Efraín por parte del padre, responde a la incapacidad de éste último, como representante del sector hegemónico, de adecuarse a la nueva realidad económica y social" (the father's blocking of María and Efraín's love speaks to the father's own inability, as a representative of the hegemonic sector, to adjust to the new economic and social reality; 183). As previously noted, Rodolfo Borello and Sylvia Molloy have also written perceptively about the father's abuse of patriarchal power.

11. *Aves sin nido*, the most canonical and reproduced novel in Matto de Turner's oeuvre, has received much critical attention. Efraín Kristal's book provides a thorough contextualization of the novel within Peruvian intellectual history, and Ana Peluffo's *Lágrimas andinas* is an excellent analysis of Matto de Turner's social and intellectual projects, writing, literary milieu, and reactions to concepts of race, ethnicity, nationalism, gender, and modernization. Francesca Denegri's *El abanico y la cigarrera* is an important resource for understanding Peru's nineteenth-century female writers and their intellectual interlocutors. Antonio Cornejo Polar writes about the representation of different ethnicities, races, and social classes; Fernando Arribas García investigates the novel as a work of *indigenismo*, as does Tomás Escajadillo. Numerous authors have examined the representation of gender, including Joan Torres-Pou, César Valverde, Gloria Hintze de Molinari, and particularly Ana Peluffo. Other critics treat the construction of families and parenting, such as Elisabeth Austin and Armanda Lewis, and I have written elsewhere of fatherhood in Matto de Turner's fiction (2011). Susana Reisz investigates feminist discourse in Matto de Turner. Catherine Davies (2004, 2005), Michelle Farfán, and Friedhelm Schmidt write about modernity in the novel; Davies (2005) also discusses spatial representations, as does Álvarez.

12. Sara Beatriz Guardia, Ana Peluffo, and Elena Peregrina write of the way in which Matto de Turner employs the characters of both Marcela and Lucía to voice her social critique. Guardia explains, "El enfrentamiento entre los buenos y malos, entre los poderosos y los indios, se focaliza en la figura de dos mujeres, la buena, dulce y culta Lucía Marín, y la india buena, Marcela Yupanqui. Juntas emprenden acciones de resistencia" (The confrontation between good people and evil ones, between the wielders of power and the indigenous, focuses on two women, the good, sweet, and cultured Lucía and the good Indian Marcela Yupanqui. Together they initiate acts of resistance; 271). Similarly, Peregrina argues that it is women who, independently of their socioeconomic status, work to defy existing social structures, and Peluffo affirms that there is a feminine sentimentalism that fuses

feminist rhetoric and pro-indigenous discourse in order to emphasize that women of different races and classes suffer in common (89).

13. See Del Castillo Carrasco 142–45; Denegri 2004, 79–85; Kristal 131–34; Peluffo 176–82 and 252–54; and Pinto Vargas 141–81.

14. Efraín Kristal explains that Matto de Turner, like her mentor Manuel González Prada, "was anti-oligarchical and pro-industry" (152) and that she believed that "social justice could only be brought about through the action on an industrial sector" (153). Fernando's work for a mining company represents Matto de Turner's wish for industrialization that would incorporate Indians into the workforce more productively.

15. Davies notes that by paying Marcela with money Fernando earns from the mines, Lucía "remodels the local political economy. She threatens the state (equated with barbarism) from within the domestic interior (civilization)" ("Spanish-American Interiors" 35).

16. Likewise, Peluffo avers, "Matto de Turner pone tanto énfasis en la identidad doméstica de sus personajes femeninos para demostrar que desde el espacio doméstico del hogar las mujeres podían expandir las fronteras de la subjetividad por medio del ejercicio de actividades aparentemente incompatibles entre sí" (Matto de Turner puts so much emphasis on the domestic identity of her female characters in order to show that from the domestic space of the home women could expand the frontiers of subjectivity by engaging in activities that were apparently mutually incompatible; 82).

17. Guardia notes, "El intento de negociar más allá del espacio privado y doméstico, desencadena la violencia que causa la muerte de Marcela Yupanqui y de su marido" (The effort to negotiate outside private, domestic space unleashes the violence that causes the deaths of Marcela Yupanqui and her husband; 271).

18. Jaime Concha's introduction to the Ayacucho edition of *Martín Rivas* remains an illuminating reading of the novel's economic structures. Patricia Vilches (2005), Mónica Meléndez, Nicolás Salerno Fernández, and Laura Janina Hosiasson analyze specific aspects of bourgeois and lower-class culture in the book.

19. Mario Hamlet-Metz examines the influence of French literature and culture on Blest Gana and *Martín Rivas*, and Hosiasson comments on the influence of Scott, Zola, Dickens, and Stendhal on Blest Gana.

20. I have written elsewhere of this dynamic (Skinner 2011).

21. See Hosiasson (9) and Meléndez for more on each family's parties.

22. In chapter 3 we will see further references to the supposed dangers posed by overeducated or very intelligent women.

23. For a much fuller analysis of the ways in which discourses about domesticity and motherhood circulated in nineteenth-century Spanish America, see chapter 3.

24. For more on Ancona's career as a historian, see Castillo Canché and Savarino.

25. The man "fue a colocarse bajo la sombra de un naranjo que extendía sus ramas fuera del recinto en que su dueño lo había plantado" (stationed himself in the shade of an orange tree that held its branches out of the area where its owner had planted it; 10).

26. Esteban, too, is cognizant of this power dynamic; early in the novel he lingers at Dolores's house after Pablo has left, explaining that "si me hubiera ido juntamente con el señor Pablo, éste habría visto mi casa" (if I had left with Mr. Pablo, he would have seen my house; 55). The only way to stay safe from Pablo's intrusions is to hide one's dwelling place.

27. Although Pablo offers to give Dolores ownership of the house in which she has been living, she rejects this; although that house is more suited to her class and ethnicity, it is not apparently her place either, "earned" as it was by sexual trade.

Chapter 3. Constructions of Domesticity

1. See, among others, Dabove, De Castro (2002), and especially Larsen. Some critics, such as Faverón Patriau and Paulk, also take issue with Sommer's strong readings of the novels she presents.

2. See Armstrong for an insightful discussion of the construction of female subjectivity in domestic narrative. As she writes of the production of domestic fiction and etiquette manuals in eighteenth-century England, "domestic culture actually worked as a principle of continuity that pervaded the social surface to provide a stable conceptual framework within which these 'outside' changes [in the economy and society at large] appear as so many variations on the sexual theme" (94).

3. For example, in an article titled "El trono de la mujer," the editors wrote, "Los verdaderos amigos de la mujer son aquellos que en lugar de querer convertirla en rival del hombre, procuran ensanchar el círculo de su noble entendimiento y se afanan por remover todos los obstáculos que se oponen al perfecto cumplimiento de su encomienda de amor sobre la tierra, es decir la caridad, cuyo centro es la familia propia y cuya circunferencia la forma el género humano todo: he aquí la magnífica y santa misión de la mujer y es verdad que no ha menester otra" (Woman's true friends are those who instead of wanting to turn her into man's rival, manage to enlarge the circle of her noble understanding and strive to remove all obstacles opposed to the perfect execution of her reign of love over the earth, that is to say charity, whose center is the family itself and whose circumference is formed by the human race: here is the magnificent and sainted mission of woman, and it is true that no other is necessary; 347).

4. For more on Torres and his career as a historian, see Pineda Soto.

5. For example, in 1902 Torres wrote, "Vuestra misión en el hogar es de paz, de dulzura, de condescencia, de abnegación y debéis estar siempre dispuestas a sacrificaros, si con ello agradáis a los que os rodean" (Your mission in the home

is one of peace, sweetness, sacrifice, and you should always be ready to sacrifice yourselves, if by doing so you please those who surround you). *La Mujer Mexicana*, no. 9 (1902): 73n9.

6. Similarly, a few months later Julián Logol responded to calls for women's rights by asking rhetorically: "¿Sabéis cuáles son los sagrados derechos de la mujer? Hélos aquí: el derecho de tener siempre el alma abierta al bien, de purificar los corazones donde el mal acaba de germinar, el derecho de consolar, de rogar y de amar. [...] El derecho de olvidarse de sí misma, de vivir y morir por aquel a quien ama, de embellecer para ellos esta vida material con su dulce sonrisa y sus cantos de amor. ¡Mujer! Esos son los derechos de que tú debes hacer eso todos los días. Bendice la misión que te ha tocado en suerte, pues ningún papel es más noble que el tuyo, no sueñes con otro, y no pidas más" (Do you know what woman's sacred rights are? They are the right to have the soul always open to the good, to purify those hearts where evil has just taken root, the right to console, plead, and love... . The right to forget about herself, to live and die for him whom she loves, to embellish for those this earthly life with her sweet smile and songs of love. Woman! Those are the rights which you should exercise every day. Bless the mission you have been given, for no role is more noble than yours. Don't dream of another, and don't ask for anything more). *La Mujer Mexicana*, no. 11 (1902): 15n11. Logol points to women's sacred, not secular or political, rights, and the rights he adduces are instead responsibilities and duties associated with the emotional and moral realm. Women should also be satisfied with these duties and not seek a different or additional role in life. "No pidas más," he writes sternly in an apparent response to increasing calls for female political emancipation, after softening his strictures by telling them that they have the noblest role of all to play.

7. "La verdadera mujer debe tener todas las cualidades que hacen el hogar, en cuanto es posible, un lugar de reposo; y es menester, por tanto, que tenga juicio y mérito suficiente para evitarle a su marido, hasta donde alcance, las molestias inherentes al matrimonio, y más que todo, hasta las dudas más insignificantes. Ha de procurar la esposa hacerse agradable a los ojos y al gusto del marido [...]. El hombre necesita estar en contacto con una inteligencia despejada, con un espíritu vivo y jovial [...] una dulce ternura. (The true woman ought to have all the qualities that make the home, as much as possible, a place of repose; and so it is necessary that she have the sufficient judgment and merit to shield her husband, as far as she can control, from the inherent bothers of marriage and, more than anything else, even the least significant doubts. The wife must make herself agreeable to her husband's view and taste [...]. A man needs to be in touch with a clear intelligence, a lively spirit, [...] a sweet tenderness; *Femina* February 5, 1911, 1).

8. See such critics as Cruz, Conway, Schmidt (1999), Sommer, and Ruiz, for example.

9. It is thanks to the unstinting efforts first of Montserrat Ordóñez (1941–2001) and now of Carolina Alzate that so many of Acosta's early serials, which would otherwise go unnoticed, are being republished in more widely available book form.

10. For example, when Lucía returned to her father's hacienda, "veía que el termómetro moral de la hacienda subía y mejoraba notablemente bajo sus cuidados, con lo cual sentía un noble orgullo y una profundísima satisfacción" (she saw that the moral temperature of the hacienda was rising and improving noticeably under her care, for which she felt a noble pride and the most profound sense of satisfaction; 237).

11. For more information on Gorriti's life, see Yeager. For more literary criticism on Gorriti's work, see Batticuore, Meehan, Salgado, and the collections edited by Fletcher and Iglesia.

12. The fact that no one else in the story other than Wenceslao sees or interacts with Isabel suggests that she may, in fact, be a vengeful spirit rather than a human being.

13. See Armillas Tiseyra for an extended discussion of the sacrificial discourses in "La hija del mazorquero" and their connections with national rhetoric and anti-*rosista* doctrines. See Huesca for a discussion of the relationship between the female subjects of the story and Gorriti's concept of modernity.

14. See Scott for more about the women (and several men) whose recipes appear in *Cocina ecléctica*.

Chapter 4. Women's Education

1. The exact place and periodical remain unclear; *La emancipada* could have appeared in *La Unión* in Cuzco, in *La Unión de Piura* (rather more doubtful), or in *Crónica del Colejio de la Unión* in Quito (Rodríguez-Arenas xix).

2. See Garabedian, Szir, and Lida for more information on the numbers and types of periodicals appearing in Argentina, especially in Buenos Aires, during the nineteenth century.

3. See Sternbach for an analysis of Guerra's essays and Mizraje for a discussion of Manso's life and career. Manso developed a particular expertise in pedagogical theory and, among other activities, translated the work of Horace Mann into Spanish. In 1854 Manso also published *El Álbum de Señoritas*, which appeared for a scant six weeks.

4. See Frederick 18–21 for more on *La Camelia* in general. Frederick also provides a helpful analysis of the magazine's three-part masthead, which included the phrases "¡Viva la confederación argentina! ¡Libertad! No licencia; igualdad entre ambos sexos"; "Siendo flor—se puede vivir sin olor"; and "Siendo mujer—no se puede vivir sin amor" (Long live the Argentine Federation! Liberty! No

license; equality of both sexes; Being a flower—one can live without scent; Being a woman—one cannot live without love). For more on Argentine women's magazines of the period, see Masiello 1994, 53–68.

5. In 1869 Sarmiento also initiated the first census, which revealed that of the total population of 1,836,490, fewer than 20 percent could read (360,683 people), and even fewer (312,011) could write (Auza 70).

6. *La Alborada del Plata*, December 9, 1877.

7. For more about *El Museo Literario*, see Melo and Bedoya Sánchez.

8. Dancing is highly approved, horseback riding tends to produce disastrous results, and swimming is acceptable only in the complete absence of any danger.

9. *Museo Literario* 1 (6 November 1871): 44.

10. *Museo Literario* 1 (19 June 1871): 25.

11. As Jil de Martínez puts it, "Que se nos ponga en igualdad completa con el hombre, en idéntica aptitud para todas las funciones, y todas nos habremos perdido en un confuso laberinto: el templo del hogar doméstico quedará desierto, sumido en las tinieblas, y apagado el fuego sagrado de su altar" (Should we be placed in complete equality with men, in identical aptitude for all functions, we will all have been lost in a confusing labyrinth: the domestic temple of the home will be deserted, sunken in twilight, and the sacred fire of its altar extinguished; 209). *Museo Literario* 1 (3 July 1871): 25.

12. For a detailed analysis of the ways in which the participants at the *veladas* discussed women's education, see Clark.

13. For more on *La bella limeña*, see Castañeda Vielakaman and Toguchi Kayo and Cárdenas Moreno.

14. "Poco simpatico sería, la que debe ser toda sensibilidad y ternura, dirigiendo una batalla, luchando con una fiera, o elevándose en un globo a las regions etéreas" (She who should be all sentiment and tenderness would be rather unappealing leading troops into battle, fighting a wild beast, or levitating in a balloon to the ethereal regions of the sky; 41).

15. At the August 16, 1876, salon, Delgado read his non-gender-specific piece "La educación del niño," in which he did not make such pronounced use of emotionally connected phrases and vocabulary; his opinion there is most frequently given in passive or third-person constructions.

16. *Perlas y Flores: Semanario Comercial Obsequiado a las Familias*, October 31, 1885; cited in Balta.

17. See Infante Vargas for a description of the periodicals intended for a female audience in nineteenth-century Mexico.

Chapter 5. New Technologies, New Work

1. See Porter for more on the ways in which nineteenth-century factory owners in Mexico deployed discourses of female morality.

2. Schivelbusch ascribes the practice of reading while traveling to the train journey in particular, saying that the velocity of railway travel turned the reality of landscape into a picturesque panorama and allowed for "the traveler's gaze [. . . to] move into an imaginary surrogate landscape," the book (64).

3. Catherine Davies notes that Naomi Lindstrom summarizes most critical reactions to the train episode when she cites both Antonio Cornejo Polar and John Brushwood as believing that the scene should have been omitted entirely (2005: 323).

4. Davies argues that the train *is* modernity and that it "leads the enlightened away from the rural pre-modern past to the progressive urban coast" (2005: 324).

5. *La Ilustración Guatemalteca*, October 1, 1896.

6. For more on Edwards's publishing career, see "Agustín Edwards MacClure" (*Memoria chilena*).

7. See Donoso Rojas for a history of the telephone industry in Chile.

8. While the 1907 Chilean Census did not include telephone operators as a separate category, it did count telegraph operators and found that 24 percent of all "telegrafistas" were women (Lavrín 89).

9. For more on *Zig-Zag*'s content and context, see "Entre el hogar y las letras: *Familia* (1910–1928) (1935–1940)."

10. Francine Masiello writes that "*Oasis en la vida* plantea por primera vez la autonomía femenina en el campo de la literatura, a la vez que defiende la independencia económica de la mujer soltera" (*Oasis en la vida* suggests for the first time feminine autonomy in the field of literature, at the same time that it defends the economic independence of the single woman; "Voces de(l) Plata" 45).

11. For more on de la Barra's life, see Berg (2007), viii.

12. The first edition of *Santa* of 5,000 copies sold out, as did the second printing in 1905 of 3,000 copies. By 1918, 18,000 copies had been sold (Glantz 41). *Santa* has also been the object of considerable critical attention. Glantz places the novel in its sociohistorical context. Several critics address the genre of naturalism, including Joan Torres-Pou, Ellen Mayock, and Jessica Shade Venegas, who reads the novel's representations of urban space in order to question *Santa*'s relationship to European naturalism. Javier Ordiz examines social and gendered norms and naturalist discourse. Sabine Schlickers and Rodrigo Cánovas explore nationalism and *Santa*, and Salvador Oropesa and David Gier discuss the Mexico-Spain relations represented in the novel. The numerous pieces collected in *Santa, Santa nuestra*, edited by Rafael Olea Franco, to celebrate the centennial of the book's publication provide insights about the novel's publication history, the themes of prostitution

and the city, and the novel's relation to and influence on other texts. Gender roles and prostitution are analyzed by critics such as Adela Pineda Franco, Debra Castillo, and Elzbieta Sklodowska.

13. As Ordiz notes, Gamboa critiques "los efectos nocivos que una modernidad que ve como laica, dehumanizada y mercantilista, está teniendo en su progresiva implantación en el país" (the noxious effects that a modernity that he sees as secular, dehumanized, and mercantilistic has during its progressive implantation in the country; 14).

14. As Rodrigo Cánovas writes, "En el burdel se confecciona un producto, tal como en una cobrería o taller" (In the brothel a product is created, just as in a factory or workshop; 85).

15. Katherine Bliss details the legal requirements of prostitution in Mexico City (28).

16. Writing of this period in Mexico City, Michael Johns points out, "The public spent more money in [bullfighting] arenas than in all the city's theaters, museums, circuses, and parks combined" (86).

Selected Bibliography

Primary Sources

Acosta de Samper, Soledad. "La aptitud de la mujer de ejercer todas las profesiones." Spain/Colombia, 1893.

———. *La Biblioteca del Hogar*. Bogotá, Colombia, 1892.

———. *El corazón de la mujer*. Bogotá, Colombia, 1869.

———. *Una holandesa en América*. Ed. Catharina Vallejo. Havana: Fondo Editorial Casa de las Américas; Bogotá: Ediciones Uniandes, 2007.

———. *Laura*. Bogotá, Colombia, 1870.

La Aljaba. Buenos Aires, Argentina, 1830–31.

Altamirano, Ignacio. *El Zarco*. Mexico City, written mid-1880s, published posthumously 1901.

Ancona, Eligio. *La mestiza*. Mérida, Mexico, 1861.

Blest Gana, Alberto. *Martín Rivas*. Santiago, Chile, 1862.

La Camelia. Buenos Aires, Argentina, 1852.

Duáyen, César. *Mecha Iturbe*. Buenos Aires, Argentina, 1906.

———. *Stella*. Buenos Aires, Argentina, 1905.

El Eco de Ambos Mundos: periódico literario dedicado a las señoritas mexicanas. Mexico City, 1873.

Familia: revista mensual ilustrada dedicada solamente al hogar. Santiago, Chile, 1910–28, 1935–40.

Gamboa, Federico. *Santa*. Mexico City, 1903.

Gorriti, Juana Manuela. *Cocina ecléctica*. Buenos Aires, Argentina, 1890.

———. *Oasis en la vida*. Buenos Aires, Argentina, 1888.

———. *Panoramas de la vida*. Buenos Aires, Argentina, 1876.

———. *Sueños y realidades*. Buenos Aires, Argentina, 1865.

———. *Veladas literarias de Lima, 1876–1877*. Buenos Aires, Argentina, 1892.

Gutiérrez Nájera, Manuel. "En el Hipódromo" and "La novela del tranvía." *Cuentos frágiles*. Mexico City, 1883.

La Ilustración Guatemalteca. Guatemala City, 1896–97.

Isaacs, Jorge. *María.* Bogotá, Colombia, 1867.

Lectura y Arte. Medellín, Colombia, 1903–6.

Matto de Turner, Clorinda. *Aves sin nido.* Lima, Perú, 1889.

La Mujer. Bogotá, Colombia, 1878–79.

La Mujer Mexicana. Morelia, Mexico. 1901–5

El Museo Literario. Bogotá, Colombia 1871.

El Perú Ilustrado. Lima, Peru, 1887–92.

Repertorio Salvadoreño. San Salvador, 1888–94.

Riofrío, Miguel. *La emancipada.* Quito, Ecuador, in *La crónica del Colegio de la Unión,* 1863.

Semana de las Señoritas Mexicanas. Mexico City, 1850–52.

Violetas del Anáhuac. Mexico City, 1887–89.

Zig-Zag. Santiago, Chile, 1905–64.

Secondary Sources

Aguirre Gaviria, Beatriz Eugenia. "Entre el desafío y la sumisión: dos revistas femeninas de Colombia y México en el siglo XIX." Diss., SUNY, Binghamton, 1995.

"Agustín Edwards MacClure (1878–1941)." *Memoria chilena.* http://www.memoriachilena.cl/602/w3-article-93378.html. Accessed April 10, 2015.

Aldaraca, Bridget. *El ángel del hogar: Galdós and the Ideal of Domesticity in Spain.* Chapel Hill: U of North Carolina P, 1991.

Alonso, Carlos J. *The Burden of Modernity: The Rhetoric of Cultural Discourse in Spanish America.* New York: Oxford UP, 1998.

Alvarado, Lourdes. *Educación y superación femenina en el siglo XIX: dos ensayos de Laureana Wright.* Mexico: Universidad Nacional Autónoma de México, 2005.

Álvarez, Raúl. "Ideologización del espacio en *Doña Perfecta* y *Aves sin nido*: La oposición campo-ciudad." *Decimonónica* 1.1 (Fall 2004): 1–15.

Alzate, Carolina, ed. *Laura, Constancia y Una Venganza: tres novelas de Soledad Acosta de Samper.* Bogotá: Universidad de los Andes, 2013.

Arango-Keeth, Fanny. "Tradición narrativa de la escritora latinoamericana del siglo XIX: escritura palimpséstica y subversión cultural." *RLA: Romance Languages Annual* 10.2 (1998): 432–39.

Ardao, Arturo. "Assimilation and Transformation of Positivism in Latin America." *Positivism in Latin America, 1850–1900: Are Order and Progress Reconcilable?* Ed. Ralph Lee Woodward Jr. Lexington, MA: Heath, 1971. 11–16.

Arias, Consuelo. "Representations of the Feminine in Modernismo: The Figure of the Exotic Woman." Diss., Princeton University, 1995.

Armillas Tiseyra, Magalí. "Beyond Metaphor: Juana Manuela Gorriti and Discourses of the Nation under Juan Manuel de Rosas." *Latin American Literary Review* 84.42 (2013): 26–46.

Armstrong, Nancy. *Desire and Domestic Fiction: A Political History of the Novel.* New York: Oxford UP, 1987.

Arribas García, Fernando. "*Aves sin nido*: ¿novela indigenista?" *Revista de Crítica Literaria Latinoamericana* 17:34 (1991): 63–79.

Austin, Elisabeth. "Reading and Writing Juana Manuela Gorriti's Cocina Ecléctica: Modeling Multiplicity in Nineteenth-Century Domestic Narrative." *Arizona Journal of Hispanic Cultural Studies* 12 (2008): 31–44.

Auza, Nestor Tomás. *Periodismo y feminismo en la Argentina, 1830–1930.* Buenos Aires: Emecé, 1988.

Azzoni, Gabriela. "Fernández de Kirchner: 'Me siento la madre del país, la madre de todos los argentinos.'" *La Nación*, March 28, 2014.

Balta, Aída. *Presencia de la mujer en el periodismo escrito peruano (1821–1960).* Lima: Universidad de San Marcos de Porres, 1998.

Baltar, Rosalía. "En su teatro, sobre el viento armado. . . ." *Espéculo: Revista de Estudios Literarios* 29 (2005).

"El Barrio Dieciocho." http://www.memoriachilena.cl/602/w3-article-591.html. 2014. Web. September 27, 2014.

Batticuore, Graciela. "Historias cosidas, el oficio de escribir." *Mujeres y cultura en la Argentina del siglo XIX.* Ed. Lea Fletcher. Buenos Aires: Feminaria, 1994. 30–37.

———. "Itinerarios culturales: dos modelos de mujer intelectual en la Argentina del siglo XIX." *Revista de Crítica Literaria Latinoamericana* 22.43–44 (1996): 163–80.

———, ed. *Mujeres argentinas: el lado femenino de nuestra historia.* Buenos Aires: Alfaguara, 1998.

———. *La mujer romántica: Lectoras, autoras y escritores en la Argentina: 1830–1870.* Buenos Aires: Edhasa, 2005.

———. "Rereading Fiction by 19th-Century Latin American Women Writers: Interpretation and Translation of the Past into the Present." *Translation Perspectives* 6 (1991): 127–33.

———. *El taller de la escritora. Veladas Literarias de Juana Manuela Gorriti: Lima-Buenos Aires (1876–1892).* Rosario: Beatriz Viterbo, 1999.

Bedoya Sánchez, Gustavo Adolfo. "La prensa como objeto de investigación para un estudio histórico de la literatura colombiana: balance de historiografía y establecimiento del corpus." *Estudios de Literatura Colombiana* 28 (March–June 2011): 89–109.

Berg, Mary G. "La época moderna en las novelas de César Duáyen." *Mecha Iturbe.* By César Duáyen. Buenos Aires: Stockcero, 2007. vii–xx.

———. "Prólogo." *Índole (Novela Peruana)*. By Clorinda Matto de Turner. Buenos Aires: Stockcero, 2006. ix–xxv.

Bliss, Katherine. *Compromised Positions: Prostitution, Public Health, and Gender Politics in Revolutionary Mexico City*. University Park: Pennsylvania State UP, 2001.

Borello, Rodolfo. "Sociedad y paternalismo en *María*." *Cuadernos Hispanoamericanos* 562 (April 1997): 67–79.

Bourdieu, Pierre. *The Field of Cultural Production*. Ed. Randall Johnson. New York: Columbia UP, 1993.

Bruhns, Karen Olsen, and Karen E. Stothert. *Women in Ancient America*. Norman: U Oklahoma P, 1999.

Brunner, José Joaquín. *América Latina: cultura y modernidad*. Mexico: Grijalbo, 1992.

Bulmer-Thomas, Victor. *The Economic History of Latin America since Independence*. Cambridge: Cambridge UP, 1994.

Bushnell, David, and Neill Macauley. *The Emergence of Latin America in the Nineteenth Century*. New York: Oxford UP, 1998.

Cacua Prada, Antonio. *Historia del periodismo colombiano*. Bogotá: Ediciones Sua, 1982.

Cánovas, Rodrigo. "Lectura gratuita de la novela *Santa*, de Federico Gamboa." *Revista Chilena de Literatura* 59 (November 2001): 81–98.

Cárdenas Moreno, Mónica. "Seminario *La Bella Limeña* (1872): ¿espacio de libertad o encierro para la mujer peruana del siglo XIX?" *Cloture et monde clos dans les cultures ibériques et ibéro-américaines*. Ed. Dominique Breton and Elvire Gómez Vidal. Bordeaux, France: Presses Universitaires de Bordeaux, 2011.

Castañeda Vielakaman, Esther, and Elizabeth Toguchi Kayo. "Las románticas en un semanario del siglo XIX: *La Bella Limeña* (1872)." http://www.cemhal.org/publicaciones1f.html. Accessed July 13, 2014.

Castillo, Debra A. "Meat Shop Memories: Federico Gamboa's *Santa*." *Inti* 40–41 (Fall 1994–Spring 1995): 175–92.

Castillo Canché, Jorge I. "La enseñanza y el concepto de la historia en la obra de Eligio Ancona." *Revista de la Universidad Autónoma de Yucatán* 230 (2004): 40–60.

Cavalaro, Diana. *Revistas argentinas del siglo XIX*. Buenos Aires: Asociación Argentina de Ediciones de Revistas, 1996.

Chambers, Sarah C. "Letters and Salons: Women Reading and Writing the Nation." *Beyond Imagined Communities: Reading and Writing the Nation in Nineteenth-Century Latin America*. Ed. Sara Castro-Klarén and John Charles Chasteen. Baltimore: Johns Hopkins UP, 2003. 54–83.

Clark, Emily Joy. "Addressing Women's Education in Lima in the Late Nineteenth

Century: The *Veladas Literarias* and Beyond." MA thesis, University of North Carolina, Chapel Hill, 2011.

Concha, Jaime. "Prólogo." *Martín Rivas*. Caracas: Ayacucho, 1977.

Conway, Christopher. "Lecturas: ventanas de la seducción en *El Zarco*." *Revista de Crítica Literaria Latinoamericana* 26.52 (2000): 91–106.

Cornejo Polar, Antonio. *Literatura y sociedad en el Perú: la novela indigenista*. Lima, Peru: Centro de Estudios Antonio Cornejo Polar, Latinoamericana Editores, 2005.

Coromina, Irene S. "El destino de la mujer transgresora en tres cuentos con desenlace fantástico de Juana Manuela Gorriti." *Espéculo: Revista de Estudios Literarios* 43 (2009).

Cruz, Jacqueline. "La moral tradicional y la identidad mexicana vistas a través de los personajes femeninos de *El Zarco*." *Explicación de Textos Literarios* 22.1 (1993–94): 73–86.

Dabove, Juan Pablo. *Nightmares of the Lettered City: Bandits and Literature in Latin America, 1816–1929*. Pittsburgh: U Pittsburgh P, 2007.

Davies, Catherine. "On Englishmen, Women, Indians, and Slaves: Modernity in the Nineteenth-Century Spanish-American Novel." *Bulletin of Spanish Studies* 82.3–4 (2005): 313–33.

———. "Spanish-American Interiors: Spatial Metaphors, Gender, and Modernity." *Romance Studies* 22.1 (March 2004): 27–39.

Davies, Catherine, Claire Brewster, and Hilary Owen. *South American Independence: Gender, Politics, Text*. Liverpool: Liverpool UP, 2006.

De Castro, Juan E. *Mestizo Nations: Culture, Race, and Conformity in Latin American Literature*. Tucson: U Arizona P, 2002.

———. *The Spaces of Latin American Literature: Tradition, Globalization, and Cultural Production*. New York: Palgrave Macmillan, 2008.

De Friedemann, Nina S., and Mónica Espinosa Arango. "Las mujeres negras en la historia de Colombia." *Las mujeres en la historia de Colombia. Tomo II. Mujeres y sociedad*. Ed. Magdala Velásquez Toro, Catalina Reyes Cardenas, and Pablo Rodríguez Jiménez. Bogotá: Grupo Editorial Norma, 1995. 32–76.

Del Castillo Carrasco, Daniel. "Un deseo de historia: notas sobre intelectuales y nacionalismo criollo en el siglo XIX a partir de *La Revista de Lima* (1859–1863)." *El hechizo de las imágenes: estatus social, género y etnicidad en la historia peruana*. Ed. Narda Henríquez. Lima: Pontificia Universidad Católica del Perú, 2000. 99–195.

Denegri, Francesca. *El abanico y la cigarrera: la primera generación de mujeres ilustradas en el Perú*. Lima: Centro de la Mujer Peruana Flora Tristán, 2004.

———. "Desde la Ventana: Women 'Pilgrims' in Nineteenth-Century Latin American Travel Literature." *Modern Language Review* 92.2 (1997): 348–62.

Díaz Balsera, Viviana. "*María* y los malestares del paraíso." *Hispanófila* 123 (May 1998): 37–53.

Domenella, Ana Rosa, and Nora Pasternac, eds. *Las voces olvidadas: antología crítica de narradoras mexicanas nacidas en el siglo XIX.* Mexico City: El Colegio de México, 1991.

Donoso Rojas, Carlos. "De la Compañía Chilena de Teléfonos de Edison a la Compañía de Teléfonos de Chile: los primeros 50 años de la telefonía nacional, 1880–1930." *Historia* 33 (2000). Web. Accessed August 31, 2015.

Efrón, Analía. *Juana Gorriti: una biografía íntima.* Buenos Aires: Sudamericana, 1998.

Elbert, Monika M. "Introduction." *Separate Spheres No More: Gender Convergence in American Literature, 1830–1930.* Tuscaloosa: U Alabama P, 2000. 1–25.

Engelbert, Manfred. "Problemas de periodización: 'modernidad,' 'romanticismo' y 'realismo' en *Martín Rivas* y *María*." *Aleph* 16 (2000): 37–53.

"Entre el hogar y las letras. *Familia* (1910–1928) (1935–1940)." *Memoria chilena.* http://www.memoriachilena.cl/602/w3-article-3415.html. Accessed April 3, 2015.

Escajadillo, Tomás. "*Aves sin nido*: ¿Novela 'indigenista'?" *Revista de Crítica Literaria Latinoamericana* 30.59 (2004): 131–54.

Farfán, Michelle. "Un análisis de la modernidad en *Aves sin nido*, de Clorinda Matto de Turner." *Hipertexto* 1 (Winter 2005): 55–63.

Faverón Patriau, Gustavo. "Judaísmo y desarraigo en *María* de Jorge Isaacs." *Revista Iberoamericana* 70.207 (2004): 341–57.

Ferreira, Rocío. "De la cocina ecléctica a la novela ecléctica: pasión, (des)amor, género, nación y melodrama en las novelas de Mercedes Cabello de Carbonera." *Literatura y otras artes en América Latina: Actas del XXXIV Congreso del Instituto Internacional de Literatura Iberoamericana.* Comp. Daniel Balderston et al. Iowa City: U of Iowa P, 2004. 159–76.

———. "La participación de las intelectuales peruanas a fines del siglo XIX: nación, educación, y el salon literario." *Lucero: A Journal of Iberian and Latin American Studies* 9 (1998): 40–55.

Fletcher, Lea, ed. *Mujeres y cultura en la Argentina del siglo XIX.* Buenos Aires: Feminaria, 1994.

———. "Patriarchy, Medicine, and Women Writers in Nineteenth-Century Argentina." *The Body and the Text: Comparative Essays in Literature and Medicine.* Ed. Bruce Clarke and Wendell Aycock. Lubbock: Texas Tech UP, 1990. 91–101.

Florián Buitrago, Maribel. "La construcción de las esferas femenina y masculina en *María*: un discurso llamado a ordenar las relaciones de poder y dependencia entre los sexos." *Jornada Andina de Literatura Latinoamericana* 2006. Web. June 7, 2011.

Frederick, Bonnie. *Wily Modesty: Argentine Women Writers, 1860–1910.* Tempe: Arizona State University Center for Latin American Studies Press, 1998.

French, William E., and Katherine Elaine Bliss, eds. *Gender, Sexuality, and Power in Latin America since Independence.* Lanham: Rowman and Littlefield, 2007.

Garabedian, Mariano, Sandra M. Szir, and Miranda Lida. *Prensa argentina siglo XIX: imágenes, textos y contextos.* Buenos Aires: Teseo, 2009.

García Canclini, Néstor. *Hybrid Cultures: Strategies for Entering and Leaving Modernity.* Trans. Christopher L. Chiappari and Silvia L. López. Minneapolis: U Minnesota P, 1995.

García Pabón, Leonardo. *De Incas, Chaskanawis, Yanakunas y Chullas: estudios sobre la novela mestiza en los Andes.* Alicante, Spain: Universidad de Alicante, 2007.

Gerber, Elisabet. *Comunicación y política: análisis de la campaña política de Michelle Bachelet.* Santiago, Chile: Centro de Competencia en la Comunicación, 2005.

Gier, David. "El elemento español en *Santa,* de Federico Gamboa." *Revista Canadiense de Estudios Hispánicos* 23.1 (Fall 1998): 132–43.

Girona Fibla, Nuria. "Ser de escritora, ser de escritura: memorias de Juana Manuela Gorriti." *La mujer de letras o la letraherida: discurso y representaciones sobre la mujer escritora en el siglo XIX.* Ed. Pura Fernández and Marie-Linda Ortega. Madrid: Consejo Superior de Investigaciones Científicas, 2008.

Glantz, Margo. "Federico Gamboa, entre *Santa* y Porfirio Díaz." *Literatura Mexicana* 21.2 (2010): 39–49.

Greenberg, Janet. "Toward a History of Women's Periodicals in Latin America: A Working Bibliography." *Women, Culture, and Politics in Latin America: Seminar on Feminism and Culture in Latin America.* Ed. Emilie Bergmann et al. Berkeley: U California P, 1990. 182–231.

Grzegorczyk, Marzena. *Private Topographies: Space, Subjectivity, and Political Change in Modern Latin America.* New York: Palgrave Macmillan, 2005.

Guardia, Sara Beatriz, ed. and introd. *Mujeres que escriben en America Latina.* Lima, Peru: Centro de Estudios La Mujer en la Historia de America Latina (CEHMAL), 2007.

Guerra Cunningham, Lucía. "Visión marginal de la historia en la narrativa de Juana Manuela Gorriti." *Ideologies and Literature: Journal of Hispanic and Lusophone Discourse Analysis* 2.2 (1987): 59–76.

Gutiérrez Girardot, Rafael. *Modernismo.* Barcelona: Montesinos, 1983.

Habermas, Jürgen. *The Structural Transformation of the Public Sphere: An Inquiry into a Category of Bourgeois Society.* Trans. Thomas Burger with Frederick Lawrence. Cambridge: MIT P, 1989.

Hale, Charles A. "Political and Social Ideas in Latin America, 1870–1930." *The Cambridge History of Latin America.* Vol. 4: *c. 1870 to 1930.* Ed. Leslie Bethell. New York: Cambridge UP, 1986.

Hamlet-Metz, Mario. "Crossing the Barrier Successfully: Nineteenth-Century French Literature, Blest Gana, and *Martín Rivas*." *North Dakota Quarterly* 58.4 (1990): 89–95.

Heredia, Nadine. "Heredia: el poder de las mujeres es un poder que hace la diferencia." *RPP Noticias*, March 8, 2014.

Hintze de Molinari, Gloria. "Género e indigenismo." *Cuadernos Americanos* 13.2 (March/April 1999): 103–13.

Hosiasson, Laura Janina. "Blest Gana, Martín y el calavera." *Revista Chilena de Literatura* 75 (November 2009): 259–69.

Huesca, Eva París. "La nación como formación discursiva y la dimensión femenina del proceso de la modernidad en 'La hija del mazorquero' de Juana Manuela Gorriti." *Mester* 38 (2009): 45–56.

Iglesia, Cristina, ed. *El ajuar de la patria: ensayos críticos sobre Juana Manuela Gorriti*. Buenos Aires: Feminaria, 1993. 28–44.

Infante Vargas, Lucrecia. "De lectoras y redactoras: las publicaciones *femeninas* en México durante el siglo XIX." *La república de las letras: asomos a la cultura escrita del México decimonónico. Vol. II. Publicaciones periódicos y otros impresos*. Ed. Belem Clark de Lara and Eliza Speckman Guerra. Mexico: University Nacional Autónoma de México, 2005. 183–94.

Iriarte, Josefina, and Claudia Torre. "Juana Manuela Gorriti: *Cocina Ecléctica*: 'Un si es no es de ajo molido.'" *Mujeres y cultura en la Argentina del siglo XIX*. Ed. Lea Fletcher. Buenos Aires: Feminaria, 1994. 80–86.

Johns, Michael. *The City of Mexico in the Age of Díaz*. Austin: U Texas P, 1997.

Jrade, Cathy L. *Modernismo, Modernity, and the Development of Spanish American Literature*. Austin: U Texas P, 1998.

Kristal, Efraín. *The Andes Viewed from the City: Literary and Political Discourse on the Indian in Peru, 1848–1930*. New York: Peter Lang, 1987.

Kristeva, Julia. *The Powers of Horror*. Trans. Leon S. Roudiez. New York: Columbia UP, 1982.

Lagos-Pope, María-Inés. "Estructura dual y sociedad patriarcal en 'María.'" *Revista de Estudios Colombianos* 8 (1990): 12–20.

LaGreca, Nancy. *Rewriting Womanhood: Feminism, Subjectivity, and the Angel of the House in the Latin American Novel, 1887–1903*. University Park: Pennsylvania State UP, 2009.

Lander, María Fernanda. *Modelando corazones: sentimentalismo y urbanidad en la novela hispanoamericana del siglo XIX*. Buenos Aires: Beatriz Viterbo, 2004.

Larsen, Neil. *Reading North by South: On Latin American Literature, Culture, and Politics*. Minneapolis: U Minnesota P, 1995.

Lavrín, Asunción. *Women, Feminism, and Social Change: Argentina, Chile, and Uruguay, 1890–1940*. Lincoln: U Nebraska P, 1995.

Lergo Martín, Inmaculada. "Mujer y literatura en el Perú del siglo XIX." *Escritoras y escrituras* 2.11 (October 30, 2011): 1–9.

Lewis, Armanda. "Orphan Discourse and the New Ethic in Women's Narratives of 19th Century Peru." *Latin American Literary Review* 38: 75 (January–June 2010): 46–65.

Lewis, Colin M. "Industry in Latin America before 1930." *The Cambridge History of Latin America*. Vol. 4: *c. 1870–1930*. Ed. Leslie Bethell. Cambridge: Cambridge UP, 1986. 267–323.

Lindstrom, Naomi. "El convento y el jardín: la búsqueda de espacios alternativos en *Sab*." *Decimonónica* 4.2 (Summer 2007): 49–60.

Loewe, Ronald. *Maya or Mestizo? Nationalism, Modernity, and Its Discontents*. Toronto: U Toronto P, 2010.

Martin, Leona S. "Nation Building, International Travel, and the Construction of the Nineteenth-Century Pan-Hispanic Women's Network." *Hispania: A Journal Devoted to the Teaching of Spanish and Portuguese* 87.3 (2004): 439–46.

Martínez, Agustín. *Figuras: la modernización intelectual de América Latina, 1850–1930*. Caracas: Fondo Editorial Tropykos, 1995.

Martínez, José María. "Biografía, hibridez literaria, elitismo social y modernismo en algunas crónicas desconocidas de Manuel Gutiérrez Nájera." *Anales de Literatura Hispanoamericana* 37 (2008): 161–203.

———. "El público femenino del modernismo: las lectoras pretendidas de Amado Nervo." *Actas del XIV Congreso de la Asociación Internacional de Hispanistas, IV: Literatura hispanoamericana*. Ed. Isaías Lerner, Robert Nival, and Alejandro Alonso. Newark, DE: Cuesta, 2004. 389–96.

Masiello, Francine. *Between Civilization and Barbarism: Women, Nation, and Literary Culture in Modern Argentina*. Lincoln: U Nebraska P, 1992.

———. "Introduction." *Dreams and Realities: Selected Fiction of Juana Manuela Gorriti*. Trans. Sergio Waisman. Ed. Francine Masiello. New York: Oxford UP, 2003. xv–lx.

———, ed. *La mujer y el espacio público: el periodismo femenino en la Argentina del siglo XIX*. Buenos Aires: Feminaria, 1994.

———. "Voces de(l) Plata: dinero, lenguaje y oficio femenino en la literatura femenina de fin de siglo." *Mujeres y cultura en la Argentina del siglo xix*. Ed. Lea Fletcher. Buenos Aires: Feminaria, 1994. 38–46.

Massey, Doreen. *Space, Place, and Gender*. Minneapolis: U Minnesota P, 1999.

Mayock, Ellen. "Naturalist Ambiance in Zola's *L'Assommoir* and Gamboa's *Santa*." *Excavatio: Emile Zola and Naturalism* 13 (2000): 292–98.

Meehan, Thomas C. "Una olvidada precursora de la literatura fantástica argentina: Juana Manuela Gorriti." *Chasqui* 10.2–3 (February–May 1981): 3–19.

Mejía, Gustavo. "Prólogo." *María*. Jorge Isaacs. Caracas: Ayacucho, 1978 [1867].

Meléndez, Mariselle. "Obreras del pensamiento y educadoras de la nación: el sujeto femenino en la ensayística femenina decimonónica de transición." *Revista Iberoamericana* 64.184–85 (1998): 573–86.

Meléndez, Mónica. "La tertulia y el picholeo: la colonia y el cambio social resuenan en *Martín Rivas*." *Hispanófila* 144 (2005): 61–73.

Melo, Jorge. "Las revistas literarias en Colombia e Hispanoamérica: una aproximación a su historia." 2006. http://www.jorgeorlandomelo.com/bajar/revistas_suplementos_literarios.pdf. Accessed July 16, 2014.

Miller, Nicola, and Stephen Hart, eds. *When Was Latin America Modern?* New York: Palgrave Macmillan, 2007.

Mizraje, María Gabriela. *Argentinas de Rosas a Perón*. Buenos Aires: Editorial Biblos. Biblioteca de las Mujeres. 1999.

Molina, Hebe Beatriz. *La narrativa dialógica de Juana Manuela Gorriti*. Mendoza, Argentina: Editorial de la Facultad de Filosofía y Letras de la Universidad Nacional de Cuyo, 1999.

Molloy, Sylvia. "Borello Paraíso perdido y economía terrenal en *María*." *Sin Nombre* 14.3 (April–June 1984): 36–55.

Navarro, Marysa, and Virginia Sánchez Korrol. *Women in Latin America and the Caribbean: Restoring Women to History*. Bloomington: Indiana UP, 1999.

Olea Franco, Rafael, ed. *Santa, Santa nuestra*. Mexico: El Colegio de Mexico, 2005.

Ordiz, Javier. "En los márgenes del Naturalismo: mujer, religión y sociedad en *Santa*, de Federico Gamboa." *Iberoamericana* 9.35 (September 2009): 7–17.

Oropesa, Salvador. "Hacia una identidad nacional: la relación México-España en *Santa* de Federico Gamboa." *RLA: Romance Languages Annual* 8 (1996): 627–32.

Ortiz Mesa, Luis Javier. "La sociedad colombiana en el siglo XIX." *Las mujeres en la historia de Colombia*. Vol. 3. Ed. Magdala Velázquez Toro. Bogotá: Editorial Norma, 1995. 169–203.

Osborne, Peter. "Modernity Is a Qualitative, Not a Chronological, Category." *New Left Review* 1 (March/April 1992): 192.

Palermo, Zulma. "Mujer y mundo: recuperación novelada de un personaje histórico." *Alba de América: Revista Literaria* 5.8–9 (1987): 171–79.

Paulk, Julia. "Foundational Fiction and Representations of Jewish Identity in Jorge Isaacs's *María*." *Hispanófila* 162 (2011): 43–59.

Peluffo, Ana. *Lágrimas andinas: sentimentalismo, género y virtud republicana en Clorinda Matto de Turner*. Pittsburgh: Instituto Internacional de Literatura Iberoamericana, 2005.

Peregrina, Elena. "Las mujeres construyen naciones: *Aves sin nido*." *HiperFeira* 8 (2005). Web.

Pineda Franco, Adela. "La que mata y la que muere por segunda vez: Algunas escenas del imaginario amenazado del Porfiriato." *Revista Iberoamericana* 71.210 (January–March 2005): 77–90.

Pineda Soto, Zenaida Adriana. "Mariano de Jesús Torres y sus aportaciones a la historia." *Tzintzun: Revista de Estudios Históricos* 20 (July–December 1994): 47–67. Web. Accessed September 3, 2014.

Pinto Vargas, Ismael. *Sin perdón y sin olvido: Mercedes Cabello de Carbonera y su mundo.* Lima: Universidad de San Martín de Porres, 2003.

Poderti, Alicia. "La nación imaginada: trayectos ideológicos y ficcionales en el espacio andino." *Ciudadania y Nacion.* Ed. Roland Anrup and Vicente Oieni. Gothenburg, Sweden: Institute of Iberoamerican Studies, University of Gothenburg, 1999. 107–22.

Pollock, Griselda. *Vision and Difference: Feminism, Femininity, and the Histories of Art.* New York: Routledge, 1988 [2003].

Porter, Susie S. *Working Women in Mexico City: Public Discourses and Material Conditions, 1879–1931.* Tucson: U Arizona P, 2003.

Pratt, Mary Louise. *Imperial Eyes: Travel Writing and Transculturation.* New York: Routledge, 1992.

Radcliffe, Sarah. "Geographies of Modernity in Latin America: Uneven and Contested Development." *When Was Latin America Modern?* Eds. Nicola Miller and Stephen Hart. New York: Palgrave Macmillan, 2007. 21–48.

Ramos, Julio. *Desencuentros de la modernidad en América Latina: literatura y política en el siglo XIX.* Mexico: Fondo de Cultura Económica, 1989.

Ramos Escandón, Carmen. *Industrialización, género y trabajo femenino en el sector textil mexicano: el obraje, la fábrica y la compañía industrial.* Mexico: CIESAS, 2005.

Rector, John L. *The History of Chile.* New York: Palgrave Macmillan, 2005.

Reisz, Susana. "When Women Speak of Indians and Other Minor Themes . . . Clorinda Matto's *Aves sin nido*: An Early Peruvian Feminist Voice." *Renaissance and Modern Studies* 35 (1992): 75–94.

Reyes, Lisa D. "The Nineteenth-Century Latin American National Romance and the Role of Women." *Ariel* 8 (1992): 33–44.

Rodríguez, Ileana. *House/Garden/Nation: Space, Gender, and Ethnicity in Post-Colonia Latin American Literatures by Women.* Durham: Duke University Press 1994.

Rodríguez-Arenas, Flor María. "Ideología, representación y actualización: el Realismo en *La emancipada* de Miguel Riofrío (1863)." *La emancipada.* Buenos Aires: Stockcero, 2005 [1863]. vii–li.

Rosenberg, John. "From Sentimentalism to Romanticism: Rereading *María.*" *Latin American Literary Review* 23.43 (January–June 1994): 5–18.

Royo, Amelia, ed. *Juanamaría, mucho papel: algunas lecturas críticas de textos de Juana Manuela Gorriti*. Salta: Ediciones del Robledal, 1999.

Ruiz, José Salvador. "El laberinto de la aculturación: ciudadanía y nación mestiza en *El Zarco* de Ignacio Manuel Altamirano." *Revista de Critica Literaria Latinoamericana* 31.61 (2005): 23–36.

Salerno Fernández, Nicolás. "Origen, configuración, y representación de las capas medias en el siglo XIX en *Martín Rivas* de Alberto Blest Gana (1862)." *Contracorriente* 11.1 (Fall 2013): 1–38.

Salgado, María A. "Juana Manuel Gorriti: una escritora decimonónica ante el discurso de la enfermedad." *Hispanic Journal* 17.1 (1996): 56–67.

Savarino, Franco. "La transición al positivismo en *Historia del Yucatán* de Eligio Ancona." *Historias* 45 (March/April 2000): 67–83.

Schelling, Vivian. "Introduction: Reflections on the Experience of Modernity in Latin America." *Through the Kaleidoscope: The Experience of Modernity in Latin America*, ed. Vivian Schelling. London: Verso, 2000. 1–36.

Schivelbusch, Wolfgang. *The Railway Journey: The Industrialization of Time and Space in the 19th Century*. Berkeley: U California P, 1986.

Schlickers, Sabine. "*Santa*, texto fundador ambivalente de la patria mexicana." *Santa, Santa nuestra*. Ed. Rafael Olea Franco. Mexico: El Colegio de Mexico, 2005. 145–58.

Schmidt, Friedhelm. "Amor y nación en las novelas de Ignacio Manuel Altamirano." *Literatura Mexicana* 10.1–2 (1999): 97–117.

———. "Harriet Beecher Stowe y Clorinda Matto de Turner: escritura pedagógica, modernización, y nación." *Iberoamericana* 1:4 (2001): 133–46.

Scott, Nina M. "Juana Manuela Gorriti's *Cocina Ecléctica*: Recipes as Feminine Discourse." *Recipes for Reading: Community Cookbooks, Stories, Histories*. Ed. Anne L. Bower. Amherst: U Massachusetts P, 1997. 189–99.

Sedgwick, Eve Kosofsky. *Between Men: English Literature and Male Homosocial Desire*. New York: Columbia UP, 1985.

Shumway, Nicolas. *The Invention of Argentina*. Berkeley: U California P, 1991.

Skinner, Lee. "Constructions of Domesticity in Nineteenth-Century Spanish America." *Hispanic Journal* 21.2 (Fall 2000): 409–20.

———. "Family Secrets: Incest in Jorge Isaacs's *María*." *Hispanic Review* 76.1 (Winter 2008): 53–69.

———. "The Functions of Landscape in Jorge Isaacs and Soledad Acosta de Samper." *Symposium: A Quarterly Journal in Modern Literatures* 68.1 (Spring 2014): 12–24.

———. "Material Lusts: Socio-Economic Desires in Nineteenth-Century Spanish America." *Bulletin of Hispanic Studies* 88.7 (2011): 795–809.

Sklodowska, Elzbieta. "'No vayas a creerme santa . . .': dominación visual y control narrativo en *Santa* de Federico Gamboa." *Symposium* 50.2 (Summer 1996): 114–31.

Sommer, Doris. *Foundational Fictions: The National Romances of Latin America.* Berkeley: U California P, 1991.

Sosa, Carlos Hernán. "En los umbrales del texto: prólogos y legitimaciones, de dicatorias y complicidades (notas sobre el uso del paratexto en algunas escritoras argentinas del siglo XIX)." *Verba Hispánica* 13 (2005): 59–68.

Spicer-Escalante, J. P. "The 'Long Tail' Hypothesis: The Diachronic Counter-Metanarrative of Hispanic Naturalism." *Au Naturel: (Re)Reading Hispanic Naturalism.* Ed. J. P. Spicer-Escalante and Lara Anderson. Newcastle upon Tyne: Cambridge Scholars, 2010. 11–36.

Stansell, Christine. *City of Women: Sex and Class in New York, 1789–1860.* New York: Knopf, 1986.

Sternbach, Nancy Saporta. "'Mejorar la condición de mi secso': The Essays of Rosa Guerra." *Reinterpreting the Spanish American Essay: Women Writers of the Nineteenth and Twentieth Centuries.* Ed. Doris Meyer. Austin: U Texas P, 1995. 46–56.

Suárez de la Torre, Laura. "La producción de libros, revistas, periódicos y folletos en el siglo XIX." *La república de las letras: asomos a la cultura escrita del México decimonónico.* Vol. 2, *Publicaciones periódicos y otros impresos.* Ed. Belem Clark de Lara and Eliza Speckman Guerra. Mexico: University Nacional Autónoma de México, 2005. 9–25.

Subercaseaux, Bernardo. *Historia del libro en Chile (alma y cuerpo).* 2nd ed. Santiago: LOM Ediciones, 2000.

Toranzo de Penín, Amabilia. "Vinculaciones entre la vision femenina y la autobiografía en *Cocina ecléctica* de Juana Manuela Gorriti." *Escritura femenina: diversidad y género en América Latina.* Ed. Gloria Hintze. Mendoza: Universidad de Cuyo, 2004. 49–74.

Torres-Pou, Joan. "La ficción científica: fábula y mito en *Santa* de Federico Gamboa." *Crítica Hispánica* 17.2 (1995): 302–9.

Twinam, Ann. "Estrategias de resistencia: manipulación de los espacios privado y público por mujeres latinoamericanas de la época colonial." *Las mujeres en la construcción de las sociedades iberoamericanas.* Eds. Pilar Gonzalbo Aizpuru and Berta Ares Quieja. Mexico: Colegio de Mexico, 2004. 251–69.

Urraca, Beatriz. "Juana Manuela Gorriti and the Persistence of Memory." *Latin American Research Review* 34.1 (1999): 151–73.

Valverde, César. "Masculinidad y nación en la narrativa decimonónica: el caso de *Sab* y *Aves sin nido.*" *Torre de Papel* 8.2 (1998): 39–72.

Velázquez Toro, Magdala. *Las mujeres en la historia de Colombia.* Vol. 3. Bogotá: Editorial Norma, 1995.

Venegas, Jessica Shade. "Heterotopic Space and the Limits of Naturalist Discourse in Federico Gamboa's *Santa*." *Symposium* 63.4 (Winter 2009): 251–64.

Vergara, Magda. *El discurso femenino de Juana Manuela Gorriti*. Diss. U Virginia, 1993. Web. October 15, 2010.

———. "In Defense of Motherhood: Juana Manuela Gorriti's Ambivalent Portrayal of a Slave Woman in *La Quena*." *Romance Notes* 36.3 (1996): 277–82.

Vilches, Patricia. "Rocín-antes: La vestimenta, el lujo, y lo material como referentes de ascendencia social y espacio económico en la nobleza espiritual de Don Quijote y Martín Rivas." *Nueva Revista del Pacífico* 50 (2005): 157–76.

Yeager, Gertrude M. "Juana Manuela Gorriti: Writer in Exile." *The Human Tradition in Latin America: The Nineteenth Century*. Ed. Judith Ewell and William H. Beezley. Wilmington, DE: Scholarly Resources Press, 1989. 114–27.

Zea, Leopoldo. *El positivismo y la circunstancia mexicana*. Mexico: Fondo de Cultura Económica, 1985.

Index

María (Isaacs)—*continued*
work-related activities at home in, 36;
sewing and its manifestations in, 31–32,
36; significance of house space in, 32–33;
space of house as essentially female in,
31; spatial configurations subverted and
undermined in, 30, 39
Marisabidilla: Herrán y Tejada on, 117, 118
Market capitalism: in Gamboa's *Santa*,
173–74; Gorriti's *Oasis en la vida* and,
161–65; women's traditional roles and, in
Guzmán's "Amor a las ocupaciones del
hogar," 86
Marketplace: writers and influence of,
13–14, 19
Marriage: in Acosta de Samper's *Laura*,
88–90; in Acosta de Samper's *Una holandesa en América*, 92, 93; in Altamirano's
El Zarco, 80, 81, 82; arranged, in Riofrío's
La emancipada, 106, 107, 110, 111; in "Consejos a una novia" (*Familia* magazine),
159–60; "El vértigo de la vida" and, 159,
160; Guzmán's ideas of, in "Amor a las
ocupaciones del hogar," 83; political
agendas expressed through allegory of, 70
Martí, José, 13
Martínez, Agustín, 10
Martín Rivas (Blest Gana), 15, 30, 49–58,
62, 68; class in, 51, 52, 53, 58; duality of
public/private spaces and gender norms
in, 50–51; economic concerns, gender,
and, 53; economic structures in, Concha's
introduction to Ayacucho edition and,
180n18; European literary models and,
49; fashion and objectification of women
in, 54, 55; French enculturation in, 49;
liberal uprising of 1851 in, 56–57; liminality in, 50, 58; *paseo* (leisurely stroll) and
commodification of women in, 53–54, 55;
picholeos in, 52; privatization of the family
and, 55–56; reiteration of boundaries
between private and public in, 58; setting
of, and echoes of European and North
American texts, 49; *tertulias*, or salons in,
51–52, 53, 55; transgression of public/pri-
vate divide in, 56–57; violation of societal

norms associated with private spaces in,
52–53
Massey, Doreen, 30; on domestic space, 32;
on spatiality and gender, 26
Massification of labor: in Duáyen's *Mecha
Iturbe*, 165
Mass transit: employment and, 151
Matto de Turner, Clorinda, 13, 14, 131; "anti-
oligarchical and pro-industry" stance of,
180n14; *Aves sin nido*, 15, 16, 30, 39–49,
59, 62, 68, 148–50; *El Búcaro Americano*
edited by, 130; *El Perú Ilustrado* edited by,
29, 45, 150; homage to Ricardo Palma,
149
Mayan orality: Spanish literacy and, in
Ancona's *La mestiza*, 61, 62
Mecha Iturbe (Duáyen), 16, 165–69; clocks
and scheduling in, 167; egalitarian vision
of society in, 165; partnership between
progressive men and women in, 167;
quasi-immigrant women as feminine
ideals in, 165; railway system in, 166;
scientific progress in, 168; technological
and social change in, 166
Mechanization: writers, dismantled system
of patronage, and, 13
Men: condemnation of restrictive patriarchy
in Riofrío's *La emancipada*, 109; critique
of public corruption in Matto de Turner's
Aves sin nido, 43–44, 45–48; pensions of
war veterans, 6; permeability of interior
and exterior barriers and, 27; reading
and, *Lectura y Arte*, 22, 23, 24, 24
Mérida, Yucatán: Eligio Ancona's *La mestiza*
set in, 30
Mestizaje: interior decoration of homes in
Matto de Turner's *Aves sin nido* and, 45
Mestizo laborers: debt peonage of, 6
Mexican Revolution, 79
Mexico: access to education and ruling
class in, 133; Altamirano's *El Zarco*,
80–82; Ancona's *La Mestiza*, 58–68;
Diario de Méjico founded in, 75; *El Eco
de Ambos Mundos* in, 76–78; Gamboa's
Santa, 169–74; Gutiérrez Nájera's "En el
Hipódromo," 19–21; *La Mujer Mexicana*

LEE SKINNER is associate professor of Spanish in the Department of Modern Languages and Literatures at Claremont McKenna College. She is the author of *History Lessons: Refiguring the Nineteenth-Century Historical Novel in Spanish America,* and she has published articles and chapters on diverse topics in nineteenth-century Spanish America.